STEVE SMITH'S MEN

STEVE SMITH'S MEN

BEHIND AUSTRALIAN CRICKET'S FALL

GEOFF LEMON

Hardie Grant

BOOKS

Published in 2018 by Hardie Grant Books,
an imprint of Hardie Grant Publishing

Hardie Grant Books (Melbourne)
Building 1, 658 Church Street
Richmond, Victoria 3121

Hardie Grant Books (London)
5th & 6th Floors
52–54 Southwark Street
London SE1 1UN

hardiegrantbooks.com

A catalogue record for this
book is available from the
National Library of Australia

Steve Smith's Men
ISBN 978 1 74379 509 5

Cover design by Luke Causby/Blue Cork
Cover images: Adobe Stock, Michael Dodge/Stringer
Typeset in 11/17 pt Sabon by Kirby Jones
Printed by McPherson's Printing Group, Maryborough, Victoria

Some sections of this text are adapted from the author's prior publications
with the ABC and The Roar.

The paper this book is printed on is certified against the Forest
Stewardship Council® Standards. FSC promotes environmentally
responsible, socially beneficial and economically viable management
of the world's forests.

Geoff Lemon superbly documents
and dissects the fiasco that tore
Australian cricket asunder.
JIM MAXWELL

Typical Geoff Lemon writing.
Evocative. Sad. Funny. Insightful.
Revelatory. Bloody brilliant.
PETER FITZSIMONS

Geoff Lemon interviews Patrick Cummins at the Wanderers, Johannesburg, March 2018. (Photograph: Adam Collins)

About the Author

Geoff Lemon has covered cricket as a writer and broadcaster since 2010, including touring with the Australian men's and women's teams since 2013, for outlets including the ABC, BBC, *Wisden Almanack*, *The Guardian*, *The Cricketer*, *The Saturday Paper* and Cricinfo. He has worked on radio and television in Australia, England, New Zealand, South Africa, India, Sri Lanka, the Caribbean, Ireland and the UAE, and hosts cricket podcast *The Final Word*. His writing outside sport appears in places like *Best Australian Stories*, *The Monthly* and *Meanjin*. He's editor of one of Australia's oldest literary publications, *Going Down Swinging*, and formerly directed the National Young Writers Festival. His previous books were the essay collection *The Sturgeon General Presents*, collaborative novel *Willow Pattern*, and poetry collection *Sunblind*.

Contents

Chapter 1

LEGEND TO THE FALL

Australia's 45th Test captain has always been more ice than fire. But after yanking his helmet off, raising both arms, and turning through a slow circle to every section of the Gabba, Steve Smith found he needed something more to express what was raging through him, a torrent of emotion seeking release. He faced his teammates in the grandstand, screamed an affirmation whose words were unimportant next to their expression, and beat his clenched fist against his chest as though hammering in a marker.

The first Ashes Test of 2017 wasn't the first time he'd done this. Nine months earlier, starting a tour of India with another century, he'd reacted the same way. But overseas excursions get relegated to the back corners of pubs and attention spans, so this was new to the home-only crowd.

It wasn't just the behaviour, it was the visual. The whole impression. Smith was always called boyish, but where for others it can be a compliment, he genuinely still had the air of a kid. It didn't end with his pizza-faced teenage photos or his chipmunk-cheeked Test debut, but carried into the second half of his twenties. In his blazer at the toss, he always looked like he was playing truant from a pricey private school. When Australia lost, a friend of mine would joke that the captain wasn't allowed to stop for Macca's on the way home.

In Pune and in Brisbane, though – and nowhere in between – Smith pulled off his helmet to reveal a broad headband. His fair hair was soaked with sweat into a darker shade, and his previously chopped style was longer, swept to one side in something of a Brylcreem wave. He had found, dare we say it, a dash of heartthrob.

Then there was his playing style. Where once it had been flurry and flourish, this was batting by abnegation. The Gabba track was underprepared and spongy thanks to weeks of cloud and rain. Pune had been a dust-pit where balls were ragging from minute one. On both he played with Zen calm, letting turning balls beat his edge, putting close calls out of mind, evaporating risk and ignoring his opponents hour after hour. Both times, he waited until exhausted bowlers made mistakes. He pounced on every one.

In India, where Australian teams so seldom prosper, this set up a winning start to a series. In Brisbane, his first Ashes in charge, it took his team from peril to advantage. The roar from this understated player showed how much these innings mattered. The ferocity was new. It showed what it meant to have stepped up as captain. This was graduation from boy-man to leader.

We'd known he was good, but 2017 was when Smith became supreme. Three centuries in a series in India, while his main rival, Virat Kohli, barely made a run. Three more hundreds within the first four Ashes Tests. To use the bluntest metric, his batting average was now the second-best-ever at 63.75. There was no longer any doubt he was the best Test batsman in the world. One-time rivals like Joe Root were left in the dust. The streak, the dominance, were truly insane. 'We're watching Bradman here,' said the Australian Broadcasting Corporation's lead radio caller, Jim Maxwell. Watching on from the back of the box, Jim was shaking his head in disbelief.

Everyone made that comparison at some point during the summer. Of course Smith was a mile off Bradman's famous 99.94, because the old maestro had him well covered in scale: where Smith made hundreds, Bradman made triples. But Maxwell's comparison was literal and technical, referring to Smith's use of feet and wrists to open up gaps in the field wherever he wanted and manipulating bowling with three different shots for each ball. It was about depth of control and the impotence of opponents. And it was about frequency: from his first hundred onward, Bradman made one every 1.75 Tests. After that summer's Melbourne Test, Smith was second with 2.13.

The maddest part was that this wasn't a purple patch, no simple hot run of form. Smith was well into his fifth year making these kinds of runs. He'd zoomed up to 23 Test hundreds in 2017, catching Gilchrist, Taylor, Hussey, Mark Waugh, Boon, Harvey and Langer. There were only seven Australians ahead of him, Ricky Ponting leading with 41. He could have walked out of cricket that New Year's Eve ranked as one of the greats, and he was still only 28 years old. The thought of what he could do – how much longer he could prosper – was enough to make a stats fan light in the head. I remember muttering it out loud at the MCG: 'There is no way Steve Smith won't break that record. He could catch Ponting in three years.'

Barely two months after raising the Ashes trophy with a personal series average of 137.4, Steve Smith sits in the Cape Town media centre looking stark and harried under lights. He asks for a cameraman's halogen spots to be turned down, literally shrinking from their glare. What a metaphor. Then a stilted confession, one that soon turns out to be half lies. World attention explodes.

He comes down from his hotel next morning with sunglasses covering dark-ringed eyes. Chris Barrett, an old-school journo from *The Sydney Morning Herald*, grumbles with distaste as he's ordered to pap the Australian captain with a phone camera. A couple of days later, captain no more, team polo replaced by plain white t-shirt, Smith is buried in a phalanx of bright-vested security guards hustling through Johannesburg's OR Tambo International Airport. At the other end of that flight, white t-shirt replaced by black suit, he chokes out sobs and apologies in a curtained-off airport vestibule in Sydney.

He won't be wearing his Australian uniform again for at least a year, and is banned from the captaincy for two. Contracts are torn up around the world. The previous time India toured Australia, Smith and Kohli each made four hundreds head to head. In the season to come Kohli will take the stage alone.

It is a fall of staggering proportions. In a few short weeks the Australian captain goes from best in the world to bottom of the chasm. Through it all rings one endless question. How the hell did it come to this?

Chapter 2

CAUGHT ON TAPE

You know it's serious when Mluleki Ntsabo isn't smiling. The South African Broadcasting Corporation commentator is small in stature and huge in energy, beaming a high-wattage grin as he booms away in English on the main mics or Xhosa on the update line. But as I walked into the broadcast area on the third afternoon of the Cape Town Test in March 2018, he came bouncing round the doorway behind me like a rubber ball, rebounding off the far wall, his face stern as he rushed along. 'Did you see?' he asked with urgency. 'Cameron Bancroft has something on the ball.'

We piled into our commentary box where the ABC and SABC were running a joint broadcast. On the gantry outside our window were the three lead Supersport camera operators, adjusting and aiming their artillery-sized lenses, making fine calibrations beyond our understanding. They were chattering away on their walkie-talkies, co-ordinating with the other cameras all around the ground. There were close to 30 cameras overall, each with a part to play.

It was Bancroft they had followed first, tipped off to the possibility of shenanigans and tracking his every movement with or without the ball in hand. An hour or so later, they had the shot. Cricket lenses have 76× to 95× zoom, able to shoot from the grandstand to track a single bead of sweat running down a batsman's face. 'Through this extensive framing latitude, every dramatic on-site sensation can be captured', is how Canon describes it. Too true. Bancroft was holding the ball in his left hand, scrubbing his cupped right palm and fingers over the leather as though battling an unforgiving doorknob. You could see the pressure he was applying by the white flush of his knuckles. The fix was on.

But the broadcasters wanted more. Something explicit. What better way than to have the suspect provide it? So they sat on the original footage for a few minutes, setting up the cameras. One for the coach, Darren Lehmann, watching from a Rapunzel window up in the team rooms. One for the reserve player, Peter Handscomb, surrounded by discarded pads and gloves down at the side of the field. Cameras on the captain, vice-captain, umpires, and half a dozen on Bancroft himself. Then the final ambush: just after Pat Cummins had finished a spell in the 42nd over, the original close-up of Bancroft's scrubbing hand flashed onto the ground's big screens.

The Australians poked their heads into the trap immediately. Lehmann made a radio call to Handscomb, who trotted onto the field and spoke to Bancroft. The young fieldsman, heart plunging through his shoes, already knew exactly what was going on. Meanwhile, third umpire Ian Gould was watching television monitors and jumping on his own walkie-talkie from up in the grandstand, prompting on-field umpires Richard Illingworth and Nigel Llong to wander over to each other for a chat. So Bancroft did what any kid shoplifting a Milky Way would do: he shoved the evidence down his pants.

Most apprentice petty thieves don't have quite the same battery of surveillance devices awaiting their every move. The initial footage was replaying as the umpires moved over to Bancroft. He produced the soft black bag for his sunglasses, claiming that was all he had in his pocket. Strictly speaking this was true. Sandpaper in the jocks, though, was about to cause more discomfort than the immediately physical.

The second lot of footage hit the screen: the long shot of Bancroft watching the umpires coming together, then turning his back to them. Cut to the close-up, and the super slow-motion capture of the waistband pop: this camera that usually depicts the vibrations in a cricket bat at the moment of impact, or the faintest twitch of glove on ball, was instead capturing 150 frames per second of a drawstring being tugged, frantically enough to turn the slow version into an incongruously extravagant flourish. A magician's fling of the hand, the cord springing out, two ends separating, then trailing, trailing, the smoke coils of downed aircraft. The magician in his haste proved to have no magic at all; not the slightest hint of sleight of hand in the way he took a bright yellow square from his pocket, thoroughly unpalmed, and pushed its incriminating colour into hiding.

It was a confession, signed unwittingly but indelibly. Yet as obvious as it was, it was hard to believe. It was hard to believe it could have been so obvious.

There is a human tendency at events of significance to gather, to legitimise our experience together. We can't risk some spectacular misinterpretation; we look to others to confirm a city burning before our eyes. So commentators from every television and radio station crammed into the small break room in the broadcast centre. The previous morning its lone occupant had been Shane Warne, face down among some errant cables to take advantage of a break, snuffling awake with an imprint of the industrial grey carpet mottling one cheek. Today, though, everyone who wasn't on air was crowded in here: Shaun Pollock, Allan Border, Jim Maxwell, Kepler Wessels, Brendon Julian, arrayed around the widescreen television to watch the footage repeat and repeat.

There was no doubt or defence in the slow-motion ballet of elastic. As we watched, another shot was shown with even more detail. Bancroft's hand on the ball, close-up on his fingers. Index and middle knuckles parting for a second, for a millimetre, an aperture just enough for the camera's aperture to swoop through. A frozen flash of yellow proving beyond equivocation that his hidden treasure had been applied to the ball.

Admittedly, it can seem absurd to imbue this action with such drama. But altering a ball can alter the course of a match, the worth of a legacy, the history of the game. This ball would alter some of the world's most prominent careers.

Ball-tampering has always been a dark art. Bowling teams try to manage their sole weapon into its most dangerous state, but use methods retaining some vestige of deniability, or at least the mitigation of spontaneity. To use foreign objects brought onto the field for that purpose was something else. No Australian player had ever been charged with tampering, and now came a case that wasn't even marginal. This was proper cheating. To be caught so fully, so squarely, and looking so amateur in the attempt, just capped it off. And if we knew anything, it was that the least experienced player in a team wouldn't develop that plan on behalf of ten colleagues of his own accord. This story was going to be huge.

Back on the gantry, the cameramen were high-fiving each other at the sting. Supersport's TV director leaned back in one of the hinged chairs set outside, swinging back and forth in contentment with his arms crossed and a toasty smile. 'Our guys did a very good job today,' he said in his thick Afrikaans pronunciation, all plosives and alveolar trills. 'A very good job.'

When the bust happened the match had been poised. South Africa's star batsman AB de Villiers was at the crease. His team was 175 in front in their second innings, and two wickets down, but Australia's pace leader Mitchell Starc had induced two collapses in the opening Test of the series with reverse swing. The ball had just been thrown to Starc for a new spell, and was in the reverse-swing hotspot at 43 overs old.

Once the subterfuge became bloody-obvious-fuge, the Australians had to suffer through another session of play. Faces were glum and minds distracted. Smith spent time off the field: who was he speaking to? What did he know? Was strategy afoot, or was he curled up in a toilet stall? David Warner filled in as captain, calling a video review to dismiss Faf du Plessis. Warner wouldn't be implicated that day but would be central later. Handscomb filled in at slip, taking a catch. He had been implicated but would later be cleared. One other wicket fell, taking the total to five, the match slipping away by stumps with de Villiers still there and the lead at 294.

But the score was no longer a big factor in Australia's glumness as they left the field. They knew the trouble that had been circling was coming in to land. The standard radio and television interviews were denied, at least by their side. South Africa's opener Aiden Markram, who had been batting with de Villiers when the trap was sprung, used his 23 years of age to play a very straight bat as I interviewed him for ABC. 'As a batter you're in your own zone and your own tunnel vision. I wasn't aware of it at all. I wasn't even aware of it as I got out. I've not been exposed much to it. I haven't played many first-class games, and haven't played much Test cricket. I'm still very young and naive in things like these, and I think it may be a blessing in disguise.'

He took the same tack with the press conference that followed, speaking at length to a full room. But the room wanted the other team's young opener: Bancroft in his eighth Test. The question was whether it might also be his last. Markram wrapped up and still there was no sign from Australia. There had been a message that someone would show. So we waited. Twenty minutes, half an hour, three quarters. From the full-length windows on the fourth floor of the North Stand, Cape Town's sky fell away into darkness, the seemingly immutable bulk of Table Mountain dissolving, the cricket ground vanishing until all that was left were our own reflections coming back at us in a blaze of light.

After nearly an hour there was movement on the far side of the ground. You had to stand up against the glass to see through the glare. Distant figures came down the steps, then onto the grass. As they crossed the oval we could make out two white-clad forms, Bancroft and Smith still in their playing gear. On their right was media manager Kate Hutchison, hands in her jumper pockets as she hunched forward. On the left, team manager Gavin Dovey in a grey suit. Trailing him was security manager Frank Dimasi, his long peaked hood pulled over his head. Shoulders were rounded and feet slow. From outside, the press box windows high in the grandstand were glowing gold, but those approaching would have felt little warmth or welcome.

Chapter 3

TEAM SMITH

This book is not a detective story. It won't give you every detail of what happened in the Cape Town dressing rooms. When it gets released, Steve Smith, David Warner and Cameron Bancroft will still have careers to salvage – bans will end, comebacks will begin, and it will remain in their interest to avoid any detail of what happened or how it came to pass. They will stay vague and speak in platitudes. Under the omerta of professional cricketers, their teammates will do the same. Only once careers finish will talk begin. Someone can write the comprehensive history then.

Nor is this book a moral judgement. It's not about berating sportsmen for cheating, but trying to understand what I heard and saw across that South Africa tour and the five preceding years. It's the story of how a team hit a wall and burst into flames.

Australian cricket's engine was purring until its core group of greats retired in 2007 and 2008. From there it began to sputter and conk out. Ricky Ponting's team was beaten by South Africa at home in 2008–09, England away in 2009, then England at home in 2010–11. Michael Clarke lost South Africa's next visit in 2012, two Ashes tours in two years, and got whitewashed away by India and Pakistan. There were highs, like Australia's own whitewash in Mitchell Johnson's Ashes followed by a crazy win in South Africa, plus the home World Cup win of 2015. But increasingly it was a team prone to malfunction and collapse.

As Smith took over for the 2015–16 home summer, he lost all of his senior players within two Tests. Opening bowlers Johnson and Ryan Harris, wicketkeeper Brad Haddin, batsmen Clarke and Chris Rogers, all-rounder Shane Watson: six first-choice picks gone in a flash, and the new captain severely understaffed. He had two proper batsmen in himself and Warner, an underrated off-spinner in Nathan Lyon, and two excellent quicks in Mitchell Starc and Josh Hazlewood. Those three bowlers carried the show, as James Pattinson and Peter Siddle battled injury, Jackson Bird showed promise, and Chadd Sayers couldn't break into the starting XI.

The batting was frailer. Adam Voges was a senior stopgap who averaged 542 against the West Indies but too small a fraction of that in tougher conditions. Usman Khawaja was supreme at home and pizza on tour. Glenn Maxwell smashed it domestically but only got Tests in Asia. The team switched and swapped like a barn dance, a parade of raw players or players not given time or players who were never up to snuff: Joe Burns, Moises Henriques, various Marsh brothers, Nic Maddinson, Hilton Cartwright, Callum Ferguson, Matthew Renshaw, Peter Handscomb.

Smith's full-time reign started by mugging New Zealand at the Gabba, but faltered once batting got tricky at the first day-night Test in Adelaide. Australia got lucky when an umpiring howler all but gave them the series 2–0 rather than 1–1. Voges beat the West Indies on his own. A winning 2016 tour to New Zealand was the best performance, but was proven a false dawn five months later with a whitewash in Sri Lanka, embarrassed across three Tests on turning tracks. Losses to South Africa in Perth and Hobart made it five Tests in a row, and the last of them being a thrashing made it panic time again. Half the team was sacked and a new side got a consolation win in Adelaide. It was desperate stuff: Ferguson and bowler Joe Mennie were dumped on debut, Burns and Voges for lean patches, and wicketkeeper Peter Nevill for being too quiet behind the stumps.

A home loss against Pakistan had never happened before, but Australia still had to sweat. Pakistan nearly chased 500 at the Gabba and nearly drew in Melbourne, some late Starc magic pulling a win out of the fire both times. The 2017 tour of India saw a better fight than Clarke's team had managed four years earlier, but Smith's mob still lost across four Tests after winning the first by a mile. Bangladesh were treated as easybeats, which nearly bit Australia in the arse as Lyon and Warner narrowly salvaged a 1–1 draw.

By this stage Cummins had proven he was the natural pick as the third fast bowler. He'd been a Messiah figure, in that people had been waiting years for his return; Cummins had played one Test as an eighteen-year-old all the way back in 2011, awarded man of the match in a win in Johannesburg, then had missed the next six years with a laundry list of injuries. He'd finally returned in 2017, leading the line in Asia while Starc and Hazlewood juggled injuries of their own.

That was Smith's team running into the Ashes: young, unsure, unproven, made up of one excellent bowling quartet and two quality batsmen, with little else mortaring the bricks and even less in reserve. By Smith's own metrics, their previous fifteen Tests from Kandy to Chittagong had averaged one batting collapse per match.

All of which meant that by November 2017, Australia's administrators were a pile of shredded nerves. Yes, England had an even less convincing top order and a lack of pace in their bowling. Sure, their brilliant all-rounder Ben Stokes was suspended for trying to punch a man's face out the other side of his head. But even the weakest England team could spook Australia. Lyon got in the press before the Brisbane Test and talked about ending careers, but the home camp was at greater risk.

The bowlers were a lock: Starc, Lyon, Cummins, Hazlewood. So were Smith, Warner, and Khawaja at home. Handscomb had done enough to keep his place. With the last three decisions, selectors wanted to guard against criticism if it all went wrong.

Shaun Marsh had been moved on after India that April, dropped for the Bangladesh trip and not given a new contract, while Maxwell had made a century in India and scrapped useful runs in Bangladesh. But Maxwell had a reputation for loose shots and Marsh had more experience. The nervous choice won out. Renshaw had a good year as a Test opener starting at the age of twenty, but had three bad games in his Sheffield Shield warm-ups, while Cameron Bancroft's warm-up was red hot. In a fateful move, one young opener was swapped for another.

For the wicketkeeping spot, Tim Paine was the bolt from the blue. He'd debuted with Smith in 2010 but spent seven years in the wilderness after a broken finger never healed properly. In 2017 the national setup had been quietly building him back up through the T20 team, with Haddin now on the coaching staff giving close attention. Nevill had been dumped for Matthew Wade, who was more verbally aggressive. But Wade's year in the team had delivered even less with the bat and he was infamous as a keeper for bouts of iron glove.

A new keeper was required but no one had demanded the spot with runs. Going back to Nevill would have meant selectors admitting they were wrong – God forbid – and his only rival as a pure gloveman was Paine. Queensland's immaculate Chris Hartley had retired six months too early. Paine had conceived the same idea, but kept the faith long enough to catch a Hail Mary instead. The team was set but, in a nervous time, few involved would have predicted the five matches ahead.

Chapter 4

AUSTRALIA'S PREFERRED POISON

The Ashes is the story of antagonism. Months before Cameron Bancroft and his jocks got global attention, I described the relationship at the heart of the series as an 'itching, grating, sandpaper-underwear tension'. Perhaps it was a subconscious message from the future, but the image of P12 Extra Coarse bikini briefs was supposed to evoke chafing at condescension from a distant ruler. A quarter of a century before federating as a nation, Australia's colonies banded together to take on England at cricket.

The teams and their supporters had more in common racially and culturally than not, but commonality can spawn dislike as readily as divergence. Tribal loyalties scale in ever-decreasing circles, from nations and religions to provinces and sects, neighbourhoods and factions. Those most like us are so close their differences are taken as insult, a rejection of what we value in ourselves. In 2013 I took a break from the Ashes with cameraman Cam Fink to shoot football videos. Manchester was a town in red and blue binary, where scarred and knobbly City and United ultras told of running battles in the streets where they lived side by side. Without a trace of awareness, each group told us theirs was a family club, a close-knit community worth admiring, while the other was a mob of lunatics without honour. Had you dressed them in civvies they'd be comfortably leaning up against the same bar.

Cricket in the 1800s was ad hoc, but what we now call the first Test between Australia and England came in 1877 in Melbourne. Five years later, Australia's win in a standalone match at The Oval prompted the mock funeral notice from which the Ashes name and trophy arose. The jest reflected sincerity – national pride was pinned to the contest, like the jingoism attached to British military moves.

After Australia's founding win the home of Empire assumed the dominance expected, taking eight series before the colonies began to hit back in the 1890s. It was through cricket that a young Australian nation expressed its identity in the new century. After the First World War and on through Don Bradman's 1930s it began to break free of dominion, resenting an empire that had fed so many people into the mincer of Gallipoli and the Western Front. Loyalty remained when tested: when Robert Menzies announced that Britain had declared war on Germany in 1939, it was a given 'that, as a result, Australia is also at war'. The countries fought together, then lined up in opposition for the Victory Tests. But an undercurrent of ill will was always there, as it often was between the nations' militaries.

Douglas Jardine was the most famous provocateur, the classic toff who delighted in his role as villain during the Bodyline series in 1932–33. Scornful of colonials and unswerving in purpose, Jardine baited local crowds as his bowlers battered local batsmen, having masterminded the brutal tactics that hauled Bradman back from the realm of deity to mere brilliant mortal. Australian actor Hugo Weaving must have channelled some of his Jardine from the *Bodyline* television drama into his tart and implacable Agent Smith in *The Matrix*. Indeed, *The Matrix* is also an Ashes movie: Smith against his nemesis Mr (Jimmy) Anderson, the importance of choosing a shiny red pill at the start, the sequels coming too frequently, the subset of awful fans festering in a corner of the internet.

The earlier England captain Archie MacLaren refused to face Aboriginal bowler Jack Marsh in a 1902 tour match, citing race but likely hoping to prevent Marsh's thunderbolts appearing in the upcoming Sydney Test. The white establishment weakly acceded – Marsh was never picked for Australia, and barely again for New South Wales. Then you have WG Grace and Warwick Armstrong as twin titanic sources of dislike. One from each country, 30 years apart, they were like for like in spirit and in form: enormous men of equally proportioned stubbornness, using their figurative heft to bend rules into unrecognisable shapes. Expert in gamesmanship and flexible in ethics, both found the honour of conduct fell behind the honour of victory.

In part, the irritation between the countries is pantomime. On three tours to England I've met little but warmth and goodwill. When English writer Oliver Laughland moved the other way he adopted a defensive antagonism, but soon found 'it has mostly been me who is the aggressor ... The most bizarre aspect of the situation is that I find myself conforming to a national stereotype I once berated, only to learn that my preconceived ideas of another nation were just a fabrication.' The Oval crowd sang that Bradman was a jolly good fellow moments before they cheered his last dismissal. Australia's retiring contingent in 2015 received warm farewells, and as a teenage Ashton Agar approached a century at Trent Bridge in 2013, all but a few of the England supporters had switched sides to cheer him on.

But nastiness and stereotyping are pimples: it's under pressure that the juicy stuff oozes out. There are still English minds that turn to convicts and criminality, incivility and animality, ragged edges and lack of class. There are Australian perceptions of class obsession, pomp and pout, hereditary privilege and self-regard. Those things have some truth, but most are also evident in the other culture, if less recognised. Australia's self-facing myth of being egalitarian, larrikin, anti-authority, is a fiction, however pleasing, for a people reverent of wealth and prissily insistent on rules. England's self-image as civilisation's cradle is proven to be a veneer, whether by colonial depredations or a lads' trip to Spain. When you've popped an especially excrescent cyst, it pays to wipe the mirror. While you're there, it doesn't hurt to have a good hard look at the rest.

'The Ashes is the story of fast bowling,' I wrote for *All Out Cricket* magazine from the Adelaide Oval as Mitchell Johnson caught flame in November 2013. The thread is strong. Demon Spofforth (his parents called him Frederick) all but created the Ashes in 1882, his match figures of 14–90 remaining the second-best by an Australian to this day. Having stormed into England's rooms to give Grace a paint-stripping blast after the game's most famous cheat ran out a batsman who was patting down the pitch, Spofforth channelled his rage in the second innings to torpedo the English as they sailed towards a target of 85.

The Demon wasn't lightning fast, but a bowler of precision and pressure whose approach was to attack at all times. His demeanour helped: hair in peaks reminiscent of horns, eyes in a burning glare. His comrade George Giffen said that Spofforth 'has frightened more batsmen out than many bowlers have fairly and squarely beaten', while writer Rob Smyth credits him with having 'started the tradition of Australian fast bowlers using the moustache as an intimidatory weapon'.

Thirty years later, Jack Gregory and Ted McDonald started the lineage of intimidation's most brute form. One brawny and slingy, one lithe and subtle, they took apart everyone they saw in the opening Test at Trent Bridge in 1921. 'The first fast bowlers to mow down opponents in tandem', as David Frith has it, would change the way cricket was played. Nowadays the new-ball pair is standard; before Gregory and McDonald, their captain Armstrong sequestered the shiny missile for his leg-breaks. His pacemen forced even his giant ego to wander off to third man and read a newspaper.

It's illegal to publish a cricket book without a Neville Cardus quote, and on this subject the great scribe is worth his ink. 'I cannot find language yet to describe the awe-inspiring and mingled speed, power and effortlessness of his attack. Rhythmic, tawny, aquiline. The silent curving run of McDonald. Stumps flying like spears. It was bowling of havoc but also of rare beauty. It was bowling which seemed to become ignited from the burning sun above.' Gregory, in contrast, 'a giant of superb physique, ran some twenty yards to release the ball with a high step at a gallop, then, at the moment of delivery, a huge leap, a great wave of energy breaking at the crest, and a follow-through nearly to the batsman's doorstep'.

Bradman described Gregory's bowling as 'positively violent in its intensity'. The equally great quick Harold Larwood placed him 'just a little ahead of his great opening partner because he was a man of more terrifying appearance', while the duo's wicketkeeper Bert Oldfield would 'unhesitatingly hand the palm to McDonald as the greater because of his versatility and remarkable stamina'. The pair was the first proof of one thing: legend does not need longevity. They played eight Tests together, all in 1921. Their first three in Australia blew no one away. But when they got a run on in England, they won the Ashes.

That's all that pace needs. For five Tests in 2013–14, Mitchell Johnson prowled in off a shortened run, his left arm a weapon, black with tattoos. That crouch in delivery, back bent low for the slinging limb to launch, man become catapult. Once, England had laughed at Johnson's inaccuracy; now every ball leapt at nose, grille, throat, badge, shoulder, with pace that made spectators flinch. 'Part of Johnson's deal this time was that he was in our heads even when he wasn't bowling,' wrote Kevin Pietersen. 'You very seldom hear people in your own team saying that they are physically scared, but our tail-end batsmen were scared.' That fear spreads through a team in an instant. Did Johnson speak to Anderson after amputating middle stump in Adelaide, leaving the timber reeling in a gap-toothed grin? 'I thought about it. I didn't need to.'

Larwood and Bill Voce were Jardine's instruments of Bodyline: bowling at the head or ribcage with a cordon of catchers on the leg side. Decried as unsporting, it only worked when fast enough to impair judgement and accurate enough to impair scoring. In other words, you still had to be bloody good: 'Bradman would murder you if you gave him any stuff that was slightly loose,' said Larwood. Australians were more concerned with him murdering Bradman. Bodyline is the most famous series ever, but featured the only four Tests in which Larwood and Voce combined.

Typhoon Tyson destroyed Australia in 1954–55, John Snow in 1970–71, and neither toured the country a second time. Australian crowds pelted Snow with beer cans for his hostile bouncers, then cheered Dennis Lillee and Jeff Thomson for the same four years later. 'For two and a half series,' wrote the pair's captain Greg Chappell, 'they were the most lethal bowling combination that I have ever seen.' England had no answer but Tony Greig's insane counterattacking bravado and an aged Colin Cowdrey returning from retirement, swaddled in padding, mouth forever frozen in an O of pain.

Two and a half series, then Thomson busted his shoulder and was never the same. England dished back multiple threats in 2005 when Freddie Flintoff, Steve Harmison and Simon Jones screamed the ball around at 150 kilometres per hour.

They never bowled together again. Perhaps such ferocity can only exist in an instant. Perhaps an instant is all it needs. The perfect peak is remembered all the more for its brevity: a moment when the heavenly lights align.

The fear and aggression of fast bowling mirror the Ashes story. A contest where the sides want not just to triumph but to humble each other. Most current players wouldn't know much Ashes history: Bradman's average, Jim Laker's nineteen wickets, sure, but plenty would never have heard of McDonald or Gregory, Spofforth or Snow. They'd know Ian Chappell and Allan Border but not their scorelines. They may remember Steve Waugh's tons at Headingley, but would more likely start with Ponting. Yet the contest still matters. Emotion transmits more readily than information. Even if you can't name a single player, it's the story of Australia sticking it to England, of England putting an upstart in its place.

In 2017 Cricket Australia funded an Ashes doco titled *Forged In Fire*, which is also the name of a History Channel show about mediaeval weapons. The latter features men with meticulous goatees saying things like 'I'm hoping that the judges will push my axe over the limit', and 'Alright gentlemen, let's go tell our bladesmiths'. The former features cricketers like Justin Langer and Matthew Hayden breathlessly describing the significance of playing England. Literally: their breath shortens, eyes widen, bodies quiver; this is the word 'tremulous' in practical application, a sort of emotional frottage.

The long heritage isn't what weighs on players; it's the heritage all rolled together to create a feeling, a vague and generalised sense of stature and grandeur and significance. Tied in with national pride, with identity, this is so potent its provenance becomes irrelevant, or becomes baggage slowing it down. Like any worship, it is insisted upon rather than spontaneous. Every voice speaks of sanctity until no one new dares question it. To do so would be to risk reprisal in the hall of zealots. So it passes down generations, and, while it's intense for England, it's more so for Australia, still the smaller party with a bigger point to prove.

Contradictorily, Australians have also developed a sense that we're inherently better. England lapsed into 1990s hopelessness – Phil Tufnell shelling catches, Mark Ramprakash wilting in the glare – where otherwise good cricketers became Australian bywords for mediocrity. But those lows only worsen the more recent Australian fear of losing. We were willing to forgive 2005 as a classic and a fluke: ok, you were plucky and lucky and scraped home against half a bowling attack. The 2006–07 whitewash was order restored. But when England doubled up on home wins in 2009, there was genuine dismay: this was not how it was supposed to be. And when the unthinkable happened – the rout on Boxing Day 2010, a home Ashes conceded with three innings defeats – Australian cricket lost its collective shit.

Even mixed with bravado, the compulsion to prove ourselves remains. Australian cricketers know the most important contest. They know it ends careers. Those not sacked can still be sapped, deflated, their sense of failure too acute. The 2010–11 loss finished off Tim Nielsen as coach, Ponting as captain, CA's board structure, and the playing days of Simon Katich, Doug Bollinger, Marcus North and Michael Beer. Mickey Arthur was knocked off as coach before 2013 even started, while 2015 was the end for five players with a sixth soon to follow.

So antipathy remains. Fervour gives way to fever. A month before commencing in late 2017, the atmosphere had got to David Warner. When he joined Jim Maxwell in Sydney for a pre-series interview, Warner was away. 'As soon as you step on that line it's war. You try and get into a battle as quick as you can. I try and look in the opposition's eyes and try and work out, how can I dislike this player? How can I get on top of him? You have to delve and dig deep into yourself to actually get some hatred about them to actually get up when you're out there. History is a big part in this and that is what carries us on to the ground.'

Our friend Jardine would have backed Warner's sentiment, even as they glared at one another with loathing. 'We have to hate them,' said England's captain in 1932. 'It's the only way we're going to beat them.'

A win is not enough. The Ashes became about obliteration. There's a fear that if you don't destroy your opponents they might find a way back. Those watching from the stands, me and you and Laughland, can play at aggression before retreating to friendliness. But for those prosecuting the conflict on our behalf, it's easy to see how this switching of gears becomes unaffordable luxury. Under conditions of such intensity and pressure, aggression is not the slightest surprise. And so, in the weeks leading up to a new edition, David Warner went to war.

Chapter 5

DAVID

Everyone thinks they have David Warner's measure. He's a meathead thug with no self-control, or a passionate top-bloke family man who would do anything for a mate. People don't think they have the answer because they don't think there's a question. He's a statement of the obvious, something you need only behold to understand. But somewhere a fake Einstein quote must say that the true mark of complexity is when something appears simple. Having covered the Australian team since his Test comeback in 2013, I'd call Warner one of the most complicated humans in cricket.

Some readers will find that hilarious, but hear it out. Three days before the 2018 South Africa series, Adam Collins and I recorded our podcast *The Final Word*. Warner was barely off the plane from New Zealand, yet happily sat down in Durban for a longform conversation about his demeanour, legacy, upbringing, and the prospect of going into public service. His answers were thoughtful and detailed. I wrote up a positive account.

Days later, on the field in the first Test, he exploded. Having run out AB de Villiers, Warner screamed until veins bulged out of his neck like a Schwarzenegger finale. His tirade was aimed at Aiden Markram, and rather than random abuse it was roasting the young batsman for having torched his senior partner. But the look was unhinged. The huddle of teammates around him gave less an impression of celebrating than restraining him – Warner struggling towards his opponent, still yelling, frothing upwards in the scrum of bodies with the effort – like they were trying to stop a Jack Russell from wriggling out a half-open car window.

The two episodes were a contrast like night lightning. People who've made up their minds about Warner will choose their side, seeing it as the truth that proves the lie of the other. The lie could be deliberate or a misunderstanding, a confection on his part to make himself look good or on mine to make him look bad. Either way, the subject of the debate is viewed as binary. But not all divisions are irreconcilable.

Warner is aggressive, impulsive and daft. He is thoughtful, curious and more intelligent than credited. He can be objectionable and wounding, then considerate and generous. He switches between these states according to slight shifts of the wind on internal seas, and can as easily invent a rationale to justify this afterwards as plot a logical course to arrive there in the first place. He might think these are words by some wanker who doesn't know him, or he might feel gratified at being understood. He might feel either or both depending on the day.

People dismiss him as an idiot for behaviour that could just as well reflect a complexity whirring behind the obvious.

My favourite description of him came from *The Guardian*'s Barney Ronay during that comeback in Manchester: 'Warner had looked bristlingly malevolent in his brief stay at the crease – but then his default setting is bristlingly malevolent: no doubt he potters around his local Tesco Metro bristling malevolently.' Cricket writers have since adopted 'bristling' as Warner's Homeric epithet, and why not, it fits him body and soul: the moustache you could scrub potatoes with, the compulsive yapping to anyone in earshot, the strut and bustle on the pitch, the pull shots like a Venus fly-trap snapping shut. The small and powerful frame, flesh packed so densely that the inside of his body seems to be straining the skin to get out, dynamo legs driving faster than should reasonably be allowed.

He bristled into international cricket in January 2009, a bullet-headed miniature with a spiky crew cut in a Twenty20. I was at the Melbourne Cricket Ground that night to watch this kid who had never played a first-class game walk to the middle in an Australian shirt. There's a stat so good it gets repeated whenever someone mentions that innings: Australia's first ever Test in 1877 was the only other time a player with no first-class record had turned out for a national team. Such anomalies were a matter of necessity in the slapdash world of colonial cricket, where teams were assembled using word-of-mouth recommendations of whichever players happened to be within reach of a telegram. Renewing the anomaly in the twenty-first century made a perfect origin story for a player who would never be conventional.

Cricket's new format created a new batch of pioneers making things up as they went along. The first edition of the Indian Premier League had finished seven months earlier. The state teams of Australian domestic cricket were three years from being shaken into fluorescent city avatars. The national team started out in 2005 treating T20 as a joke, playing the inaugural international against a New Zealand side in 1980s fancy dress while Glenn McGrath pretended to bowl underarm. Ricky Ponting made 98 not out and hated every minute of it. Four years later, Warner was the next experiment, a new kind of player for a new style.

Dale Steyn was at his peak, lightning fast. Makhaya Ntini and Jacques Kallis were already South African greats. Johan Botha and Albie Morkel would go on to play more than 500 T20s between them. Warner destroyed them all. That early stage of his evolution was about dumping everything into the leg side. A swivel, a closure of the hips, and he would snap across the line to pace, sometimes dropping to one knee against spin. There was occasional nuance – a standard leg glance, and a shorter ball down the same line that saw Warner catch up, close the face to leg, and gently trampoline it off the full blade over backward square for six. There was one foreshadowing of his future when he opened the face and chopped behind point. But mostly there was pure on-side violence, as he carnaged everything into the stands so hard he made a verb out of it. It only ended, in a moment of symmetry that would become apparent in 2018, in the hands of AB de Villiers.

It was so much fun. This guy was a curiosity, a nobody plucked from nowhere, yet here he was demolishing the best in the world. It was like getting pulled up from the front row at a concert only to shred the solo. The fact he kept his cool was astonishing. There were 60,000 people there and he'd probably never played in front of 600. He departed to a standing ovation at the largest ground in the country, having scored 89 from 43 balls. There was no sense he would still be wearing the number 31 on his back in a decade's time, but in the moment everyone wanted a piece. The crowd wanted to see more, the commentators wanted to know where he'd been, and the administrators wanted to know when they could get him playing next.

Journalists hunted the background story. Peter Lalor, chief cricket writer at *The Australian*, knows the heart and pulse of Sydney better than just about anyone. He explained Warner's area to the uninitiated after driving south to meet this new sensation's family.

It's hardscrabble there. To the east is Maroubra beach. Outsiders surf the waves at their own peril for the Bra Boys are territorial and violent. Graffiti on an outflow pipe and the cliffs announces this area is for 'locals only'. To the west are the industrial container terminals of Botany Bay and low-flying planes landing at Mascot airport.

Matraville is an odd space, caught in the middle, a former soldier settlement that's too far from the beach, too far from town and too down at the heel to have been caught up by the gentrification along the rest of the Eastern Suburbs. This pocket between the jail, the rifle ranges, the beach and the docks remains flint-eyed, wary and waiting for something better to happen. ['Generation Warner', *The Cricket Monthly*, May 2015.]

Something already was for Warner: his first IPL deal had landed via the Delhi Daredevils even before his Australian debut, though his night out at the MCG meant he arrived at the Feroz Shah Kotla in April with a lot more clout. By the end of 2009, with that first season's cheque in the bank, his brother, Steve, rocked up to a second-grade game at Chatswood Oval driving a white Range Rover – the kind of car worth well north of a hundred grand – with the customised plates DW31.

It was Ferris Bueller time: life moves pretty fast. 'As a kid I had to do everything at home with my brother, because my parents worked all the time,' Warner recalled on the podcast. 'All the normal things, dishes, ironing. And once I was able to work, I went and worked, because we needed that money to pay the bills.' Australia's public flats are not the Harlem projects, and Warner doesn't inflate a hard-knocks narrative, saying his childhood was no-frills but lacked nothing important. While he wasn't in the so-called pathway as early as some, he was playing for New South Wales by Under-17s, made the Under-19 World Cup squad, and scored a state rookie contract. But it was still a cricket upbringing of harder scrabble than most, and that Matraville flintiness remained.

One illustration was as funny as it was instructive. When I interviewed a range of people in Sydney grade cricket, three players with no connection nominated Warner as the second-worst sledger they had ever encountered. Of course I asked who came first. 'Steve Warner,' they all replied without hesitation. It wasn't a punchline. David's brother had a reputation of being even looser in behavioural matters, and others who saw him play think he was more naturally talented too. The whole family was involved at Easts Cricket Club, with parents Howard and Lorraine volunteering in the canteen. The tenet for both sons was that you played as hard as you could, and there was never any doubt this included ripping into opponents on the pitch.

Ultimately, those Sydney players subscribed to the maxim that all's fair as long as you have a beer at the end of the day. But it's mandatory to call someone 'a lovely bloke' after criticism, and it's notable that they recall Warner's on-field angst as standing out. As described by its targets, his sledging was blunt force and relentless. The soundtrack to your day at the crease was a stream of slurs so limited in variety they could have formed a kind of Morse code. 'At least,' smiled one respondent, 'you had no doubt whether he thought you were a cunt.' Fitting that *The Kaboom Kid* books – the sponsored children's series about good-natured Little Davey whose most creative aspect is crediting Warner as the author – are listed as both 'juvenile' and 'fiction'.

This was the player unleashed on Test cricket in 2011. His first captain, Michael Clarke, encouraged and defended his approach. His on-field angst blossomed, then outgrew the boundary line; by May 2013 he was brawling on Twitter with old-school journos Crash Craddock and Malcolm Conn, and in June he lamped England batsman Joe Root on the chin while hammered six ways from Sunday in a Birmingham trash palace. Luckily the alcohol that inspired the punch also rendered it ineffective. With the Ashes looming, Warner was suspended and his coach Mickey Arthur was sacked, Cricket Australia deciding Arthur lacked control of the team. His replacement, Darren Lehmann, would go on to make that a virtue.

Lehmann was as supportive as Clarke – fair enough, since Warner had got him the job. 'We can't control what's happened in the past,' said Lehmann sagely, while promising 'very much so a clean slate.' Warner went to Zimbabwe for a reserve tour, smashed 193 against South Africa A, and had a running verbal brawl with wicketkeeper Thami Tsolekile. Steve Warner hopped in with his own brand of help, firing shots on Twitter at his brother's teammates, at CA, and to defend Arthur as having been an 'escape goat'. David was back for the Manchester Test having missed all of two games, and back in his preferred opening spot by the second innings. He made 41 there, 71 in Durham, and was a first-choice player from then on.

His Chatswood Oval spirit thrived through the 2013–14 Ashes, including a press-conference swipe that Jonathan Trott was 'scared' and 'weak' before the England batsman quit the tour with a mental health issue. Warner was backing up the talk with runs now, and carried both on to South Africa, including twin tons at Cape Town. 'That was definitely the most abuse we've got on the cricket field,' said de Villiers of the series. 'Australia made a conscious effort to be verbally over the top.' After Faf du Plessis described the Australians as swarming batsmen like 'a pack of dogs', Warner literally barked him off the field when next dismissed. As for the beer-at-the-end-of-the-day rule, the South Africans declined a post-series refreshment. Less than a year later, in January 2015, Warner snarled at India's Rohit Sharma to 'speak English' during a multilingual argument, showing no awareness afterwards of its racist connotations. The late Kiwi batting master Martin Crowe jumped on Cricinfo to give what might be the strongest blast from any former player to a current one.

> Warner can play, but he is the most juvenile cricketer I have seen on a cricket field. I don't care how good he is: if he continues to show all those watching that he doesn't care, he must be removed, either by Cricket Australia or definitely by the world governing body. The more he gets away with it, the more others will follow his pitiful actions. Already we see one or two of his team-mates enjoying being close to his hideous energy.
>
> What must the talk be in the opposition dressing rooms about how to combat this daily occurrence? Do you stand up for yourself when confronted with Warner's spit and expletives or do you turn a blind eye? I dread to think, and it shouldn't be a choice. The officials must step in now. ['Why cricket needs yellow and red cards', Cricinfo, January 2015.]

The problem was, other people did care how good he was. CA boss James Sutherland gave one of many scoldings: 'He has worked very hard on his leadership and behaviour over the past twelve months and I have told him very clearly that instances like this only serve to set back the progress he has made. Quite simply, he needs to stop looking for trouble.' But his coach Lehmann gave one of many shrugs: 'David's an aggressive character and we support that … We've got to make sure we play hard but fair, and don't cross the line. We're always going to teeter pretty close to it, that's just the way we play.'

Plenty of authority figures had failed to make Warner listen. Sutherland's deputy, Michael Brown, had personally booted

Warner out of the Australian Cricket Academy in 2008 for ill-discipline, yet when Brown rang in 2009 about Warner's T20 selection the batsman didn't remember who he was. We're talking a master of stubbornness: go back to the story of the junior coach who made him bat right-handed for a season to limit his attacking shots, or Greg Chappell repeatedly kicking him out of the nets for Australia A because he wouldn't stop slogging. In the end Warner was so good that people let things slide. After his right-handed foray he reverted to the left and broke the club's season record. On that A tour, nets or not, he smashed 341 runs in three innings, including a knock of 82 off 57 balls. He was out stumped.

Around the Rohit stoush, though, things off the field were changing. In September 2014, Warner's daughter Ivy Mae was born. In April 2015, in the narrow window between the World Cup and the IPL, he married Candice Falzon. And between those joyous, life-affirming events, he saw his close friend Phillip Hughes die. Hughes was batting for South Australia in November 2014 when a bouncer struck him in the neck, with Warner a few metres away in the New South Wales slip cordon. The vision of Hughes staggering and falling is imprinted on the memory of anyone who saw the broadcast, so one can only imagine how it lives on with the friends and teammates who saw it first-hand.

That impact isn't often considered. Warner, Shane Watson, Nathan Lyon and Brad Haddin all had to carry on in the Australian team. They had to keep playing at the SCG, standing in the middle where it happened. We've seen Warner touch Hughes's bronze plaque as he goes out to bat, and gesture in acknowledgement when he reaches his friend's final score of 63. Before the Adelaide Test a week after Hughes's funeral, Warner found himself unable to train, unsure whether he was spooked by being hit or overcome with grief. When Australia won the toss he smashed seven boundaries from his first fifteen balls, saluted the sky on 63, and went on to twin hundreds in an emotionally fraught match. He also got fined by the match referee for a fight with Virat Kohli and Shikhar Dhawan.

That summer, former New Zealand fast bowler Iain O'Brien posited that Warner's blow-ups might be linked to PTSD. But the batsman was no more antagonistic than he had been through his career. It's more likely that grief influenced him in the opposite direction, even if it took a while to filter through his system. By the time Warner arrived for a tour of the West Indies in late May 2015, with his wedding and another successful IPL behind him, a shift had taken place. Or at least he forced one by committing to it publicly.

Before the Tests he announced he'd quit drinking – a significant move for a renowned pisshead. After a subdued period on the field he confirmed he'd quit sledging too. His canine side, he implied, had been urged by senior personnel: 'In the past I've been someone who's been told to go out there and do this and do that, but at the end of the day I've got to look after myself … If I don't want to be that instigator, I don't have to be that instigator.' Lehmann and Clarke smacked this down, insisting Warner had always instigated his instigation. At the very least, though, their constant backing and defending implied approval.

Warner wasn't just quiet on the field. Teammates on that West Indies tour say he all but refused to speak to them for the duration. He hinted at it himself, citing self-preservation: 'In the everyday world, everyone knows that sitting down and having a conversation with someone can be draining and energy-sapping.' It was bizarre nonetheless for colleagues who were suddenly being blanked in hotel hallways. You could never say Warner didn't commit.

He stayed quiet in England in 2015, both with willow and tonsils – he made a fifty in each Test, but the first four came when matches were all but decided. Runs piled up in season 2015–16, with a fast double-hundred in Perth and two hundreds in Brisbane. The latter was a rare feat: Ponting and Sunil Gavaskar were the only other batsmen to make twin tons on three occasions. By now Warner was vice-captain and voicing concomitant responsibility: 'Now that my daughter's one year of age, I've got to set an example and be a role model to her. So I've got to calm down a little bit.' His second daughter, Indi Rae, was born in January 2016, and that year Warner went on to make seven One-Day International centuries, cracking the code of the 50-over format that had been his least comfortable for Australia.

This included captaining in Sri Lanka while Smith rested. Here Warner showed what he could do as leader, his relentlessly upbeat approach turning the tour around after a Test whitewash. On rough tracks they won four of five one-dayers and both T20s. Under Smith, Glenn Maxwell had been pushed to the national fringes and hadn't made the ODI squad. For the T20s Warner chose him to open, perhaps sympathetic to another pigeonholed attacking player. Maxwell blitzed Sri Lanka by batting through an innings for 145 not out, then creamed 66 from 29 balls to knock off a chase on his own.

By the time the ODI team travelled to South Africa that October, Warner had gone full Reverend. Having added meditation and mindfulness regimes to his sobriety, he was extolling the approach of life coach John Novak, who had told him to respond to any negative thought or comment with three affirmative ones. 'It's more about being a bit more positive and proactive, taking a more positive approach on everything I do, and trying to negate the negative stuff around and conserving energy for processing while you're out there in the heat of the battle and getting your job done, and being grateful for everything we've got,' he said, laying this on his teammates forcibly enough to earn his preacher nickname. As ever, his approach to behavioural patterns was headlong.

Australia lost that series, and again to South Africa in the late 2016 Tests at home. Warner made decent runs, then a big hundred against Pakistan on Boxing Day, and another before lunch on the first day in Sydney. The latter feat put him on another rarefied batting list, joining Bradman, Victor Trumper, Charlie Macartney and Majid Khan. 'The mystique around centuries in a session is well established, but rarest of all is the first session of a Test,' wrote Collins.

The innings illustrated how Warner's batting had evolved. Where his wham-bam T20 debut had been sixes in the slog zone, his hundred runs on this day came almost entirely through point. His technique had been moving this way for a while: getting up on the balls of his feet, riding the bounce, chopping square on the off side. A misread shot would get a single, a timed one would get a boundary. If the bowler pitched fuller he could come forward and lash through cover. Wider, he could steady and flay the square drive. Shorter, he could lean back and uppercut over slip. But even on that decent length, where Test bowlers try to spend most of their time, he could milk or punish the slightest error in width all day. 'It's hardly a shot kids will dream of playing,' ran Collins's report, 'but it is where Warner makes his money.'

That was Warner's start to 2017. Like a true disciple of meditation, the great self-believer had done away with ego. Everything was falling in place, even Pakistan's bowling. Making money was the least of his worries. In the second half of that year he cleared his final technical hurdle: he had never been awful in Asian conditions but only made middling scores, never entirely sure how to tackle serious spin. Against Bangladesh in August he found a method, scoring centuries in back-to-back Tests against Tigers who were newly ferocious at home.

Before that tour came the episode that could have been the defining one of Warner's career: his advocacy in the pay dispute between Australia's cricketers and managers. While this was distorted in some quarters as greedy athletes wanting more cash, the international players at the top of the financial pile had nothing to gain. The lower end of the domestic scene was supposed to miss out. The most privileged needed to stick up for the least powerful. Top players knew they would cop grief for speaking out, but didn't flinch. Plenty did their part, but it was Warner who effectively acted as the shop steward in a union brawl. The problem child couldn't have acted as more of a leader.

But it was never as simple as a Bull-to-Reverend redemption. Warner had always had good aspects on show. Like that comeback Test at Old Trafford, when he spent the whole match being barracked by the crowd for punching Root, especially when he muffed a video review in his first innings. He regarded this as fair penance, as did Clarke in stationing him in the deep. 'He has gone some way towards winning over the locals by accepting and even relishing their raucous abuse, whether shadow boxing on the boundary or applauding a rendition of the theme from Rocky,' Andy Wilson reported.

'I'm not well liked at the moment but this morning was quite entertaining down there,' said Warner when he was put up for a press conference. 'I had a little chuckle. It's not every day you walk out on the field and get booed. But you've got to embrace it. Obviously it was all my fault. I know what I did was a terrible thing.' He smiled genially throughout and when asked about the catch that ended his innings, he had the perfect response. 'Yeah, hooked another one to Rooty,' he said to surprised laughter. 'Of all the people on the field. It was quite comical. I'll just wait to read Twitter a bit later.' Partly it was good PR, but you felt the thermostat in the room rise a few degrees.

When asked about anything technical, Warner's eyes light up and he tucks into his answer. He discusses tactics and how he can counter them with positioning and shot selection. He's deeply engaged with his game and relishes detail. Plenty of sportsmen are unfairly served by the assumption of stupidity, but there are some where the stereotype fits. Warner isn't one of them – in person, an intelligence burns within.

Of course there are areas where he's uneducated, but he's aware of those shortcomings and the work it would take to address them. When a topic interests Warner he locks on and won't let go. He lacks some tools but no curiosity. During a night out, meeting a journalist who'd worked in finance, Warner gave an hour-long grilling then got on the phone to his adviser. He's interested in Indigenous disadvantage in his area of Sydney, and jumped at community service trips to the Northern Territory during his 2018 suspension. People he's met through charity work or coaching clinics speak of him glowingly. He could still emerge as an effective advocate or campaigner – whether for good or ill depends on which ideas grab him first.

And among all this the negatives remain. In mid 2017, Warner was playing the wise old man. 'We all go through periods when young and naive,' he told Ali Martin through the confessional grille of *The Guardian*. 'It's not about stuffing up and moving on, it's about learning the ropes of being away on tour for such a long period of time. There are things you have to think about as a youngster: "What can or can't I do?" I probably didn't work that out at that stage but now I have and have a great balance on and off the field.' In November, three weeks before the Ashes, he whispered contritely to Nick Hoult of *The Telegraph*, 'I had stuff going on in my life that was inexcusable.' By this stage, he'd already spoken of hatred and war to Jim Maxwell and made a decision to get ugly again. Even to Hoult he sent up a warning flare. 'You will see the same person you have seen before. I will be out there giving my all. If I need to get out there and have some verbal banter, then I will be on it.'

The Ashes, of course, had come round again. A home series. The first since Johnson played the bruiser so convincingly that talk became irrelevant. An enforcer, to Australian thinking, was required. Matthew Wade was on his way out, the punchy wicketkeeper innately associated with verbals. Senior players felt they needed to take up the bedraggled chirp mantle. Lyon tried some trash talk, which fitted his character about as well as a mesh singlet. With some encouragement behind the scenes, Warner took it on himself once more.

'I was surprised,' said Maxwell of the salvo. 'But then I thought, that's David Warner. People get used to him, and the belligerent, bellicose statements in the way he deals with the game.' Warner was scolded, especially in the British press, as violent, confrontational, lacking perspective, offending veterans and whatever else you can think of. He rightly identified a double standard: *The Cricketer* magazine filled its Ashes preview cover with 'LET BATTLE COMMENCE', while in 2013 England captain Alastair Cook had received no censure for saying 'On the pitch it's pretty much a war'. In our podcast interview, Warner recounted doing some research to back up his grievance.

It was amazing, because I went to Google and typed in 'war'. And I looked up numerous sports stars, actors, and everything who have used the same terms in everyday stuff. It was just a beaten up thing, which is as normal.

But for me it was about how I go about my business. You have to be in the zone. What gets me up and going is a little bit of banter. It's not just an Ashes series, but the talk and the hype around Ashes. You are always going to say something in the media. That's what I love doing. What is it? The pantomime villain. If you want to be that person, you want to be. And that's me. I love that in that series. And I'll do it again if I get selected in the pending Ashes series next year.

That curious mix. Wounded dignity, self-justification, unfair malignment, mixed in a highball with the smug glee of annoying people. Clarke had said the same about playing villains in 2013. 'He loves it. He's got that aggressive approach. He won't take a step back.' The sense of injustice was a preferred fuel. The man who stood up for others in the pay dispute has been called a bully more times than one can count. And it's true: Warner targets opponents when they're outnumbered and goes harder as his team gets on top. If there's one thing bullies love, it's righteousness. They always know the rules. Find a technicality to claim they've been wronged and they can guard their own sins from interrogation: a pre-emptive strike against being held accountable.

'He has an unshakeable faith in himself,' wrote Lalor in 2015, 'at times admirable, but which at others makes him seem surly and immature like a teenager. He is, as anyone who has argued with him will discover, never wrong. If forced to a public act of contrition he will whisper moral relativisms and resentments in private.' If Warner ever felt bad about punching Root, it passed. Soon he was pushing around a story that Root had made a racist gesture, and insisting the punch had barely made contact, and blaming the repercussions on the sneaky British press. Attacking England in 2017 just needed a new set of justifications.

The Ashes can be toxic. The prospect of the series drove Warner slightly mad, or at least sang the songs to draw his madder aspect from its cave. It was as pointless as ever: 'Anyone else find this pre-Ashes trash-the-opposition talk childish? In cricket there is only ever one contest, and that is on the field,' sighed Indian commentator Harsha Bhogle. But Warner was as good as his word, snapping and snarling through his next two Test series from home shores to Durban. 'The way that we celebrate or other people celebrate should never be questioned, I don't think,' was how he brushed off distaste at his de Villiers froth-show. 'We were excited, it's a big moment in the game.' As ever in the sledging debate, the only view that mattered was from inside the Australian team.

So you're back to the same dilemma. The Warner who wants to build up teammates, or the Warner who wants to tear down opponents? Here's Warner shaping up for fisticuffs in a stairwell. Here's Warner laughing with the Dalai Lama as His Holiness honks Frank Dimasi's nose. The rap sheet speaks for itself. But the things he said on the podcast were also true, in that while he was saying them he believed every word. One truth doesn't make all else false.

'I've spent plenty of years on Warner's trail since that drive to Matraville in 2009 and can vouch that he is not wired like anyone else,' wrote Lalor. The reality is that Australia's most controversial modern player is not two sides of a coin. He's more like a handful of twelve-sided dice. Any combination of facets could be true. Any of it could change in an instant. All of those possibilities are simultaneous. He probably knows as little about them as anyone.

Chapter 6

BRISBANE

For a minute there, everything was going beautifully for England.

Starting a series in Brisbane isn't easy on the nerves. This was the 60th Test at the Gabba ground, of which Australia had lost eight. The most recent was when the West Indies used to be good, in 1988. England captain Nasser Hussain had his horror show in 2002 when he asked Australia to bat and they made a million. There was no question what his 2017 successor Joe Root would do when he won the toss. Grand old Alastair Cook, the most prolific opening batsman in the history of the game, was to stand tall at the top of the order and shepherd his inexperienced teammates through the trials of an opening day.

Plan A failed in ten minutes. Plans B through Z were heavy on a cross-your-fingers, thoughts-and-prayers approach. Having run out of batsmen, England selectors had been forced to punt on some names from county cricket. Three of the top five got picked that way for the toughest tour on their calendar. But after Mitchell Starc gave the shepherd an early exit, the sheep set about herding themselves.

Mark Stoneman was the other opener, a gently bearded left-hander of that stocky ginger type that emerges good-naturedly from the northern reaches of England. Cook's dismissal ushered in James Vince, a right-hander of darker beard and paler aspect. Between them they had ten Tests, a scratchy handful of runs, an average of 23, and had never ventured past the foggy shores of home. If they were carrying the hopes of a nation, it was only expected to be as far as the next corner.

Four Starc deliveries after Cook edged an outswinger, Vince strode into a drive to the boundary. Having calmed a few nerves, he settled into an innings whose theme stroke would not be the cover drive for four, but for three. Vince hit this repeatedly, reining himself in to avoid a miscue to slip, punching circumspectly into the gap, collecting his score by legwork rather than backlift. Stoneman crouched low and drove through midwicket when the straighter ball arrived, in the manner of the unglamorous southpaws of cricket past. When he was bowled for 53 on the stroke of tea, the lynchpin Root occupied the other end without fuss.

It seemed, if they dared to say it, easy. Vince was on 83, the cricket gods on his side, a hitherto undreamt-of hundred within reach to define an Ashes series on the first day. Then Nathan Lyon happened.

'In hindsight I wouldn't take the run,' was Vince's submission to the 2017 Statement of the Obvious Awards. His tap to cover was regulation. The single was tight but regulation. Australia had left a gap to encourage an edge. Their attacking field got a wildcard bonus.

Lyon has never offered the most poetic cricketing vision. He jangles about the field like a sack full of coathangers, angles protruding from his whites that human anatomy should not allow. But he moves well, deceptively fast and with mousetrap reflexes.

When you watch this moment back, he's on the move from point before the ball is struck. Vince's shot bounces twice on the infield turf. It sits up at cover for Lyon to swoop and gather in his right hand, low to the ground. He's bent down, off balance, on his left foot while snaring the ball and cocking his right arm in the same motion. Vince is neglecting what batsmen have been taught forever: head turned to his right, he's watching Lyon rather than laying down the full-burner sprint that would soonest make his ground. It shouldn't matter. If Lyon takes one more step to reach the ball, or one more step to steady, Vince will be fine.

Lyon doesn't.

He lands on his right foot. Aiming at the non-striker's end, which means that rather than a natural motion swinging his arm back across his ribcage as he runs right, he has to throw in the same direction he's running, twisting to the side to line up the two stumps he can see. 'If you think about where the momentum's going,' Ricky Ponting analysed later, 'when you start your throw, you can't start it at the stumps, you've got to start it on the left-hand side because the momentum takes the ball towards the stumps.'

Lyon's elbow splays, forearm moving out from his body in a flat half-circle, wrist snapping behind the ball. It is a deeply awkward action. On the replays, Vince's face is a ghostly oval framed by black. He passes Hazlewood, who is turning gradually in his bowling follow-through with canine excitement, invisible ears pricking.

Finally, the Vince forever trapped in digital amber realises his trouble, turning his head where it should have been all along. He gets in one more step. The ball bounces. He strains every hamstring sinew for a second stride at exactly the moment when he should be diving, but he hasn't set up his gait to dive. He knows he should have started faster, gone harder. Eyes fixed on the place where he should be, he sees the far stump rock back like it's winding up for a throw itself. The lights ignite, the ball ricochets, and while umpire Aleem Dar hasn't had time to get remotely side-on, he smiles and squints and nods knowingly at Lyon, the response of a man who has just witnessed an outrageous trick shot on his local pool table.

Vince was gracious in disappointment: 'He bowled pretty well, he deserved something from the day.' Lyon had, extracting far more turn than day one at the Gabba should allow. He could have had Vince on 68 had Tim Paine held a thick outside edge. But grace couldn't diminish significance. From 2–145 with a set batsman approaching a century, England were hauled back to 302 all out before lunch on the second day. Dawid Malan, the third new batsman, chipped in with 56, but slow scoring contained the damage. The visitors had blown a chance of 400 and a dominant position. The home side –

players and selectors foremost, supporters second – heaved a sigh of relief.

It dissipated when Australia batted. Cameron Bancroft nicked Stuart Broad, Usman Khawaja's pad was nailed by Moeen Ali's off-break, Warner holed out on the flip-pull that had brought him undone in the past, and Handscomb was trapped by Anderson. The score was 4–76, trailing by 226, and trouble loomed like a Queensland thunderhead.

Such was the situation when Smith's epic began. When the fourth wicket went down the captain had been batting for fourteen overs. He would stay in the middle for another 106, from after lunch on the second day to the final hour of the evening on the third, remaining unbeaten as his last teammate fell. He would take his score of 19 on to 141, facing 326 balls in the process.

The numbers, the pace, the strike rate of 43, were due to a pitch nothing like the Gabba, whose normal range is trampoline to runway. In a seasonal rarity Brisbane had seen weeks of cool weather. The Women's Ashes match at Allan Border Field had fluked one dry day after a fortnight of downpour. The Test wicket had sweated and stewed under covers, and there was little that curator Kevin Mitchell Jr could do for his farewell surface. It was spongy and tacky, the ball sticking and popping up. For less-than-express seamers like Anderson, Broad and Jake Ball, it came through slowly. You might mistime attacking strokes but avoiding them meant safety. So Smith did: eschewing risk, denying himself, tonguing over and over the mantra of patience, patience, patience.

Shaun Marsh kept him company through the long session to stumps, similarly circumspect bar the odd lash through the off side. He showed the risk of attack next morning, playing full and wide where instinct urged the cover drive. Broad rolled his fingers so the ball plugged in the surface. It caught Marsh through the shot early and lobbed to mid-off. He'd made 51, but Australia still trailed by 127.

If Smith's resolve needed strengthening that did the trick. He glanced one boundary in the session. After lunch he on-drove the occasional one that was full and straight. No matter how long England spent banging the ball in short with catchers out, he swayed away like seaweed in a current. He held back from anything in the channel outside off stump. England went through every option. Their bowling was accurate and admirable. They tried patience, then increasingly funky fields, changing lines of attack, back to wearing away in the channel. Throwing in the odd light-sabre flourish on his leave, Smith continued to Jedi them out of the contest.

With Australia 93 behind, out came Patrick Cummins batting at nine. The 24-year-old had been vital on day one. He'd ripped through Stoneman to end the partnership with Vince at 125. He'd moved the ball again to trap England's captain and best player before stumps. He got the dangerous wicketkeeper Jonny Bairstow next morning. Six years after his debut in South Africa, Cummins was finally playing his first Test at home. But the occasion didn't get to him. He looked every inch the batsman rather than the lower-order enthusiast, matching Smith's organised defence and adding a touch more attack.

He made 42 of the pair's 66, while Smith's hundred arrived with a rare cover drive through a packed field. For once it wasn't stonkingly hot. Brisbane's summer is fetid, an overripe mango whose seed is about to sprout, and the humidity was evident from Smith's sweat-drenched hair. But under heavy cloud the max in the middle reached 26 degrees. The flipside was that the bowlers stayed fresher, so Smith kept waiting them out with suffocating patience.

When Cummins finally edged after 32 overs, Smith allowed himself a few cut shots and aerial adventures with Hazlewood and Lyon. His flurry took Australia from 27 runs behind to 26 in front, his first Ashes innings as captain unbeaten. England were dying inside. They'd outfoxed each top-order batsman but one. Removing him early would have halved Australia's score of 328. Asked at stumps what the performance meant, Smith said simply, 'Everything.'

Test matches are often decided by how players respond to frustration, rather than by the performance that frustrated them. At Adelaide in 2013 Cook failed in the first innings, spent two days in the field, then impulsively hooked Ryan Harris to fine leg for 3. Brisbane this time followed the same pattern, ending with the exact same dismissal off Hazlewood for 7. Both times it showed a player whose decision-making was baked.

The sun dipped into the gap between cloud and horizon to smother the ground in orange molasses. Australia's quicks gave it everything. Bouncers flew. Good-length balls zipped past the edge until Hazlewood left Vince a squared-up, tangle-footed mess. England were two down and still in deficit. Starc clattered

Root in the helmet, the batsman jumping and ducking and fending all in one as the ball smashed chunks of protective gear loose. The Australians checked on his health then resumed the assult. On *The Final Word*, BBC commentator Daniel Norcross described the passage.

In that last hour and a quarter of the third day, when England found themselves batting and it was getting dark, and Cummins, Hazlewood, Starc were flying in to Mark Stoneman in his first Test in Australia, and England lost two quick wickets – he and Root batted for about forty-five or fifty minutes before the close of play, and it was spellbinding. I got to commentate the last twenty-five minutes, and the hairs on my arms were standing up. The noises at the Gabbatoir, the speed of the bowling, the intensity of the competition. The fact that it was the first Test and both sides had been at each other. At that stage, we had a really good Ashes series. It was the most exhilarating cricket I've ever been involved in.

The pair pushed on in the morning, but Stoneman edged Lyon for 27, and Malan the same for four. The three newbies had gone in a row, unable to back up their first attempts. Hopes lay with Root, but his pretty half-century ended as he raised it – Hazlewood again. Moeen's bright 40 would be his best for the tour, ending in an unlucky stumping when the crease line gained some lunchtime weight in being repainted. That gave Lyon three of England's left-handers, having gobbled up lefties over the previous couple of years at an average of 14.

Starc and Cummins unleashed a bouncer barrage at the tail, while Bairstow became flustered and played a ramp to Handscomb at third man. The last four wickets fell for ten runs, England had made 195, and a target of 170 was not enough on a track that was still improving.

After nine opening partners in Warner's career, Bancroft was the new man on the dance floor. The chase gave an insight into their relationship. With 34 overs left on the fourth day, the Warner of old would never have resisted launching after 170 by stumps and having an extra day off. Or at least, had he resumed in the morning with 60 to his name and 56 runs to win, he would have smashed his hundred while his partner blocked out the other end. What better way to win a Test than raining sixes on the crowd?

Instead he did neither, dragging out the innings to give Bancroft time at the crease. Warner wanted to get the new player comfortable in the middle, then to have the experience of being not out overnight and restarting the next day. The match pressure was gone, and England's bowlers were obliged to provide a high-quality net session. In five separate overs on the fifth morning, Warner took a single from the first ball and gave his partner strike. In four other overs it was the second ball, and in three it was the third. Bancroft swelled in confidence, finishing with a trio of boundaries. The new buddies were not out on 82 and 87, all simpatico, Warner not even flirting with three figures. The Bull had taken the calf into his herd.

England had been in the hunt, but twice a commanding position had slipped away. It took until the fourth morning, their second turn with the bat, before the match followed suit. 'It was the closest ten-wicket win I have ever seen,' said Norcross, smiling but serious, 'and I don't think there'll ever be a closer ten-wicket win.' One man and a couple of supporting hands had stood between England and ascendancy, then had taken it for their own.

Chapter 7

HEADBUTTING THE LINE

While the Brisbane Test unfolded, another plot line was running alongside. Part of it was comedy but another part was uglier. After play on day five, Jonny Bairstow made a statement before the usual press conferences with England captain Root and coach Trevor Bayliss. Smith and Bancroft were next, as per custom – the winning captain plus a notable player. But questions for Bancroft had little to do with his 82 runs, a score he would never top before his suspension in Cape Town.

Instead Bancroft was asked about news from the previous evening. Neroli Meadows, the Fox Sports reporter who breaks more stories than most, had reported that Bairstow had 'connected his head with the side of Cam Bancroft's head' at a Perth nightclub weeks before the Test. Stump mics had picked up Australian fieldsmen – or one, at least – berating Bairstow.

Modern cricketers know when they're in mic range, so it looked like a deliberate way to get the story out. Someone had also briefed out follow-up details: Meadows had the location, the context, the teams and people involved.

Her careful phrasing was abandoned by other outlets. 'Cameron Bancroft was allegedly attacked by Jonny Bairstow', ran a photo caption from Sydney's *Daily Telegraph* for an article saying he had 'launched an unprovoked headbutt'. It was equated to an incident with which we're familiar: 'Australian opener David Warner was famously banned for two matches for a similarly minor confrontation with England player Joe Root at a Birmingham bar four years ago.' Lalor took the same slant, saying Bancroft's comrades 'only found out this week and were incensed after a similar scuffle saw Dave Warner disciplined', while generously concluding that Warner had 'stayed out of trouble since'.

But for Bairstow there had been no fight, no confrontation, not a displeased word. There had been a soused man in a pub greeting another soused man in a pub with one of those forehead-bumps that rugby players or American college students use to vent excess testosterone before stabbing a can of beer with their keys. It was, conceded Cricinfo correspondent George Dobell, 'an almost inexplicably strange greeting, it is true. Unless, perhaps, you are a stag.' But he put it down to Bairstow being 'a well-meaning, likeable but perhaps slightly socially awkward fellow. Think of Alan Partridge trying to fit in'. Bairstow's manly bonding attempt had clunked harder than intended – presumably not aided by the 'ridiculously delicious cocktails' advertised by the venue – at which point he apologised and they carried on drinking. It was a non-event. At least until Bancroft had mentioned it during the Test and someone had seen it as ammunition.

England already had an image problem thanks to all-rounder and IPL millionaire Ben Stokes punching on with strangers in a Bristol street a month before the Ashes. The worst part of the story may have been his choice of venue – Mbargo is the kind of nightclub dive that keeps the Red Bull trade afloat, and Stokes had left at 2 am in exactly the state required to tolerate the joint for more than half a minute. His drunken punching was as precise as Warner's, but he threw a lot more and the ones he landed did some damage. In Australia, a social rejection of street fights had been drilled into public consciousness after a string of one-punch deaths, especially in cricket since former Australia player David Hookes was killed by a security guard outside a Melbourne pub. Stokes and the question of when England might reinstate him created a point of ongoing angst and let Australians assume a position of moral superiority.

Bairstow's story therefore needed clarifying. Unfortunately Bairstow wasn't the man for the job. 'We were just in the bar having a good laugh and a good evening out, it was very enjoyable. Cameron and I enjoyed the evening and continued to do so. There was no intent nor malice about anything during the evening.' All those words, yet no hint of what had actually happened. 'I think Jonny's been very clear about that,' said Root. *Brrrrp,* incorrect. It was up to Bancroft at his first press event, facing a room of reporters and photographers whirring and tapping away. Ben Horne for the Murdoch tabloids cut to the chase. 'I remember it very clearly,' Bancroft answered, trying to control a smile. 'We'd just won a Shield game for WA and one of our values is to celebrate success.' A euphemism for a bunch of cricketers getting shitfaced: it was funny already.

BANCROFT: At the same time that coincided with the English team arriving in Perth for the tour game. It was very friendly mingling the whole night. Some of our players knew some of the English players. As the night progressed, it was great to be able to meet some of those guys. I got into a very amicable conversation with Jonny and yeah, he just greeted me with a headbutt kind of thing. I was expecting a handshake, it wasn't the greeting of choice I was expecting. That was the way that I took it, there was certainly no malice in his actions and we continued having very good conversation for the rest of the evening.

HORNE: Did he apologise to you that night or subsequently?

BANCROFT: Obviously at the time he said sorry. For me personally, it was just really weird. It was so random, I certainly didn't expect it coming. A handshake or a hug would have been something I would have expected more than a headbutt. But as I said, there was certainly nothing malicious about his actions. I just took it as – I don't know Jonny Bairstow, but he says hello to people very differently to most others. As I said, we got along for the rest of the night quite well. I let it go and moved on from it. It was fine.

Tom Collomosse from *The Evening Standard* wasn't having any more vagueness, nor Mike Colman from *The Courier-Mail*. We wanted a goddamn diagram.

COLLOMOSSE: I realise this sounds a bit ridiculous but did he headbutt you like that [accompanied by a Liverpool kiss mime], straight forward, or like that [makes a little nudge] – because we can't actually work out what happened.

BANCROFT: Whatever your imagination pictures it as is probably what it would be. I didn't wake up –

COLLOMOSSE: Well, we'd picture it as knocking someone over.

BANCROFT: He didn't knock me over. I've actually got the heaviest head in the West Australian squad. It's been measured. There's an actual measurement for it. So, just took the blow quite well and moved on from it. It was a good hit. Play on.

COLMAN: Trevor Bayliss said it was a long way from being a headbutt. He said there's a headbutt and there's what happened to you. The headbutt is totally different. Could you, perhaps, define on a one-to-ten basis the difference between what happened to you and a headbutt?

BANCROFT: Well, he connected with my head, with a force that would make me sort of think, 'Wow, that's a bit weird.' And yeah, that was it.

COLMAN: Was it the top of his head that hit you in your nose, or what happened?

BANCROFT: Well, headbutts clash with heads. When he made the decision to do that, it meant our heads collided.

MEDIA MANAGER: I think we've clarified it now.

COLMAN: Well, no, because a headbutt, it can break your nose, it can put you in hospital. So where did the top of his head hit yours?

BANCROFT: Yeah, it hit my head.

COLMAN: But where?

BANCROFT: My head. It hit me there. Forehead. There you go.

By this point Smith had dissolved into giggles. Months later the internet would gleefully assemble before-and-after shots of the pair laughing in Brisbane and moping in Cape Town. At the time, though, it felt genuinely goodhearted. Bancroft was doing Bairstow a favour – explaining the scenario, laughing it off, bringing a friendly tone, and defusing it on the spot, when a straighter response could have dragged it out longer.

But it was also true that Australia had used the situation tactically. 'Sources within the England camp were baffled by the story and suspect it is all part of a co-ordinated Australian campaign to undermine them using sensitivity about off field behaviour,' wrote Nick Hoult in Britain's *Telegraph*. 'Cricket Australia did not want to become involved last night but England suspect the Australians have allowed their media to fire bullets for them.'

If that was the plan, it worked. For England any attention meant pressure. 'Are we disappointed a small incident gets brought up in the press? Yes. It's a distraction. There will be further discussion within the camp,' said Bayliss. Behind closed doors the coach was 'incandescent', reported BBC commentator Jonathan Agnew, while director of cricket Andrew Strauss had 'gone into the team room and delivered an absolute rocket'. Bairstow's ghosted *Daily Mail* column said 'the fuss was exactly what Australia wanted.'

Amateur Sherlocks may be tracing back a few threads. The headbutt happened when Bancroft was under the radar in state cricket, but came out weeks later during his first Test. 'Talking to some of the Australian boys,' said Bairstow, 'they didn't know anything about it until just before some of their players made comments to me.' So who was Bancroft most likely to share that story with? Well, who was his new big brother at the top of the order? Then there was Lalor's piece, which must have had input from somebody: that 'teammates' were incensed, that 'teammates' believed the incident was like 2013. Which teammates would instantly think of Root getting clocked in the Birmingham Walkabout four years earlier?

Whose voice was on the stump mic? Warner's. Who was the type to speak for his whole team? Warner. Who held fastest to grievances? What was that line about moral relativisms? Which Australian player, on hearing Bancroft's story, would be least likely to laugh at an anecdote and most likely to decide it was a crime demanding restitution? Who wanted to 'find a way to dislike' the opposition?

All the while a darker story was swirling. After the Test, various voices suggested it had also included a different strain of sledging. 'There's a lot that's gone on that I think the England players are quite upset about, and rightfully from what I've heard. [Things that] quite frankly shouldn't be on a cricket pitch,' said Bairstow's wicketkeeping predecessor Matt Prior. The version circulating on tour was remarkably consistent. Writer Andrew Miller would later voice a 'widely held view that a line was crossed where Jonny Bairstow in particular was concerned', while Nasser Hussain implicated Warner. Local media gestured at it: 'The nature of those comments have not been revealed though social media is awash with speculation,' wrote Andrew Wu for *The Sydney Morning Herald*.

Some of that speculation involved the death of Bairstow's father, David, but the guess was wild. Voices closer to the action indicated a more generic strain of attack, but it must have involved slurs of sufficient intensity that they would create a furore if reported. Nobody wanted to break the story. Journalists sat on it uneasily. The England camp didn't want drama, the Australian camp didn't want publication, so no one could get a proper source. There was a general sense that pursuing it would be kicking a wasp's nest. In the end someone usually takes a deep breath and winds up the boot. But in the climate of November 2017, it felt like we were all waiting for someone else to go first.

The closest it came was before the Adelaide Test, when Smith was asked pointedly whether he was sure everything in Brisbane had been above board. 'I think everything was fine, it was played in good spirit,' he said, assuring us his personal line remained uncrossed. That didn't jibe with Bairstow's newspaper column, which confirmed that 'other things' had been said in Brisbane besides headbutt chat, 'but what they were is staying there. We move on. Hopefully it's gone now. I'm not making an issue of it. Only if they are said again would the matter go further.'

Still no one would even hint at the subject. The rumours affected the series anyway. The Australians reached Adelaide with the tale bubbling and knew there was a danger it would spill: they took some of the heat out of that contest immediately, leaving England to be aggressors in the field. Weeks later in

Melbourne, when asked about sledging in the series, Warner obliquely admitted there had been 'maybe one occasion where it's gone a little bit too far'. It was a curious utterance from someone not prone to conciliation, but he offered nothing further. Nor had anyone from England in the meantime. It would do nobody any good, both sides still seemed to agree, to let that particular pot boil over.

Chapter 8

ADELAIDE

December 2017

Adelaide Oval may be the only venue in the world to hold a full-pack press conference with its groundsman. Television crews set up to ask Damian Hough how much grass is on the wicket and what it'll do under lights. Sport is full of spooky intangibles: serious pundits get paid large sums to tell us with straight faces which team had greater hunger, whose level of heart really stood out, who rated highest on the passion index. We twist correlative environmental factors into causatives every day of the week – the bus breaking down on Tuesday clearly affected Sunday's result. But cricket pitches must be one of the most woo-woo Ouija-board soups in the sporting world.

Curators are alchemists, commentators are astrologers: the former meld arcane physical ingredients with heat, moisture and time, and still have little idea how it's going to turn out; the latter interpret the result using generalisation, assumption, history and hindsight. We guess blindly then filter events through that lens. If you don't rate the batsman, it was flat. If a spinner did well it was a Bunsen. Low score without wickets: dead. With wickets: unplayable. Physicists are rarely involved, but pitch talk is so vague it's difficult to prove anything wrong. What if an unplayable track is played well? The day-night format is the Pitch Wanker Expansion Pack. More grass to protect the pink ball could add seam movement. More polish might swing longer. Moist evening air might hoop. Or none of those things might happen, but we'll use confirmation bias to blot that out.

Day-night cricket also gives the Adelaide Test an unmatched energy. It feels different in the lead-up, anticipation of a varied flavour. Down King William Street or its parallel boulevards through the central city, people spill out of pubs at 10 am pretending it's 2 pm, then roll down to the cricket at 2 pm pretending it's 10 am. Over the river, under the eucalypts, but half the people don't take their seats, heading instead for the grass tennis courts down the western side, watching big screens under acres of shade cloth and bunting by the vodka bar, Pimm's bar, champagne bar, wine tent, beer hall. It's a carnival day as much as a match.

On the first afternoon the coin fell for Root again. In Brisbane the idea he would choose to bowl was a punchline. In Adelaide he was serious. It's worth noting that mocking Nasser Hussain – or any captain who bowls first to lose – is nonsense. History shows a minimal margin: teams batting first have 52 per cent of the wins. The difference is in the teams. On the pitch where Hussain's bowlers gave Matthew Hayden 300 runs, Hussain's batsmen had an innings for 79. Had they done that first, we'd say they sucked at batting. We'd never blame the captain or the toss.

Root may have been right. The pitch may have been freshest at the start, bookended by a perilous evening. But conditions only count if players use them. Broad and Anderson couldn't. A pair of bowlers closing on a thousand Test wickets must know a bit, but their careers seem to constantly feature annoyed pundits asking why they keep bowling short. At Adelaide less than a third of the pair's opening spell was full. The ball was back of a length, angled in to the body – bowling to keep down runs, not threaten wickets. It was a bewildering waste of a chance at seam and swing.

The breakthrough had more to do with stop–start cricket from rain delays. Four balls after tea Warner barbecued Bancroft, luring him halfway down on a misfield then sending him back. Chris Woakes had time to steady, aim and fire down a stump and a half from mid-off. He then supported Root in a way the senior bowlers hadn't, pitching up with bounce to clip Warner's edge for 47.

Smith and Khawaja reached 138 by dinner, but afterwards Khawaja flashed to gully. A year earlier, in the renovated post-Hobart team against South Africa, Khawaja had played his best innings, batting through two night sessions after filling in at the last minute as an opening batsman, and making 145 over the course of three days. His cornerstone was avoiding his pet shot on Adelaide's seaming track: through the whole innings he didn't drive a cover boundary from pace. A year later that restraint deserted him for a middling 53, having already been dropped by Stoneman hooking on 44.

'Sure, Jimmy Anderson made the delivery deviate away from the left-hander to invite the error,' wrote Adam Collins for *The Guardian*. 'But it is hardly revelatory that he would be doing just that. He has not picked up 500-plus wickets rolling them down nude. Up to that stage Khawaja had edged or missed a quarter of the England paceman's offerings to him. If a lairy cover drive on the up to start the dangerous final session was his answer, he was probably addressing the wrong question.'

Smith, meantime, was building up a head of emotional steam. He had barely got off the mark before dinner when he gave Broad precise directions on how best to go forth and multiply. England saw the signs and wound him up further. Smith had swiped back before the game after Anderson criticised Australia in a newspaper column. 'It's interesting coming from Jimmy calling us bullies and big sledgers. I think he's one of the biggest sledgers in the game, to me in particular. I remember back in 2010 when I started and I wasn't any good, he was pretty happy to get stuck into me then.' In came Anderson to short straight mid-off, right where Smith wanted to stand as non-striker.

For someone as ritual-heavy as the Australian captain, being forced to stand wider upset him, as did every entanglement when the ball came that way. Anderson riled him with smirking silence, while Smith lost any remaining cool to the point that Aleem Dar had to stand between the two and give a lecture. Soon afterwards Smith on 40 edged an in-ducker onto his stumps from debutant Craig Overton. England had thrown a stick in the spokes of the run machine.

The best bowling came in the last session, but without reward as Handscomb battled through nineteen overs with

Shaun Marsh to stumps. 'This morning was overcast skies and a bit of moisture,' Overton explained on the decision to bowl. 'They're only going at 2.7 an over. If we get early wickets in the morning, we're confident.' Handscomb was out the next day before a run was taken, the score was 5–209, and Australia would end the innings at a run rate of 2.9. The problem was that rate would stretch across 149 overs. The English weren't expecting an epic from Shaun Marsh.

To be honest nobody does: it's the batting equivalent of the Spanish Inquisition. 'Shaun Fucking Marsh' is a message I've received verbatim from more than one person over the years. Shaun F Marsh (middle name Edward), a player who enraged as easily as he tantalised. Who promised so much, inscrutably refused to deliver, then came good in the middle of the night two years later on the other side of the world with a suddenness and surety that stunned even himself. At each of his occasional and brilliant hundreds, nobody has seemed more surprised than Marsh, running down the pitch with the expression of a man who has just realised he's giving a speech to his school assembly naked.

Australia's cricket establishment spent the best part of twenty years obsessed with the Western Australian. One of those left-handers whose best game emits an audible purr, he had every shot and looked gorgeous playing them. In 2003 he impressed a good audience with one of his perfect days against a full-strength New South Wales. Steve Waugh was national captain and called it 'the best innings I have ever seen from a nineteen-year-old'. Future selector Mark Waugh watched alongside. Future coach Justin Langer roomed with Marsh and predicted he would play a hundred Tests. The other factor was pedigree: Marsh's dad, Geoff, was a Test batsman and coach. His kids grew up in Australia's change rooms. Surely they were bound to don the cap?

The mix of birthright and potential was intoxicating. Marsh had six hundreds in eleven first-class seasons by 2011, yet got the call when Ricky Ponting's baby daughter created a vacancy. He scored a hundred in Kandy and kept his spot for Colombo, beginning a long game of musical chairs with Khawaja. In Cape Town he made a polished 44, hurt his back, and made a duck batting at number ten. A month later he got a home series against an expired Indian team. In the plum spot at first drop against a busted-arse bowling attack surrounded by teammates racking up double and triple hundreds, he contributed 0, 0, 0, 3, 3 and 11. The Marsh sequence was set: a melange of sporadic brilliance, epic failure, ill-timed injury, unmerited call-ups and batting-order pinball.

A cat burglar of selection, his specialty was getting into Australian teams from the outside. Where others had to bang down doors Marsh slipped through an air vent. Most egregious was the South Africa trip in 2014. Since India he'd averaged 25.8 in first-class cricket, including five hits for Australia A without topping 30. There were 33 players ahead of him for Sheffield Shield runs that summer. Yet chairman of selectors John Inverarity, a fellow Perth boy, somehow stood up in public and put his name to the following glorious justification: 'He seems to be fit and striking the ball very well. When he plays well he's a fine player and we're hoping that he can play at his potential. He's in a good space at the moment, Shaun.'

With no claim to be there and no form to draw on, Marsh naturally carved up the world's best pace attack for 148. It was a staggering innings, so casual he might have taken guard on a banana lounge. The second Test he made twin ducks. The third he made way for Shane Watson. 'Shaun Marsh is the ultimate enigma,' wrote Malcolm Conn. 'I saw him make a fantastic hundred, a pair and be dropped in a three-Test series. Covered all bases.'

High, low, comedy, tragedy. Marsh became injury cover: Michael Clarke's spine, Chris Rogers' scone, Khawaja's hammy. He was desperate for redemption on India's next visit, crawling to 99 in Melbourne as he should have been bashing declaration runs, scuttling any chance of a win, then running himself out in a panicked bid for his century. He was parachuted into the 2015 Ashes to strengthen the batting, made 0 and 2, and got skyhooked out, having added Australia's Trent Bridge 60 to the Cape Town 47 on his CV.

Next Khawaja injury, November 2015, Marsh sealed a tricky chase against a seaming ball under lights to beat New Zealand. He cashed in against West Indies for a Test-best 182, was squeezed out by Khawaja anyway, then replaced him in Colombo in 2016. Shifted from the middle order to open, he made another ton, kept his spot for the home season, and broke his finger in the first match.

He was back in the middle order for India 2017, Khawaja not trusted in spinning conditions. It was classic Marsh again: two worldly half-centuries, 197 balls apiece in grenade conditions, surrounded by scores of 0, 1, 2, 4, 9 and 16. He was dropped for Bangladesh in August and missed a national contract, and his time at last looked done. Then came the Ashes.

Of course people got annoyed, as the years passed and the recalls began to make cats look hard done by. Partly it was the gulf between promise and delivery – no one would be so mad if they hadn't seen his best. Partly it was hereditary privilege, the way he and his brother Mitchell were given so many more opportunities. The pair, wrote Crash Craddock in 2012, 'have been mollycoddled all their lives and Shaun, in particular, has got away with telling half-truths to his parents, friends, coaching staff and administrators forced to probe his turbulent private life.' He was a silent presence on the field but an enthusiastic one in Perth's party scene. Local reporters referred to him and state teammate Luke Pomersbach as the Chemical Brothers. WA cut Pomersbach in 2011 'after repeated drug and alcohol issues'. Marsh's real brother at eight years younger was arriving on the scene: the two were dropped by the Perth Scorchers in 2012 after a messy night out before a match.

Justin Langer as WA coach helped turn that aspect around, and in Adelaide, Shaun paid a return on all his credit. From a vulnerable position he assumed Smith's role from Brisbane. When the captain couldn't, he did what Smith had done. Steeping himself in patience, waiting out the bowlers, taking advantage with a late assault, and remaining unbeaten. He reached his fifty at a strike rate of 37, untroubled by runs. When England occasionally bounced him, his hooks were crisp. The fullest balls met off-side drives. Straight ones were picked off with clip or glance. Off-breaks were an outlet, quick on his feet down or back. Everything else met thin air or the broadest blade.

It couldn't have hurt that he'd been prescribed contact lenses before the match. An optometrist sponsor tested the team as a joke and was stunned to find Marsh was mildly short-sighted. The other medical issue was Tim Paine worrying a short ball had newly mangled his dodgy finger. 'I remember not wanting to take my glove off because I didn't really want to know. It was literally my second Test back in, and I thought, "This would be great, all over again."' He pushed on with a typically belligerent wicketkeeper's innings, helping add 85 before it was Cummins again with a stand of 99.

By the second session they were batting for time, wanting to go at England in the dark. Marsh raised his hundred, then was dropped at slip when Cook and Vince dived into each other to symbolise England's match. Party time came after dinner with a hundred-metre-long bomb from Broad down the ground before Smith called them in. It was an exclamation mark at the end of a novel, the batsman 126 not out, night fallen, Australia 8–442 declared.

Marsh had now scored centuries all through the order: opening in Colombo, first drop in Kandy, number four in Johannesburg, five in Hobart, six here. He would add another at five in Sydney, capping his most consistent series for the national team before resuming scorecard obscurity in South Africa. This, though, was his moment – the one he could hold with pride however his career might turn out. In Brisbane he'd been essential support; in Adelaide he was the headline act. Across two Tests he had produced key innings at key times, swinging not just matches but the Ashes. By the time he was done, Root's team in Adelaide had spent more overs in the field than Hussain's at the Gabba.

The night stint was rained short, but England offered little in daylight. At 5–132 came another Lyon moment. Moeen checked a drive to mid-on, mistimed but safe. Except the bowler was in motion, horizontal. From round the wicket, wide on the left-hander's off side, he landed with ball in hand a metre off the pitch to leg. A photographer caught him at full stretch, parallel to the ground. But this was nothing so stilted as Superman's rigid Americana. Lyon had one leg drawn up at the knee, louche, like he'd just rolled over amid the late morning's rumpled sheets. Having always resembled Leisure Suit Larry, he was now fielding like him. His head was turned, left arm stretched out, fumbling for something on the bedside table. The physics of it were impossible, the effect shoulder-shruggingly casual. There was never any doubt. Moeen was walking before he'd landed.

Within minutes meme artist Ethan Meldrum had edited Lyon's dive into Michelangelo's *Creation of Adam*. Instead of the Almighty descending from a cloud to touch his progeny's hand, a Canberra off-break bowler imparts the spark of life with a pink Kookaburra. Such was the excitement Lyon was generating for those watching, and the confidence he was pumping through his team. Not long ago you would never have associated that quiet player with swagger. Now it was coming off him like pheromones.

England fumbled to 227, still trailing by 215, but the evening session created a dilemma Smith hadn't had a quiet moment to consider. Should he enforce the follow-on to have a crack at them at night, but risk blowing out his bowlers if England went deep the next day? Or should his batsmen tackle the night session, pile up a lead, wear out the other bowlers, and give his own a longer rest and a fourth-innings pitch? In the end Smith did what Australian captains do in bowling conditions: backed his batsmen to tough it out.

Batting at night isn't easy. The glare of floodlights makes the ball tricky to pick up. The fluorescent pink dye flares out, easy to see the glow but harder to read the trajectory. Every now and then a ball slithers through; batsmen pick things up a fraction later, and a fraction is all it needs. The crowd gets raucous, having had all afternoon to load up. The new ball in its coat of lacquer glistens on-screen like a freshly sucked gobstobber. There is a perception, as yet unsupported by science, that it swings more readily after dark. Out of Anderson's hand it did. 'Being able to bowl rather than follow on was a gift that kept on giving for the 35-year-old,' wrote Collins, 'as he attacked the hosts' edges and stumps until they were routed.'

Australia was 4–53 by stumps, two nicked off and two leg-before. Smith overturned a dismissal when Anderson pitched outside leg, but that only let Woakes trap him instead. He'd made 6. Lyon as nightwatchman milked a groin injury to waste time, which was less explicit than it sounds. But he fell after the restart, as did Handscomb a second time. Paine and Starc holed out, Marsh got a serpentine ball onto his stumps, and Anderson had his first five-for on Australian soil. Done for 138, no Australian had more than 20.

That still left England 354 to get, the sort of target only ten teams have chased in nearly 2300 Tests. But Smith was simmering in his own juices, stewing on the thought that he might have made the wrong call. His face was pure angst after declining a review against Cook that would have smashed leg stump, even though his next review got the same batsman at little cost. As Root and Malan built a partnership through the evening, Smith blew both his reviews in three balls, then dropped Malan at slip. The Barmy Army taunted him at each appeal, hundreds of sunburnt English arms making the T signal of the review system he could no longer use. It was Cummins who soothed him before stumps. Angle and jag slipped through the left-handed Malan and the bails lit up.

Four days down, four wickets down, 176 on the board, 178 more to win, England's captain on 67. The chase highly unlikely on a fifth-day pitch, but a chance remained. Ahead lay sixteen hours of not knowing, imagining every scenario, revelling in the future's obscurity. For the neutral it was the beauty of a game that could swing one way and then the other. For England, it was hope. For Australia it was less positive. Afterwards Smith admitted the prospect had kept him awake deep into the fourth night, wired to the point that he needed tranquillisers to grab some patchy hours of rest.

The best remedy was the shiny pink pill out of Hazlewood's hand. Next day, possibility and potential collapsed back to reality. The Barmies hadn't finished their opening chorus of Jerusalem before Woakes – a nightwatchman but with nine first-class hundreds – got the thinnest edge to the second ball bowled. Next over, one kept so low it scraped the underside of the toe of Root's bat. Starc charged through the rest.

'I was a little bit nervous last night,' Smith admitted when the cause for nerves had passed. 'It's been a pretty tough twenty-four hours. It's all part of being captain of your country. Sometimes you're going to make the wrong decision. It's part of a learning experience. I'll reflect on some things I can improve in my leadership and captaincy.'

It was all a bit silly. Saying he'd made the wrong decision didn't add up, neither from him nor those watching. We were back to hindsight wisdom, as with Root at the toss. Just because a decision hadn't gone as planned didn't mean it was wrong – the other decision mightn't have worked either. A captain can choose the right tactic and still have players screw it up. Tactics are decided on the balance of probabilities, but no one can foresee the future.

Had Smith enforced the follow-on and watched England sail through an evening, there would have been calls for his head when Starc had blown an Achilles tendon bowling at 6–380. The first two night sessions hadn't been deadly, so there was no guarantee the third would be. Even with England bowling well, most of the wickets fell the next afternoon in bright sunlight, and the ball kept swinging as it had under lights. And, even being smashed in their second innings, the Australians had put the match out of reach. England's chance of a chase was slim from the outset. The score was 2–0, and the home team had done far more worrying than it deserved.

Chapter 9

PERTH

We're watching Bradman here. Bradman-like. The way he threads the field. It reminds me of some film taken by Clarrie Grimmett, the great leg-spinner, of the Ashes in 1930 and 1934. In a few frames you can see Bradman. It's an extraordinary cameo picture of being able to weave the ball through the field. That's what Smith did there.

Just using his wrists. Not heaving the ball around the place. Using his ability to judge the length. Particularly on the pull shot. Didn't he judge the length. Just back and bang. I'm telling you, he's like Don Bradman.

Jim Maxwell doesn't date back far enough to know first-hand, born a couple of years after Bradman's last Test in 1948. But he's watched a lot of cricket since. Great players adapt to conditions, and Smith in Perth was the opposite of Smith in Brisbane. Craig Overton had dismissed Warner and Bancroft cheaply, but Smith smacked his third ball against the seamer for four. When people speak of batsmen being wristy they mean through midwicket or mid-on. Smith was using his wrists to open the blade through cover. Nine of his thirteen boundaries by the end of the second day went through the posh side. He would only seem to reach halfway to the ball, then would whip the bat outward through the line.

His Brisbane strike rate had puttered in the 30s, Perth purred at 75. His control was supreme. Of 122 balls faced on the second day he missed one leg-glance, while CricViz analysts tracked him as attacking 30 per cent of balls faced, more than any specialist in the match. Even his scarce edges went down and through the cordon to score, as did some of his horizontal strokes. 'That was almost the Bradman late cut, if Jim was still on,' said Simon Katich on ABC radio later in the day. 'That's how it used to go, isn't it, the fielders all clapping as the ball went past them? They just look clueless as to how they're going to get him out. There are times when you're watching someone playing a level above. You see it sometimes with a player going back to state cricket, and they're too good for it. He's like that, but in a Test match.'

Smith finished the day in sight of another hundred, but no one had overnight jitters. 'Wherever we went last night, people were talking about him,' said Gerard Whateley the next morning. 'And they were all talking about a double century. He was on ninety-two but they couldn't see it fall short. Which is ridiculous.'

During the Adelaide post-mortem a few days earlier, the chief sportswriter for Britain's *Telegraph* had a question for Joe Root. 'One of the pluses is you've managed to unsettle and disrupt Steve Smith. Kept his scores down, sledged him pretty heavily. Do you think you've left a mark on him in some way?' Paul Hayward asked. 'He's a good player,' said Root. 'He'll come back I'm sure with some sort of reply.'

Each year before a WACA game, media outlets went through a pantomime about whether we would see one of the pitches of old, a cracking monstrosity of viper bounce with the Fremantle Doctor sending the ball on parabolas. The truth is the WACA had lost those traits when the square was re-laid in the early 2000s because the soil and grass mix couldn't be mimicked. This Ashes edition was at least more lively than some recent dead efforts. It helped when a whole pace attack could top 145 kilometres per hour. While Starc and Cummins were known for speed, Adelaide had been Hazlewood's fastest average match in three years. In Perth he kept going up through the gears. Add the benefit of being the most accurate, and Hazlewood's bouncer was the fiercest of the three. It zeroed in on the batsman's grille like a *Top Gun* sidewinder.

Such was the barrage England had to face in the first session. Vince and Stoneman, who if joined together sound like a detective who isn't afraid to get his hands dirty, battled it out after Cook fell early. At the end of the session Hazlewood went full to exploit Vince's weakness for the cover drive, then after lunch he crashed Stoneman in the helmet, rattling the batsman enough that he edged Starc a few overs later. But the pair had absorbed the day's most punishing bowling to let Bairstow and Malan flourish.

Malan took on the short stuff, Bairstow evaded it, and both dispatched full balls when they came. The outfield was on

Ritalin compared to the damp sod in Brisbane. As Bairstow punched to cover, Jim called: 'They'll get one. Maybe two. Puts in the dive. Maybe four! Yes. That's the beauty of this ground. You beat the infield and the ball just seems to gather pace.' Malan broke Lyon's stranglehold on left-handers, holding him at bay until weary short balls could be picked off. The lefty was dropped at slip on 92, then raised his hundred. 'To be honest I thought I was going to cry. The boys said I was quiet but I was trying to keep the tears in.' Bairstow celebrated his own hundred the next morning by headbutting his helmet.

The partnership was 237, the score 4–368. But after Malan charged Lyon and sliced a catch on 140, England's next five batsmen made 22 between them. Given how easy it had looked for that one partnership, England faced the dire prospect that 403 wasn't enough. Smith by stumps gave them no cause for comfort.

Ever seen a team start a day 200 runs ahead and still felt like they were in trouble? Before the series former Aussie skipper Ian Chappell gave his assessment. 'It is the extra pace of Starc and Cummins that I am basing Australia's superiority on. In Australia if you are struggling for wickets you can always resort to a bit of short-pitched stuff and that is more easily done with genuine pace. England has a good attack but I am just not sure how they will go if the Kookaburra isn't doing much.'

The third-day pitch had bounce. It had pace. It carried a bowler's work through clean to the wicketkeeper. But batting in these conditions is like drinking Fernet: fierce if you're unaccustomed, delicious once you acquire the taste. Australia's captain relished it. 'Because the track is faster, he likes that pace onto the bat,' said Katich. 'The bounce is true and the ball isn't deviating. In Brisbane it wasn't coming on, and in Adelaide it was moving. Whereas here he can just play through the ball.' Whateley described the same while indulging his fondness for drama: in Brisbane, Smith 'ceded to the conditions, the terms, the state of the game. On this pitch he's bent it absolutely to his will'.

With his hundred in the bag, Smith switched modes from domination to durability. The first day of his innings included thirteen fours and a six in 92 runs, the second had twelve fours in 137. But he made up the difference in relentless ones and twos. Root became so desperate that merely hitting the pad brought a review. Twice. The second was a no-ball.

Smith was eternal. I wrote of him that day as the Nefud Desert, with Omar Sharif and Peter O'Toole surveying the trek ahead.

'There is no rest now short of water, Lawrence. On the other side of that.'
'And how much of that is there?'
'I am not sure. But however much, it must be crossed before tomorrow's sun gets up. This is The Sun's Anvil.'

By the 95th over, Root had gone leg theory. The field was open from point to mid-on while short catchers crammed next to the non-striker and at midwicket, with others in the deep. Broad wasn't short enough, Smith on his toes punching through the open acres. 'England are gawwwn, mate. They're gawn,' was Katich's distillation. They still led by 53 runs.

That fell before tea. A deficit grew. Smith began tiring but all he had to do was remain, easing to his double-century while a new force was at work. Mitchell Marsh had taken over from Shaun in the first session and stuck around. He was different to his brother: taller, right-handed, a whacker more than a stroke maker, an all-rounder whose medium pace had been the justification for his recall. In truth he'd so recently had a shoulder operation that he couldn't manage more than a few gentle overs. But selectors needed cover for breaking one of Australia's pointless rules: that you don't change a winning side. Peter Handscomb had been worked out by Anderson while Marsh had been in form for Western Australia. With a game at the WACA, no one could have engineered a better chance for him to succeed.

Marsh has always hit the ball like he wants to crack it open and feast on the goo inside. But he was heavy and unsophisticated, his only mode to plant one hoof down the track. Facing spin he was a Clydesdale trying to pick blackberries with its teeth. Facing pace everything was front foot: pull, cut, defence, throwing hard hands at the ball. He made 87 in his second Test in 2014 and never looked like getting near it again. He was a slogger batting too high, and with games on the line he was a liability. By the time his shoulder blew out in March 2017, he was statistically the worst number six batsman in Test history.

The injury turned out to be a blessing. He couldn't bowl and had months to fill, so he started from scratch with batting coach Scott Meuleman. 'I got back from India and sat down post-surgery and I was in a pretty bad place with my cricket. He got a hold of me and changed my game. Changed the way I play, the way I defend, the way I think about the game. I finally worked out after eight years that I can't just plonk on the front foot, I have to start defending off the back foot and playing off the back foot.'

Six months later the renovations were on show. His decision-making was as crisp as his feet. He defended when needed, attacked when able, was balanced for either. The power remained, his strikes echoing around the WACA. If Smith was the anvil, Marsh became the hammer. He hit thirteen boundaries in the final session to Smith's three, imposing himself at the crease like only the physically enormous can. His straight drives and thrash cuts were brutal and beautiful, his late cuts showed finesse. There wasn't much else, it was a simple game played immaculately. Fielders spread. Wheels fell off. More than three years after his Test debut, he was *on*, that feeling when you know you're watching a player on the best day of their career. He breezed through the 90s for the first time, liberated from doubt, as Whateley captured it for the wireless.

He charges off towards the crowd, towards the pavilion. How Mitch Marsh has craved this moment. A Test century, on his home deck no less. It is the most exuberant celebration you would see for the milestone. A kiss of the badge, a hug for his captain, and a lifetime ambition achieved. The relief pours off him as the excitement rushes in. One hundred and thirty balls, seventeen boundaries, he has been a commanding presence, Mitch Marsh, this afternoon. And still they stand at the WACA and applaud.

Exuberant, alright: his celebration was pure, built of delight, like a Labrador trying to wag its way into your lap. He ran because he didn't know what else to do, following the ball behind point towards the boundary. 'I'm not a jumper,' he said later, and his heavy frame backed the statement. He wrenched his helmet off his enormous head (scientifically proven to weigh less than Bancroft's), swung his bat and helmet forward in each hand, and roared. Malan had been too overcome to express anything. Marsh would have split down the middle had he tried to keep it in.

By stumps he was 181, Smith 229, and Australia 549 – a lead of 146. England's quicks were so spent that Moeen had bowled a long spell of off-spin from the Fremantle Doctor end, squandering the world's most coveted paceman's breeze for the simple expedient of not being hit for six upwind. Cook was so tired crossing the ground after play that he dragged his kit bag obliviously through a TV interview. He was celebrating his 150th Test match, having enjoyed his 100th at the same ground in 2013–14.

Anderson dug deep on the fourth morning to get Marsh without addition and Smith for 239, but there were Cummins and Paine to follow. Australia declared after lunch with a wicket remaining and 662 on the board. Biblical rain crashed over Perth all night, the ground staff in a desert climate caught unprepared. Curator Matt Page was concussed by a flying tarp in a morning gale, while Root ran from it like a woodland elf fleeing a waking monster. The pitch was saturated at one end, a debacle met by a phalanx of groundsmen surrounding it with leaf-blowers. Play started three hours late with England's first-innings centurions to resume, but their rearguard lasted six balls before Hazlewood hit the wet patch and tunnelled under Bairstow's bat. The bowler took 5–48, England collecting 218 and an innings defeat.

The Ashes were done in straight sets. Marsh the younger beamed. 'I've just had to take my parachute off from parachuting into the third Test … I think it has sunk in now. Just lying in bed, I kept on looking at the scorecard. I couldn't really believe it. That's literally what I did when I got home the other night, was look at the scorecard. No highlights. Just staring at the scorecard. It might sound a little weird, but that's what happened. No press. Skimmed across a few pages in the paper to get to the racing, but that was about it.'

Smith's reaction was more complex, emotions warring on his face as he came back to the field for his radio interview after a few minutes taking deep breaths in the rooms.

It's still sitting with me a bit actually. I was crying in the sheds a bit just a minute ago, everything just sort of came out.

My first series as captain of an Ashes series, I really wanted to leave my mark and do some great things. I'm proud of my performances but I'm really proud of everyone in that room.

Our bowlers, to take twenty wickets in every game, we haven't won a toss, we've probably had the toughest of the conditions to bowl in … Each of the games they've had a foot in the door. We've had to work really hard.

It's obviously huge pressure. No matter what series you play, here in Australia we're always expected to win. That's what we expect of ourselves as well, you know? We grow up on these pitches and we know how they play and we should do well on these wickets. But an Ashes series is always that extra little bit.

Whateley finished the interview with a throw to Katich. 'We've got the guard down at last. That's Steve Smith, and I've been waiting to see that for ages.' For Marsh it was simple joy. For his captain, winning the Ashes looked a lot more like relief.

Chapter 10

FISTS AND FINGERS

By Melbourne the zip was gone from the contest, and there was none to be gained from the drop-in pitch. Warner did his bit to combat both with an attacking hundred and a fight with debutant bowler Tom Curran, who'd had Warner caught at midwicket on 99 only to reprieve him with a no-ball. 'It was just one of those things where the bowler's going to be annoyed that he overstepped the mark,' said Warner, for once speaking literally. 'He muttered something, I didn't let it go, I obviously had to bite back as I normally do. It always comes with a game of cricket. When he comes out to bat I might start going.'

The MCG is never as festive as Adelaide Oval. Even a mighty Boxing Day crowd of 88,172 can only do so much while isolated in the middle of Yarra Park with nowhere to socialise but the amphitheatre's sterile concrete bars. The cricket didn't help, dragging its arse along the carpet to 3–244 at the close. Warner's brisk 103 flattered the stodgy surface but no one else got past a crawl, while no bowler could get movement, bounce, inconsistency or pace from its brown monotony. Jimmy Anderson was his sunny Lancashire self. 'It wasn't exciting to watch. It wasn't exciting to play in, to be honest, when it's attritional like that. But that's the pitch that we've got, and we've got to put up with it.'

Smith made 76 but got a bottom edge into his stumps. Mitch Marsh and Paine went the same way, testament to the lack of pace. 'Here be drag-ons,' wrote some internet wit. If the pitch hadn't asphyxiated the contest, Cook applied the pillow to the face by keeping Australia in the field for two days, carrying his bat for 244 not out. He passed Mahela Jayawardene, Shivnarine Chanderpaul and Brian Lara on the all-time runs list, and replaced Viv Richards on a giant honour board in the Members' Stand for the highest visiting innings at the ground. Its most entertaining passage came when Stuart Broad, spooked by fast bowling after being hit in the face a few years earlier, thrashed a wild 56 at the other end. Cook noted it was the second time they'd batted together in 113 shared Tests.

A joke of a tampering story was drummed up by some outlets, using a close-up of Anderson's thumb on the ball. The bowler had been cleaning off mud under the supervision of the umpire, who was cropped from the photos. People really were bored. Rain soaked up day four, and Smith did the formalities by batting out the fifth for an unbeaten 102 that must have been the easiest of his career. The pitch 'hasn't changed over five days and I'd say if we were playing for the next couple of days it wouldn't change at all either,' he said. England had the modest pleasure of avoiding nine defeats in a row on Australian shores: 'Thanks for bringing that up,' Anderson deadpanned back at the BBC's Stephan Shemilt. 'Full of the joys of spring. Merry Christmas to you.'

In Sydney the temperature topped 40 all week, and 50 at times on the SCG. Root came down with heat exhaustion and some form of fielding poisoning. He'd fought for 83 of a solid 346, but another Australian score of over 600 would have finished off any captain. He retired on 58 the second time around and checked into hospital as England lost by an innings. The Marsh brothers scored centuries together, creating one of the moments of the summer when Shaun got so swept up in Mitchell's hundredth run that he stopped to hug his brother halfway down the pitch, before Mitch had to shove him towards the other end to stop him being run out.

The video is amazing. As the brothers set off, the dressing-room balcony is packed with applauding players: Bancroft, Warner, Lyon, Hazlewood, Khawaja, Paine in his whites ready to go in next while slurping a Zooper Dooper. When disaster nearly unfolds, everyone starts laughing. Except Smith, who jolts as though electrocuted, points frantically as though the batsmen can see him, yells at them to run, then smacks both hands to his head and visibly pronounces 'Fuck me!' Even as his teammates cheer, Smith stays frozen, a look of horror on his face that someone almost messed up in a cricket game. Only after a long pause does he shake his head with dismay before digging up a half smile.

Smith's series finished with a godly 687 runs at 137.4. It was interesting, though, that his last three knocks included the chopped-on 76 in Melbourne, then 83 in Sydney chipping a catch back to Moeen: scores which by no means warrant criticism but by his own standards were exceedingly rare. It wasn't just that Smith at that stage had more hundreds than fifties. It was that when he reached the 70s he was almost invulnerable.

From Smith's first hundred in 2013 until Melbourne, he'd passed 71 on 24 occasions and made hundreds on 22 of them. Only twice had he been out within reach of a ton. Now he'd done it twice more in three innings. The earlier numbers told of his prodigious focus and technical excellence; the later numbers said those traits had slipped. He was exhausted. This became obvious in his one-day series to follow, marooned on strike and prodding mediocre scores while England's new breed of power-hitters thrashed Australia 1–4.

Cricket Australia had exacerbated Ashes jingoism at every chance. All through the series and the Women's Ashes preceding it, the slogan had been 'Beat England'. It had taken a panel of geniuses in the marketing department to come up with that. 'What do you see as our underlying values? When we play cricket, what's our reason to exist?'

Confetti explodes, pay rises flow. Beat England. An inspiring take on the human force of will. Channelling the pure joy of sport, of camaraderie and competition, achievement and aspiration. At women's games in sleepy Coffs Harbour, boxes of Aussie gold shirts ensured every kid at the ground could carry home this message of glorious victory. The big screens showed fans and players thumping fists on ribcages over dramatic music, a military drumbeat with a chant to follow. 'Beat. England.' Then a little kid squealing it, too young to get the words: 'Bep Engin!' Adorable, now get him to break down an M16. Posters and banners were everywhere with the hashtag: change up the capitals and it said #BeatenGland, more fitting for such onanistic ritual.

In Sydney this ugliness got one last foray. Root was lucky to be passed out in the change room as Anderson took his place on a podium bristling with fists and fingers. A giant cardboard hand, painted with Australia's quarter-British flag, had four fingers raised for four Test wins. Another hand painted with the St George's cross had its fingers closed for a zero. This had been planned well in advance – we found alternative hands stashed in an SCG tunnel to cover all possible results, including a three for Australia and a lone index for England. The marketers could have saved replication by making two that simply flipped the middle digit.

Magellan, the company that would later dump its sponsorship when Australia's ball-tampering proved 'inconsistent with our values', had no problem being represented on that stage. 'I am presuming that the moment inspired you all to rush out to buy half-a-dozen Magellans in a range of colours,' wrote Greg Baum in *The Age*. With only partial sarcasm, Will Macpherson of *The Times* called the moment 'cringeworthy enough to bring into question whether all future Ashes series should be cancelled'.

This was the atmosphere in which Smith had led his team, and which his sport's governing body had spent a lot of money to create. He was told to skip the T20 series in February to rest. Warner was the Duracell bunny who would push on, while Smith would head to South Africa to set up base for four more Tests. He had navigated the most overblown series in Australian cricket, rich with the anxiety of expectation and consequence, and now was going into Australia's second-biggest rivalry for another seven weeks on tour. His break had been fifteen days.

Chapter 11

STEVEN

Australia's not very original when it comes to Test captains. We don't pick bowlers: Ian Johnson in the 1950s was the only full-timer; Ray Lindwall filled in once. We don't pick wicketkeepers: until Tim Paine met extraordinary circumstances, it was Jack Blackham in the 1800s, one sub game for Barry Jarman and half a dozen for Adam Gilchrist. Even all-rounders fell into disuse after the early decades when everyone was an all-rounder: Shane Watson had one Test; Steve Waugh and Steve Smith all but gave up bowling before being elevated.

You can find rationales – bowlers get injured more, self-management is difficult, both have another job to do – but these are only cited after the decision is made. In Australia the captain is the best batsman: Bradman to Hassett to Simpson to Lawry, Chappell to Chappell to Border to Waugh. Ponting lacked tactical range, Clarke was bad at relationships, but on batting alone both held an assumed right to lead.

By the time Smith embedded himself in the XI his ascent to captain was a formality. He had made five hundreds in little over a year before Clarke was injured in December 2014. Watson and Chris Rogers were on their last lap, and the other batsmen were Warner and the Marsh brothers. Smith set it in concrete by tonning up in all three of his understudy starts. Eight months later Clarke led Watson and Rogers into retirement, and the roster now included the 36-year-old Adam Voges, the unproven Khawaja, and a new kid in Joe Burns. Warner was made deputy in the hope it would straighten him out, but it also reflected that he and Smith were the only players assured of their spots. A team with more options wouldn't have taken the gamble.

What a rise: Steven Peter Devereux Smith, who first popped into public view as a novelty player. Already a purveyor of cricket's surrealist art, leg-spin, and an idiosyncratic thrasher with the bat, he was a chubby blond kid who played bit-part roles in quality contests like – let me just get the asterisk right – the 2009 Johnnie Walker All*Star Twenty20, a season curtain-raiser in which the actual national team took on a retiree XI whose celestial claim was reasonable when Gilchrist and Matthew Hayden opened the batting, but was becoming a real stretch by the time you hit Rhett Lockyear, Nathan Rimmington and Travis Birt. Smith wore Australian colours, but this was an era when selectors would have been happy opening the T20 bowling with a bear on rollerskates.

In his 2009–10 Shield season he crashed four hundreds and was sixth on the runs list, with several fewer games than the top five and the best average of all comers at 77.2. But people were more stirred by one innings with the ball against South Australia when he twirled down sixteen overs and took 7–64. These were the years of the spin drought, but when Shane Warne's retirement was recent enough that Australians could remember how it felt to be slaked. Smith evoked something of Warne, in his own shape and the shape of his delivery. An actual leggie? One who could take wickets in the long game? Could it be true?

He got two Tests against Pakistan in the UK, looping down the ball to good effect in the one innings where he was really required, then was a desperation pick partway through the 2010–11 Ashes. England's press and players scented his inherent comedy. Phil Walker of *All Out Cricket* summarised him as 'Impractical leg-breaks, hopeful bunts and dinner-lady hair'. It didn't help when Smith guilelessly announced he'd been given the job of telling jokes in the change room to lighten the mood. England hard nuts like Jimmy Anderson targeted that mercilessly. Picked a specialist comedian, have they? Tell us another. He looked the ultimate bits-and-pieces player, starting as a bowler clubbing runs from number eight, then batting six in a trouncing and barely getting a bowl. The ride was over, and Smith looked most likely to be remembered for his novelty middle name.

When he re-emerged in 2013 it was confusing. To be fair this was a team that had previously toured India with Victorian batsman Cameron White as its specialist spinner, but then selectors specified Smith would tour there as a back-up batsman, picked for perceived ability to play spin rather than deliver it. The third Test at Mohali proved them right with his faultless 92: in a series where Australia was monstered in Roland-Garros conditions, Smith skipped boldly down to whip quality bowling through the on-side.

We still hadn't realised that the comic relief was deadly serious. A kid who lived and breathed the game, one who'd left school at seventeen to turn pro. 'I had my mind set on cricket from when I was about ten, that's all I wanted to do,' he said during his first green-and-gold foray. Even as a short-form slogger he had higher opinions of his ability. 'To have a chance to have played already for the Twenty20 team, it's been amazing, but hopefully I'll be able to make the step up into the one-day and the Test side,' he said without hesitation. It wasn't starry-eyed dreaming but a statement of intent.

And though we'd typecast him as an all-rounder, he had no intention of a career based on leg-spin. 'I guess to get to the next level, it's my bowling that's going to get me there. There's a lot of batsmen about.' But that was just his way in. Smith had only ever dreamed of playing in Australia's top six. 'It's pretty hard getting both batting and bowling together,' he said, and it was no coincidence that as his batting stocks rose, his overs fell, until he took over as captain and all but ditched the ball entirely.

He had his good fortune, making it to the front of the India queue when four players were suspended by Clarke and Mickey Arthur for failing to submit training requests in the episode belittled as Homeworkgate. The coach ended up losing his job, but may inadvertently have given Australia one of its greats. Smith didn't get a 2013 Ashes spot but did get on new coach Lehmann's radar. A hundred for Australia A saw Smith pole-vault into the squad, then into the first Test at Trent Bridge. Rogers and Ashton Agar were also thrown into the mix, with Ed Cowan and Phil Hughes pushed down to three and six. The new boss was tipping over the toy box to see what he had to play with.

Smith started on the first afternoon during a collapse to 4–53. In those days he stood stock-still at the crease, aside from his bat cocked high and wavering in its backlift like a wasp stinger about to strike. Down it came through the ball, all flashy edges and hard drives with the blade's polish glinting in the Nottingham sun. Anderson inevitably nicked him off, but not before he'd made 53 to get Australia out of the basement and settle Hughes for a famous partnership with Agar to follow. Smith followed up with 89 at Old Trafford, then his breakthrough 138 at The Oval.

That unbeaten hundred started a glut of runs like few in Test cricket. At Perth in the back-to-back Ashes he hooked all day to slay trouble, a figure gleaming white in the heat and swivelling on his heels to deposit England's barrage through midwicket. Another at Sydney from a perilous position, then Centurion to prove himself against the world's best in South Africa. Three runs short against Pakistan in Abu Dhabi in late 2014. His first ODI hundred in Sharjah, another in Melbourne. Then his Test summer against India: four matches, four hundreds, stepping up when Clarke's hamstring went. His first Test as captain: century. His first ODI as captain: century. His first T20 as captain nearly completed the set: 90 off 53 balls.

It was like uncorking champagne from one of those Biblical bottles, something lavish and joyful that couldn't be checked.

Smith was outrageous. He did what he liked. He batted like Gumby, stretchy and bendy in every direction, a rubber man who could snap into shape with incredible force. He played wrist-flipped forehand slams down the ground and uppercut ramps over his helmet. He squeezed leaping nutmegs between his own feet. He hornpiped across the crease and fenced to third man. He got in a Cossack crouch, splayed his front leg and slapped a fast length ball over square onto the top balcony at Cardiff next to the grandstand clock. He could reach around anything outside off and divert it to leg – at one stage making Wahab Riaz bowl at third slip. Smith literally stepped off the pitch, to a ball that was still outside his pads, and flicked it square for four. Wahab's head exploded. So did people watching round the world. This was batting that was orgiastic, indecent. Someone on internet cesspit Reddit wrote: 'You can't spell Steven Smith without Semen Hits TV.'

Gradually his force-of-nature approach was supplemented by consideration and control. His 2016 struggles with the left-arm master Rangana Herath in Sri Lanka culminated in a century in the final Test in Colombo. Nine months later Smith applied those lessons in India. Herath had tormented him with the straight ball after raising spectres of turn; now Smith played straight and trusted spin to beat his bat. Through hours of near edges he remained unperturbed, his concentration monkish even before visiting Dharamsala. The result was three hundreds in four Tests, something no Australian had done in India. Three more in four Ashes matches ended 2017. Smith had every game for every place, runs against every opponent. Only Bangladesh had kept him relatively quiet.

In less than five years, Smith made 23 Test centuries from 50 starts. He topped a thousand runs four years in a row. He averaged 73.47, and as captain bumped it up to 76.45. When he won the toss and batted he averaged 113. A career of 23 hundreds is top-class: equalling Virender Sehwag, Kevin Pietersen, Javed Miandad; bettering Wally Hammond, AB de Villiers, Neil Harvey; about to catch Viv Richards. Smith was maybe halfway done.

Cricket is about incremental improvement, evolution as painfully slow as for any marine iguana hurling itself into a freezing Galapagos current. Yet occasionally, a cricketer is entirely reborn. Colin Miller went from a Netherlands club seamer to a blue-haired off-spinner crowned Test Player of the Year in a legendary side. Pietersen went from a middling South African domestic bowler to England's most prolific and damaging batsman. Smith's transformation wasn't rebirth, it was Athena springing fully formed from Zeus's head. Something so dramatic can only come from obsessive dedication: the talent plus the work to make it manifest. But if you're that single-minded from before your adolescence, how do you develop as a person?

Smith is almost impressively dull. He's pleasant, tackling his media dealings with good grace and a rehearsed kind of honesty. But after touring alongside his team for years, all I knew was that he liked cricket and Roger Federer and his girlfriend. Later he developed a fondness for New York City. He didn't have much else going on. His social media posts were PR duties. He only read self-help books. When I asked in Sri Lanka about interests outside cricket, he looked visibly constipated for a long moment before saying he might get into real estate, the most classically boring pursuit for the lost ex-sportsman. At one stage he wrote (or approved) in his colourless memoir that his agent had literally ordered him to find an interest, so Smith bought shares in racehorses and never went to see them run. When he pulled out a camera drone in South Africa, it was the first time he had indicated having an actual hobby.

Which makes it even weirder that Smith was ordered to lighten the mood in 2010. 'I've been told that I've got to come into the side and be fun. Whether it's telling a joke or something like that, it's to make sure we're all upbeat and ready to go.' They couldn't have picked a less likely candidate to bring the LOLs. If he had any joker in him, that experience would have burned it right out, exposing him to a working-over that he still resents. In 2017, when Smith said Anderson was a huge sledger, he referenced his own treatment with outward defiance. But in his voice and his expression was a shadow of a trembling lip, and you felt for that kid who had walked out there just wanting to play and got roasted instead. His youth had fooled management: this was the most intense player on the team.

One of my favourite Steve Smith moments didn't involve Steve Smith at all. In 2013 filming vox pops outside Lord's, we spotted a punter in a terrible blond wig and replica team shirt. Smith had taken three wickets to claw his team back into the game, so I barrelled up and started interviewing the impersonator as the real thing. Worse for wear after a long day, he rose to the occasion magnificently. 'Look, if I'm honest, I bowl pies, and shit gets wickets, what can I say,' came out in a classic Australian drawl. 'If Clarke had have held me back any longer I would have burst. I was dying to get amongst it. I was burning for success.' I asked what his favourite wicket had been. 'The caught-and-bowled. Because I did it all. I bowled it, and I caught it. It's all me. When the quicks were getting smacked around, I thought, there's only one guy in the side that can do this, and it's me. People call me a batsman. I call myself a cricketer.'

It's only got funnier over the years. The real Smith's every utterance is so controlled, trying desperately to do the right thing. In that interview when he'd first made the T20 side, well before anyone knew who he was, there's a moment: 'It was always pretty much cricket, I never liked school all that much.' Then a second of worry, as he realises these are not the sentiments of a Good Boy. 'I tried my hardest when I was there, and that sort of thing,' he doubles back. 'But it wasn't really sort of for me.'

At the 2015 World Cup final, Warne made headlines for his booze-focused questions to the winning players, and some gem edited a parody voiceover that has sadly vanished from the internet. It needed little exaggeration. 'How many beers are you having?' Warnie slurred to all and sundry in a growly overdub. 'Starcky, you love a fucken beer, how many tins'll you sink tonight? Forty, fifty?' But for all that the impersonator nailed Warne, he was never more painfully spot-on than for an awkwardly grinning Smith, looking typically teenage under his gold cap. Warnie asked what kind of beer he'd be slamming. In a nasal boy-tone brimming with rectitude Smith giggled, 'Oh, I'll say the sponsor's product, VB.'

All Steve Smith wanted was to win for Australia. His obsessiveness drove his success, then created a corresponding weight when he attained it. Having set his standard Smith had to keep meeting it. Having become leader of a fragile team he had to carry it. In Dharamsala, Hobart, Colombo, he held together while the rest fell apart. It wasn't fair, but Smith's temperament demanded taking everything on himself. The Fake Smith interview at Lord's had come strangely true: 'there's only one guy in the side that can do this, and it's me.'

His obsessiveness is clear when he bats, in his twitching and muttering and touching. Watch Smith in person and there's a routine you start to tick off, a rhythm to nod along to. Play the shot, walk to square. Grab pad, pad, box, helmet. Pad, pad, box. To the crease. Check the field. A bobbing knee bend, another. A couple of taps, a couple of wafts. Stillness as the bowler arrives, step across as he delivers. Everything in its right place. Perhaps that's why Smith doesn't like bowling, an imperfect art. His leg-breaks offend him like other adults regard their high-school bands. His game was about whittling away flaws. 'I think that's batting, you want to minimalise the ways you get out.'

When Smith says he loves batting, he means batting. Other players start fanging for big shots but he loves a good leave. All he wants is to face bowling for as long as possible. Anyone who has shared a net session can testify. After Melbourne's turgid Ashes draw, when the crowd sighed in relief as it was called off, Smith came in saying he wished he could have played another couple of hours. He presented it as a joke, but the truth lay beneath the smile.

What wasn't evident was the toll his concentration takes. Brisbane, Pune: because he played like this consistently, we assumed he did it easily, dropping into the zone of long-innings players like Alastair Cook. 'Most would be too mentally taxed to do it again in the second dig, but Smith isn't most people. The way he responded after reaching his hundred, tapping the helmet repeatedly as though to re-set his computer, gives an insight into the relentless machine that it powers,' wrote Adam Collins in India. But those matches did cost Smith. Nothing is easy about having missiles flung at you for hours, having to make a good decision against each one. But other players seem to put a day behind them and tackle the next. Smith carried the cumulative strain. The longer the India tour went, the more frayed he became, illegally looking for video review advice from the dressing room, spitting expletives when Murali Vijay claimed a bounce catch.

Smith has said that he reads everything published about him, which tells you something in itself. That fourth night in Adelaide, the match still live, he sat up perusing media assessments of him not enforcing the follow-on. England had the remotest chance, yet it chewed at him just as he chewed at his nails and a strip of Xanax. He's said he doesn't sleep during Test matches – another of those non-joke jokes, and one that's mildly horrifying. When he met the Dalai Lama, there was one thing the Australian captain wanted from a holy man reputed to bring peace. 'I asked him a question about sleep and how he could help me. We rubbed our noses together and he gave me some blessings, so hopefully it'll help with my sleep over the next five days.'

Smith nearly blew up his heart in Brisbane. He worried himself sick in Adelaide. He cried with relief in Perth. Implicit in his triumph was fear, worthy of being capitalised to Hunter S Thompson levels: The Fear of what would happen if he didn't make that hundred, if they didn't get that lead, if they didn't seal that Test, if God forbid Australia didn't win the Ashes at home.

'Captaincy wears down many,' I wrote for ABC when he first stepped up, 'but as unlikely as it was a couple of years ago, Smith gives every indication he's up to the job.' Just as for Australia's board members and selectors, his feats with the bat made optimism easy. Two years later, after Brisbane, I got a bit closer to the mark. 'Watching, days like this are wonderful. Playing, they aren't sustainable. The emotional load, the physical toll. You can't fight probability for that long and emerge unscathed. Even Smith can't do it every time. Carrying a team for a day can be done. For a match, maybe. Carrying one for a series could break something.'

Chapter 12

DE KOCK FIGHT

March 2018

South Africa, the dying days of summer. Jacob Zuma had been prised out of the presidency on corruption charges as inevitable as they were slow to arrive. The equally notorious and non-stick Gupta cartel was meeting a similar reckoning, its members scattering around the world and stashing their private jet to avoid its repossession. After a long India series, cricket with Australia was not front of anybody's mind, not even the taxi drivers offering polite puzzlement as we cruised up and down the coastal highway from the team hotel at Umhlanga to the cricket ground at Kingsmead.

Durban is semi-tropical, pleasant, a city hugging an endless sweep of beach while the deep blue Indian Ocean thuds untrammelled down its flank. The days start early and end in spouts of light before night falls on cheerful bars pouring out the same few bland lagers. It seems an uncomplicated place, though this proves untrue when you hear stories from within the country's biggest Indian Muslim population, having evening gatherings outside chicken shops rather than beer halls, or when you cross the inland hills to the King Shaka International Airport named for the Zulu warrior who once ruled them.

Kevin Pietersen is the city's most famous cricketing émigré. In 2018 he began the MAK Pataudi Memorial Lecture by asking his audience to 'let me take you back to Durban in the early 1980s'.

> Shimmering heat. A baked pitch and a beige outfield. Concrete slabs on which I sat transfixed watching provincial cricket of a phenomenal standard. Intensity, bravery, application, skill, relentless competitiveness. It wasn't even Test cricket but in those days it was the closest we got.
>
> Day after day I watched. Glued. Transfixed ... years later when it was clear that I would be lucky enough to make a career out of the game I love, my dad told me precisely when he knew I would succeed. It wasn't a particular shot, a special innings, or the long hours of practice. It was those lengthy summer days sitting motionless on those scorching concrete slabs.

These were whites-only matches. Cricketers like future selector Hussein Manack played in segregated leagues. Visiting South Africa, you keep being surprised afresh by the reality of how recent the age of official discrimination was. Keshav Maharaj is another Durban boy, the spinner in the 2018 Test side – aged 28, he was born before apartheid died. Of those taking the field against Australia, only Kagiso Rabada, Lungisani Ngidi, and Aiden Markram were born after Nelson Mandela's 1994 election to the presidency.

At Kingsmead the current Test would channel the hard-fought matches past rather than the contemporary city's laid-back style. 'Invariably,' wrote Greg Baum for *The Age*, 'Australians work themselves into a feverish pitch for series against South Africa'. On the fourth day, 'this mindset burst like a bomb at the run-out of AB de Villiers'.

Nathan Lyon, who broke the stumps, dropped the ball on the prone de Villiers, a petty act for which he has been charged by match officials. Warner, who had thrown it to Lyon, howled at Aiden Markram, whose hesitation had been fatal to de Villiers. It matters not whether Warner swore, only that once again he was flaunting success in the face of his opponent, who had no recourse.

In Australia's superheated calculus, de Villiers and Markram had provoked them, de Villiers by being so good, Markram by still being there. Celebration wasn't enough; it had to be almost primitive triumphalism as well. Again.

And again, Australia's motto about playing hard but fair was shown up for the facade that it is, an alibi for anything goes. ['Warner takes another big swing, trips again', Fairfax, March 2018.]

Behind the Ashes, South Africa is a close second in significance for the players and a more distant second for the public. The contest is uniformly bloody-minded and has included some of the most dramatic moments for either country. Since international cricket readmitted South Africa in 1991 after two decades boycotting its regime, Australia had never visited and lost. South Africa was conversely the only twentieth-century team to win consistently in Australia.

Durban saw Phillip Hughes take flight with twin tons at the age of nineteen. Michael Clarke broke his shoulder during a Cape Town epic, Graeme Smith broke his hand and tried to bat out a Sydney draw. Mitchell Johnson had smashed that hand, then smashed the stumps with ten balls to spare. He smashed batsmen with a dozen wickets at Centurion, and bowlers with his unbeaten 96 and 123 at the Wanderers and Newlands. Fanie de Villiers demolished Australia in Sydney chasing 118, as did Vernon Philander in the Cape Town 47. Australia hit back with an epic chase at Johannesburg, teenage debutant Patrick Cummins taking the wickets and sealing the runs. There were similar chases in 2002: Ricky Ponting at Newlands and Herschelle Gibbs at Kingsmead, a win for each. Mark Waugh's Port Elizabeth symphony was as lush as Dennis Cometti commentating it. Ryan Harris won a series at Newlands with two tailing yorkers bowled on two busted knees in the dying minutes.

But lacking Ashes hype, dollars from broadcasters and ads and sponsors and tickets don't flow as thick or fast. South Africa's home schedule has kept them from Australia's box-office window of Boxing Day and the New Year, so the series got squeezed down to three Tests, even two, meaning fewer opportunities to imprint on public consciousness. In circular fashion this suppressed future value. Through persistence at being the best, South Africa forced the 2018 tour back to four matches. For pride Australia had to beat the best properly.

Philander was waiting, partnered by new sensation Rabada, a 22-year-old who already had 120 wickets from 26 Tests. Morne Morkel was playing his valedictory series. At the other end of a career was Ngidi, as tall but twice as broad, who had towelled up a good Indian team on debut. Maharaj was the left-arm spinner, Quinton de Kock the wicketkeeper. After two years of skipping Tests, AB de Villiers was back: a game against Zimbabwe, three against India, and now this. One of the best batsmen ever across all formats, he added high-wattage star power. His experienced colleagues were Hashim Amla, Dean Elgar and captain Faf du Plessis. Finding their way were Markram, Temba Bavuma and all-rounder Theunis de Bruyn.

Warner had arrived full of cheer, bullish about this next assignment. His mad itinerary had seen him finish a Test against Bangladesh in September, go to India for a one-day series, back to Australia in October for Shield preparation, play the Ashes, roll into one-dayers through January, then captain the T20 tri-series in Australia and New Zealand. He'd led a tournament win in Auckland, accepted the trophy late on a Wednesday night, gone to the airport via the hotel, and jumped on a plane to Johannesburg to arrive part-way through Australia's practice match. Two days later he was flying to Durban with three days to prepare for the Test. 'People who know me, if I have one or two days off here and there, I am rejuvenated and refreshed,' he said.

He'd relished the chance to lead in Smith's absence. Warner had been cheerful rather than antagonistic, bouncing between his players. Australia's T20 record was poor but, as in Sri Lanka in 2016, he found a way to instil fresh energy and belief in fringe players. In Auckland, as New Zealand's openers blasted towards 243, he kept a smile on his face and an arm around his bowlers, encouraging them to forget everything but the next ball. At the innings break he grinned at his charges and told them they could chase this easily. He detonated 59 from 24 balls to start the process, and a team full of belief sailed to 245 with an over to spare. 'If there is an opportunity for me to play all three forms if the schedule dictates, I'll want to play that. And that's just how I've always been. I just like having responsibility.'

Back in the Test team, his job was being the attack dog again. But this wasn't all Warner's idea. He'd been specifically encouraged since before the Ashes, reported Robert Craddock, by a group including Lehmann, while other sources suggested the coach was not the most senior person involved. Australia put in a request to Cricket South Africa to turn down stump mics between deliveries, claiming it was ICC protocol, but this wasn't something that preoccupied other teams. The mics stayed stubbornly up in any case: chatter round the wicket came loud and clear through our radio headsets.

'That's how I play my cricket, I live by the sword and die by the sword, so I'll keep playing with that energy and making sure I'm the voice in the team,' Warner insisted. South Africa was a prestige rivalry. More confident groups would have eyed a 30-year unbeaten record on rival turf and felt cocky. For Smith's callow Australians, self-belief was less potent than fear of breaking the streak. As the series began, who knew what combination of anxiety, belief, worry and bravado was pumping through their veins.

Things didn't have a chance to heat up early. Australia batted first, which tends to postpone controversy, then South Africa got out so fast there wasn't time to develop an extended soliloquy on anyone's deficiencies. The opening day was attritional on an abrasive surface, an even 5–225. South Africa had prepared spicy green pitches for India and been beaten up by a formidable pace quartet, barely escaping with a series win. So it was no surprise that Australia's first two outings were on slow grounds – Kingsmead is the site of Sri Lanka's only win in South Africa, when Rangana Herath spun his team to victory.

Philander picked up Australia's openers with accuracy, Rabada got Usman Khawaja with seam, and Maharaj ripped a few on his way to picking up Smith and Shaun Marsh. There were starts but no finishes. Warner had made 51 but fallen at the end of the first session. On radio at stumps he was frustrated but complimentary. 'It wasn't so much getting out at lunch, but just a third wicket lost in that session. The way they bowled was great, they were up and about, set good fields, and asked questions with the ball shifting [reverse swinging] … Obviously the ball shifting after twenty-odd overs on the first day is incredible.'

The second day saw Mitchell Marsh as he was in Perth, with solid defence and crisp decision-making but against far tougher bowling. Where most pitch maps look like an acne outbreak, Philander's was a single red blemish on an off-stump line. Rabada found both types of swing with old ball and new. On the ground where he made his first-class debut aged sixteen, Maharaj landed everything. Yet starting the day on 32,

Marsh got to within a blow of a century to take Australia to an eventual 351.

Starc's campaign to promote Cummins above him succeeded, meaning the younger bowler could play the responsible hand while the senior quick was freed up to have fun. Cummins did his part in defending for most of an hour, seeing off eleven overs of the new ball that had claimed Paine. When Maharaj eventually snuck through him for 3 off 39, Starc swaggered out to break the tension with 35 off 25. Maharaj bowled him right on lunch, but the momentum had swung.

That got Marsh moving. He had blocked 28 in the session before his sandwich, but smacked 36 from 26 balls afterwards. On 96 he was second-last dismissed trying to raise his milestone, the one shot in his four and a half hours where he lost his shape. Falling away, he might still have dragged Philander over mid-on had he not tried to clear Morkel's telescope frame.

It had no bearing on the result. South Africa looked good after lunch, were three down by tea, and all out by stumps. Lyon was the masterstroke, brought on with a hard new ball. The left-handed Elgar turned across the line and looped a leading edge for another spectacular caught-and-bowled, then the right-handed Amla spliced extra bounce to short leg. In an over Lyon had passed Craig McDermott's 291 to become Australia's sixth-highest wicket taker. Bancroft under the helmet snared another, Markram fending a ribcage ball from Cummins right on tea.

For a few overs it looked like du Plessis and de Villiers would steady, targeting Lyon with a counter-attack. Then came Mitchell Starc. Picture this. Left-arm round the wicket. Extra wide on the crease, as far towards mid-off as he can legally get. He's used this angle before: Sri Lanka in Galle, Pakistan at the MCG. Usually the idea is to swing the ball in to smash stumps, creating an angle tailenders can't defend. This ball, though, is to a top-order batsman – the rival captain. It is aimed at the stumps, but late, very late, it reverse-swings *away* from the batsman, who has set up for the inswinger. It hits the pitch and jags further, too full to miss the bat, taking the edge of a defensive shot whose application and line was totally justified on all available evidence. The wicketkeeper gloves the deflection, the bowler's arm rises in victory. The ball has done a magic trick, and it is less than 28 overs old.

Magicians aren't supposed to do the same trick twice, but Starc produced the exact same delivery to get de Bruyn, then Philander. Left-handers Rabada and Morkel got inswingers, one blowing off the pad and one blowing up the stumps. In the session, Starc had bowled 34 balls for fifteen runs and taken a five-wicket haul. Lyon had turned a ball massively past de Kock's defence and ticked the top of off stump, while Hazlewood had more explosively bowled Maharaj.

Amid the wreckage, blinking as though just out of a bomb shelter, stood Abraham Benjamin de Villiers. At 71 not out he remained as lonely on the scorecard as he was that day on the field. His own batting had been supreme, cutting and sweeping and timing each stroke to perfection. Bowlers who were lethal to everyone else were defused. But his decision to trust the tail had backfired – on taking a single with Maharaj, at seven wickets down, he might have envisaged getting support to fight through to a hundred. Instead he never got back on strike, as three teammates fell in eight balls. The final five wickets had added twelve runs.

Leading by 189, Australia only needed a middling second innings. South Africa chipped away through the third day, as did the visitors, with 20s and 30s. Bancroft topped the tally with 53, important given his slender Ashes returns had brought pressure to bear. Morkel bowled consistent short stuff on a pitch that rendered it toothless. The Perth-raised Bancroft was right at home pulling and cutting, and used his feet all day against Maharaj until he was stumped. Smith fell to left-arm spin again, this time the casual offerings of Elgar. By the fourth morning South Africa were set 417 to win, one run short of the world record. Maharaj nearly got a second bag of five, but had to settle for nine in the match after the video umpire denied him twice.

Starc nicked off Elgar, Hazlewood trapped Amla, then Lyon and Warner fatefully combined. Markram stared at the ball after tapping it square, de Villiers took off without Markram's attention, then had to turn back from too far down. The shining light from the first innings was face-down in the dirt for a diamond duck; it was 'a run-out for the ages,' wrote commentator Mark Nicholas on Cricinfo, 'primarily because the defeated subject was so great a prize.' It was the same sentiment, if more gracefully expressed, as Warner would use in justifying his reaction. Five overs later, Cummins produced a thing of destructive beauty to du Plessis, severe pace that jagged in and smashed off stump, the yellow pole completing four handspring backflips before it finally came to rest. The score was 4–49, it was half an hour before lunch, and South Africa's senior batsmen had made 9, 8, 0 and 4.

A pasting looked set, but the least experienced pair held firm. Markram and de Bruyn batted till the break, composed themselves, then grew expansive after it. The young opener dominated the stand, crashing repeatedly through cover. By now Warner was fired up. The win had felt close, but these upstarts were dragging it out. When de Bruyn edged Starc to the fence, the bowler laughed. When de Bruyn smashed two more boundaries in the over, Starc was a lot less cheerful. Running verbals ensued, and a no-ball when Starc lost his run-up. The all-rounder eventually nicked Hazlewood for 36, but by then Markram had 76 and the pair had added 87.

Markram's approach was one of bonsai-tending calm. He said nothing. Smashed on the arm, he bandaged the obscene swelling and carried on. When I asked later about handling that physical and verbal assault, he just smiled. 'Look, I don't think you have much of a choice in international cricket. As the opening batter you've got to be prepared to get hit and take a few blows on the body, and then get on with it. I don't get involved with verbal things like that, I just try and offer words of encouragement for the side, and from there when I bat it's just me in my own bubble.'

That probably annoyed Australia more than anything. Warner focused on de Kock. Even as they left the field for tea he was chipping away. As the teams entered the players' race, the fuse to blow the series was lit.

Not that we knew it. We were focused on the contest. It was 5–167, a strong recovery though South Africa remained 250 adrift. But as Markram steamed to a century and de Kock pinged the boundary with regularity, thoughts of a truly absurd comeback started to twitch in the depths of our cricket souls. Markram kept up his clean hits through cover, equally comfortable off Starc or Lyon, while his partner scored almost exclusively through third man, gliding wherever the cordon wasn't.

The target came under 200, then under 150. Cummins smashed Markram on the helmet, then the elbow; Markram tucked Cummins for boundaries either side of the keeper. Lyon nearly lost a hand to a return cannonball. The crowd got more animated with each run. Until with 134 to go, Marsh ended the fun. He had barely bowled in the Ashes, but with the keeper up to the stumps to stop Markram striding out, the tired batsman prodded and Paine took a brilliant catch. In the whole modern era, Durban's track had yielded one century in the fourth innings: Gibbs in that run-chase with 104. Markram had just made 143.

The air whooshed out of the contest. Starc smashed through three batsmen in an over. Philander nicked, stumps flew to end Maharaj and Rabada, and then ... Starc was taken out of the attack. On a hat-trick. Surely the only time this has happened to a bowler. All of South Africa shares one time zone, and with Durban on the eastern edge, night comes early and without argument. The light was leaving and the umpires threatened the same. With one wicket left and the modest batting of Morkel to protect it, they wanted the game over as much as anyone. A bowler capable of 160 kilometres an hour, though, was too much.

Smith used his leg-breaks to complement his off-spinner. Morkel faced out whole overs from Lyon, stretching his giraffe legs forward to smother each ball. The stump mics were loud and clear. 'Lyon has just been unbelievable,' Jim Maxwell said as he came off air. 'Effing this and effing that, he's relentless.' The great West Indies fast bowler Michael Holding was scathing. 'I don't turn up the stump mics when I'm on commentary. I don't want to hear all the rubbish that is going on. People these days think that they are in an opera. Keep your mouth shut and play some cricket.'

After nine overs under floodlights, even the lenient umpires Dharmasena and Ravi couldn't continue. The press prepared for media conferences and articles, unable to quite write about Australia's win while faced with the peculiarity of everybody having to turn up again in the morning for one wicket. Surely the fifth day couldn't provide any news, just a pivot in the story towards the next match. At a pizza place that night with a pack of South African journos, one of our dinner companions kept disappearing outside for hushed phone calls and frantically thumbed messages.

In the morning, before we'd properly woken up, our taxi driver asked what was happening with the Australians fighting. He had more to tell us than we could tell him, and as we scrambled for our phones he flicked on the radio. There was footage, he and the news explained between them, of this David Warner fellow in a brawl.

The vision was everywhere. Warner on the landing outside the change rooms bellowing as de Kock climbed the stairs. It was bluster more than the brink of physicality, like those men antler-clashing outside pubs who make a great show of having their friends hold them back. But it was ugly enough. Khawaja and Smith did the holding, Paine pushed from in front. Twelfth man Ngidi, at twice Warner's mass, looked on quietly bemused but was well placed to interpolate himself if required. Rabada emerged giving death-stares, and out strode du Plessis wearing a towel. He didn't need anyone to speak up. 'I heard the commotion and went outside and just asked David to go into his dressing room,' was the captain's calm summary.

Exuding authority in minimal clothing is no small feat: as Stephen King wrote in his Dark Tower series, 'Eddie was doing well. The gunslinger measured just how well by the fact that he was fighting naked. That was hard for a man. Sometimes impossible.' But near-nude leadership didn't interest the world's media. They wanted to report a punch-on in a sport where that doesn't happen.

Clearly the video had been leaked: it was internal CCTV footage, clipped so it didn't show the dispute kicking off, and with no audio to convey the subject. South African team manager Dr Mohammed Moosajee had watched the vision with his counterpart Gavin Dovey after play on day four, so South African officials must already have obtained it from stadium security. A couple of hours later came the furtive dinner scramble among local journalists.

Retribution was likely a factor. Some in South Africa's camp still believed their opponents helped cause du Plessis' ball-tampering charge in 2016, after Fox Sports published a television grab of him rubbing mint residue on the ball. Suspicions were reinforced a year later by the way Bairstow's headbutt hit the headlines. The mint footage had been broadcast on TV and supposedly was first noticed by a viewer: plenty of cricket badgers are obsessive enough to do that. But even if only for Bairstow, the Australians were now swilling their own make of medicine.

De Kock was dismissed on the last day for 83, but neither he nor Warner fronted for questions. The captains waged a proxy war as the rumour mill suggested de Kock had said something about Warner's wife, Candice Falzon. 'I think both parties, from what I've heard, there was a lot of personal stuff being said. That's obviously what made it go off the field,' said du Plessis, before a polite swipe at the umpires. 'If it was happening on the field it should have been nipped in the bud.'

Smith saw a wronged party and a party in the wrong. The fight was 'regrettable' but happened because 'Quinton got quite personal and provoked an emotional response from Davey. Those things are not on from both sides. Getting personal on the field is not on, and that's crossing the line in my opinion.' What about his fellow captain's characterisation? 'Faf can say what he likes, I guess. As far as I'm aware, I don't think we got personal.' The exact cause of the dispute was avoided. 'Next time you speak to Davey you can ask him.'

By the end of his conference, after his team had pulled off an excellent win, the Australian captain had been asked a total of two questions about the cricket. 'Unbelievable,' Smith muttered as he stomped to the door. Still, it had been his teammate creating the story, and it had been a tactical blunder to keep Warner from the press. The deputy could have shown up, said he'd been angered by a rogue comment, apologised for his response, and the story would have died its natural death. Instead, when he was sanctioned by match referee Jeff Crowe the next day, there was still information withheld and the story dragged on. Mark Nicholas appealed for a game that would move past these ill-tempered sideshows.

At first, the vice-captaincy appeared to have softened Warner's hard-bitten approach to the game. But no, he's back in full voice. At least he was. Warner now teeters, just a point away from suspension, alongside Kagiso Rabada and du Plessis, both of whom were notably quiet at Kingsmead.

It is hard to fathom Warner's thinking. Clearly he likes the idea of captaincy and might well have ambitions to lead the Test team. Recently he dropped the idea of politics into a conversation about life after cricket. His leadership of the recently successful T20 campaign was wholehearted, fearless and generally laudable. Why the fuse now? Maybe he feels talismanic in this regard – 'I'm not captain but I sure still lead the way.' It would be a good thing for everyone if Crowe's action tempered Warner's more boorish side. ['It is not a softer game we look for but a kinder one', Cricinfo, March 2018.]

Over the coming weeks, the scrutiny and punishment would indeed have a lasting effect on Warner and on all those around him. One thing it didn't do was calm anything down.

Chapter 13

EASY AS ABDV

On the terrace outside the Boardwalk Hotel in Port Elizabeth there's always a sea breeze. From Durban in the far north-east you come down South Africa's long curve to the base of the continent, where the Indian Ocean gives way to the Southern. Across that water lies the frozen ghostscape of Antarctica, some 4000 kilometres distant. Cast-iron chairs, heavy so they can't be carried off in a storm, screech as tourists drag them over stone flags. That sound gouged the air, red meters flickered on sound recorders. Quietly in the corner, ironed and scrubbed in his aquamarine team polo, David Warner was ready to say his piece.

He'd fought with de Kock on March 4th. The story broke on the 5th, charges were laid on the 6th, and this interview was on the 7th for release on the 8th. The lull was inevitably filled by speculation, and now Warner's first comment would be made to a handful of reporters clustered round a patio table.

South Africans weren't invited. Gerard Whateley, who since the Ashes had moved from the ABC to SEN, had flown from Durban to Melbourne for a football event and would reach Port Elizabeth hours before the Test. The independent outlets had Peter Lalor for *The Australian*, Chris Barrett for Fairfax, Ben Horne for the Murdoch tabloids, Adam Collins for *The Guardian*, Daniel Brettig for Cricinfo, Rob Forsaith on AAP wires, and Jim Maxwell and me for ABC. Cricket Australia's three-man media crew found their tour increasingly fraught as they had to report on a scandal while effectively embedded with the team. That was the entire travelling press pack: all male, recidivist tourists, barely enough to fill a minivan.

'I think you guys are well aware that I cop it left, right and centre, especially off the field from spectators,' was when Warner got down to specifics. 'I'm used to that and it doesn't bother me. But in the proximity of my personal space and behind me, a comment that was vile and disgusting about my wife, and just in general about a lady, was quite poor. My emotional response you saw, it was just something that I don't believe should have been said … I can't see anyone else making comments the way he made them, which were outright disgusting. As I said, it's a thing you wouldn't say about any lady, especially someone's wife or a player's wife.'

The nature of de Kock's sledge was confirmed, if not the content. Warner wanted the expedience of admitting some fault but couldn't quite bring himself to say it. He sought refuge in the passive tense: things that had happened rather than things he had done. It was like the Fonz trying to say sorry. 'We honestly thought there was not a lot in it until there was a bit of video footage leaked and we had to explain ... What happened the other day was not appropriate and I responded a tad emotionally. But I think I've been fantastic the last 18 to 24 months ... The other day was probably out of line. I've seen the footage and I regret the way it played out, but for me it is how I am, and I responded emotionally and regretted the way it played out. But I'll always stick up for my family.'

The prior few days had been a circus. Warner accepted his three demerit points but de Kock contested his one point from a lower charge. He would be found guilty anyway, as was routine, but the home side was crossing its arms in protest. De Kock told his teammates he'd said nothing to Warner, before further footage proved the opposite. Bickering continued about what constituted a personal comment. Paine tried to hold the party line while retaining some shred of honesty: 'We spoke about cricket stuff and a few little things with his fitness,' was his euphemism for Warner apparently calling de Kock a 'fat fucking bushpig'.

When it first leaked that de Kock had insulted Candice Falzon, bringing Warner some defenders and sympathy, Dr Moosajee started suggesting that Warner had insulted de Kock's sister. Dalean de Kock got on Twitter herself and offered to fight Warner – another cricket sibling helping out on social media. Steve Warner kept his own counsel, unless some posts about toilet mishaps he'd encountered as a plumber were a deep metaphor. Paine lined up the first whack. 'At no stage was Quinton's family mentioned, that's one hundred per cent false. I don't know how their team manager can hear from where he's sitting ... it's disappointing that they've come out now and said a few things that are just blatantly untrue.' Warner was 'taken aback by what was accused. I think that's absolutely frivolous', while Smith insisted his players 'had absolutely no idea he even had a sister, so I think that's completely fabricated and a load of garbage to be honest'.

At the heart of the conflict was one deep-seated feeling. People didn't like an attack dog marking territory on the moral high ground. For cricket's most persistent orator to complain about talk was too much. Warner also made a tactical stumble: he said the sledge was about Falzon for vindication, but low-rent opposition fans then had a line of attack to pursue. It was quickly deduced it involved Sonny Bill Williams, a rugby player Falzon had hooked up with in 2007. It was a non-story but modern Neanderthals thought it spicy fodder. People piled onto Warner's social media accounts, while trolls encouraged them to wear masks of Williams to the match.

Gate guards were told to confiscate the masks, but when one group of spectators was stopped, two Cricket South Africa suits intervened. Commercial manager Clive Eksteen and communications boss Altaaf Kazi not only decided it would be a good idea to let the group in, but to pose with them for a photo. Barrett got the picture and broke the story, CSA issued a lukewarm apology, and CA a frosty acceptance. Kazi resigned shortly after the series while Eksteen survived a disciplinary hearing.

South Africa's players wanted nothing to do with this stuff. De Kock's snap had ceded some ground, but they felt they were more in the right than Australia. Warner had history with this team, especially du Plessis and de Villiers from 2014, and they were angry at him dictating terms. At the time, the pair denied that Durban was an extra spur. 'I think the events in the first Test match were uncalled for and unnecessary, but I won't say that fired us up,' said de Villiers. But the truth would come out later in Johannesburg, when du Plessis spoke after the series.

'I think the biggest turning point was mentally. There was a fight in the eyes, you could see in the guys' faces that they wanted to stand up to this Australian team ... I know that [kind of anger] doesn't happen a lot in cricket, and it wasn't supposed to happen. But looking back at it now, after that Test match there was a unity where we said we want to stand up to this, we want to fight against this. It was a bad incident but it motivated the team.'

As the second Test approached, South Africa were ready to rumble.

Port Elizabeth. The whole town looked like it would aid reverse swing. Rough-edged, low-rise, clad in a rainbow of brown. An old port that had boomed and slumped and was trying to rally, the classic neoliberal tale. Waterfront wrapped in battle lines of barbed wire and freeway clovers. Creative spaces sprouting among industrial detritus. The Barking Gecko pub with steel grille doors that the bartender buzzed open; once you weaved past sleeping dogs and dying poker machines you could smoke inside and a longneck was two bucks fifty. From Richmond Hill, across the bay, lines of cargo ships waited to be tended. At night they formed a glowing ellipsis dotted out into nothing, each vessel dreaming in its own little island of light.

Past the docks was Summerstrand, where in the mornings Warner and Bancroft fed their bromance by joining Mitchell Marsh's sunrise swim, running glistening from the surf. Smith sent his camera drone out to sea to snap sunsets and marine life, culminating in the most creative moment of his online life when he filmed a local bottlenose pod and dubbed an Instagram video with the song Dolphin's Cry.

South Africa's oldest Test ground is a mishmash of antique brick turrets and new corrugated tin. St George's Park has a battered prettiness and an idiosyncrasy, from the Duck Pond End whose pond is home to no ducks, to the large prints of apartheid newspapers lining the walkways as a lasting comment. Conversely, it's also the only ground to honour an apartheid-era cricketer, the Graeme Pollock Stand named in 2013. Its media boxes are hutches running off a catwalk above the indoor nets. But inside them, you genuinely call the game from on top of the sight screen. It is the most extraordinary commentary view in cricket. When a fast bowler reaches the top of his mark it feels like you can tap him on his shoulder as he pushes off.

Bancroft started with a sturdy 38 but Philander made him yet another lunchtime wicket. Warner looked a million bucks in cracking 63, threatening to shrug off his week with a hundred that would have galled the locals to extinction, but in his dismissal was proof of South African ruthlessness. Morkel's wasteful Kingsmead performance saw him dumped for Ngidi, farewell tour or not. Second ball in his third Test, Ngidi produced a peach: right-arm over, angled across, shading back in to the left-hander and doing him for pace to launch both bails. 'That's an absolute goody!' was Shaun Pollock's sweetly innocent description as Warner stayed stuck in his defensive pose for several seconds, like Gandalf if the Balrog had faked him out and snuck by on his left.

Reverse swing was the local specialty, with dry wind across a cheese-grater square. The outfield was so hard it clunked when rapped with knuckles. Dale Steyn had taken Australia apart in 2014, from an opening partnership of 126 to all out for 216. After Warner and Chris Rogers, the bottom nine made single figures. That was the game where Shaun Marsh followed up his Johannesburg hundred with two ducks in three balls.

History repeated. This time the opening stand was 98 and the total 243. Steyn had blown out the middle order with four wickets; Rabada did it with five in a spell. Prowling in with big-cat menace, swinging and seaming inward and out, he nicked or trapped Smith, both Marshes and Cummins in seven balls. Two overs later he took Starc's stumps. It was carnage that only lacked Tony Greig's pronunciation. The collapse should have been worse but Paine salvaged 61 with the tail.

Against Smith, Rabada had come wide and slanted the ball in. Smith always steps a long way across to the off side, which brings the risk of missing the ball and being leg before wicket. He explained his technique in an interview with Mark Taylor.

I used to bat on middle stump, I used to have no prelim movement and stay very still on my back foot. I knew where my off stump was, but I could be drawn a little bit wider and be able to nick. I used to get out that way a little bit. It was actually in the middle of a game, in the WACA Test match in the Ashes in 2013–14, and they were bowling quite short at me. I decided to do a little prelim movement back and across to get out of the way of the ball.

Everything just clicked into place and it felt really good, so I've continued doing it. I was probably batting on middle and leg and going to middle at that point. I moved things a little bit across to leg stump, and now I'm going just outside off stump. It's a big movement, but for me it's about trying to minimise the ways that you get out. If guys get me out lbw, I say well played, congratulations, but if I nick one off that's when I get upset at myself.

Smith skips the key: when it's straight he doesn't miss. For years, internet know-alls wrote about him being an lbw candidate as though the professional cricketers of the world hadn't thought of it. Bowlers indeed targeted his pads – and he scored thousands of runs against them because his hand-eye pickup was so spot-on.

Against Rabada, Smith missed and started walking. But the moment that followed would prove more significant than the wicket. He called for a video review, rolling the dice as the team's best batsman. From the off side of the pitch he walked towards Shaun Marsh. Rabada walked across the pitch towards cover, pumping his fists and yelling. Smith flinched when he realised Rabada was next to him, and their shoulders connected hard enough for Smith to whip his head round to confirm what had happened. As he approached Marsh, he mimed a shoulder bump.

This wouldn't matter in most sports, but cricket is militant on physical contact. Checking an injury, congratulating a milestone, making an apology – these might involve a handshake or back-pat. Bowlers get tangled with running batsmen. But the slightest deliberate contact during play was a crimson flag: immediately a Level 2 offence worth three or four demerit points. Four meant suspension, three left a player on the edge like Warner. Rabada's problem was that he had already racked up five demerits, including a charge for shouldering a batsman. If he hit eight points, he would miss two Tests – the rest of the series. With his sanction due on day four, the prospect hung over the rest of the match.

With Australia knocked over, South Africa staggered in reply. Cummins trapped Markram before stumps, and though nightwatchman Rabada was the only wicket in the next two sessions, the score barely moved. The ball was reversing, caution was paramount, and Elgar and Amla battled through 46 overs for 88 runs. After tea, when Starc produced another unplayable to spin back Amla's off stump, Australia rushed through the breach. Everyone was getting reverse: Hazlewood away for Elgar's edge, Mitch Marsh in to pin du Plessis and de Bruyn. The score was 6–183, and an Australian lead looked a chance.

Over to AB de Villiers. You often hear players say he has more time, a strange sentence which is actually true. He judges the length and pace of the ball earlier, and uses that to get in better position, making his bewildering range and unorthodoxy possible. He's faster at choosing an option, and has hands so quick he can play the ball later. You bowl, then find AB already there, mind made up and time to spare. In this innings, under proper pressure, he made top-class bowlers look like dross.

He had replaced Amla and seen Elgar disappear. Next ball he crisply drove a reversing Starc delivery through wide long-off. Hazlewood came around the wicket, landing an awkward ribcage length with a tight line whose angle took it across to off stump – a ball that you leave before nodding at the bowler. De Villiers leant back, held his bat in its backlift, waited until the ball had all but passed, then chopped it clean off the Madras Rubber Factory sticker into the cordon gap for four.

Two more wickets fell and de Villiers really took off. Cummins had been Australia's best, constantly threatening. He was thrashed three times in an over: the carve was streaky, the pull commanding, the on-drive imperious. A third man was placed, so de Villiers cut Marsh in front of point instead. Lyon was reverse-swept from round the wicket, teasing Smith into the fence. Between the flourishes de Villiers did the spade work, up and down the pitch at every chance. Toil bore fruit: Elgar and Amla hadn't built up the score but had worn down the bowlers. De Villiers started getting full tosses, two from Starc for his fifty, diverting width to third man, straightness through midwicket, all with minimum exertion and a flick of the wrists.

De Kock, who once smashed centuries in his first three ODIs, made 9 off 44 before Lyon bowled him. That took South Africa's previous five batsmen to 19 between them while the score went up by 72. The St George's Brass Band got back to full voice: a fixture since 1995, their muted pomp and cacophony comes through the effects mic on any Port Elizabeth broadcast. Umpire Dharmasena had held up play to complain he couldn't hear. The band left in protest. Crowe held negotiations, and eventually the backing tune returned as de Villiers continued his solo.

It's hard to convey the charisma of how some cricketers play the game. They hold attention and seize imagination, stake a claim to memory while others never gain that purchase. When Australia plays, the final hour belongs to Starc. He's harder to see and his quarry is tired. He sniffs the air and likes what he scents. The crowd smells the danger, every ball becomes an event. It's his time. Except this time, de Villiers mugged him for it. While de Villiers was on song, late that afternoon in the golden hour of sunlight, every person in the ground was locked on.

He swept through a Lyon leg-side trap, glanced Cummins, then leant back into an insultingly casual uppercut over the cordon for four. South Africa trailed by two runs, and Starc finally took a new ball in the 90th over. De Villiers had time for a final glide against Hazlewood and ended the day on 74. He'd faced 81 balls, compared to Elgar's 57 from 197. A deficit of 88 when he came to the crease had become a lead of twenty. 'It's not often you get into that kind of zone batting,' he said later. 'I just felt so calm at the wicket. It's so strange, your head just goes quiet sometimes.'

Next morning, Philander took his share of the strike and cuffed the first three boundaries. His partner accumulated, then resumed his boundary groove. But another factor was kicking in: the thought of reaching a century was rattling de Villiers. He'd spent two years out of the game. Drained from touring and having kids, he had left Test cricket after three ducks in a row against England. One of the most revered batsmen in the world had gone more than three years without a century.

'I was very nervous in the nineties. I don't think it showed, but I was telling Vern out there I was struggling to breathe. My legs literally went numb.' His arms were heavy, palms were sweaty. Nervous, but on the surface he looked calm and ready to launch bombs – it's just he kept on forgetting if he knew how. The whole crowd would go so loud, but before it could happen, his man was out. Cummins jammed into Philander's ribs and Bancroft took the snare at short leg. Maharaj cribbed a single. There was no time to waste. 'You only get one shot', the chorus goes, but de Villiers has dozens. An uppercut to a proper bouncer nearly soared for six.

I'd won the roster lottery and was calling on radio. His 22nd Test ton would be de Villiers' last and probably most brilliant. The only thing I'd seen in person to rival it was Virat Kohli's fourth-innings marvel at Adelaide in 2014. The difference was that Kohli made one mistake. De Villiers had six hundreds against Australia, more than any other South African; he'd passed Graeme Pollock in the shade of the Pollock Stand. 'Sometimes you don't quite realise what you have achieved until you look back. We were about to collapse like we had in Durban and it was, "Here we go again". So to get through that and score a special hundred that helped the team to victory was unbelievable. It was one of my best ever.'

The pixie dust rubbed off as Maharaj clouted sixes from Lyon. De Villiers took up the challenge against a Cummins length ball that did not even approximate deserving half of it: dropping deeper in his crease, stepping outside off, then playing a pull that was really a swat, so laid back he was half asleep, ending with his left leg raised, toe pointed balletically downward, eyes tracking the trajectory towards the St George's Brass Band. 'It's probably the first time,' said Hazlewood later, 'I've thought that even if I bowl well here I can't get him out.'

Australia dropped the field back, and de Villiers toyed with them like an orca with a seal. He would drop the ball into the deep softly enough to sprint two, then clear the fielders who were brought up. He turned down singles early in overs and found them late. When Maharaj eventually faced Starc, the spinner slapped three fours in an over. Finally he was bowled, and Smith nailed a throw from the deep to run out Ngidi. But de Villiers was unbeaten and the damage was done: from nothing he had created a lead of 136. This was a batsman who had surveyed the situation, got out his keyboard, and activated God Mode.

Australia's composure was gone. The top order crashed to 4–86. Smith went to left-arm spin again, uncharacteristically chasing Maharaj. Shaun Marsh nicked for 1. When Warner was castled, Rabada kept his shoulders to himself but yelled in the batsman's face. He was immediately charged with yet another Level 1 offence. But the steam coming out of his ears was driving the machine. His pace was severe, his control immaculate. The last-chance pair taking Australia to a slender lead was blown away either side of stumps, Rabada swinging out Khawaja in the evening and Mitch Marsh in the morning. Paine scrapped but the lead was barely a hundred. Rabada added six wickets to his first five. Ten in a match is one of the rare feats of bowling – Makhaya Ntini did it four times in 101 Tests, Steyn held the local record with five in 86. Rabada had now done it four times in 28.

South Africa's openers fell early. Paine was in our headsets with a more genial line of chat than most: 'Come on boys! Let's get another one here, and watch AB shit the bed.' Instead AB made the bed with hospital corners, sprinkled rose petals over the covers, and left your favourite book and a cuppa on the nightstand. He played carnival shots for the crowd: the reverse-swat, a delicate flick that carried an off-break onto the hospitality balcony at midwicket, another of those very rude pulls to a length ball into empty acres over square. With the finish line in sight he knuckled Lyon to short leg, the first time a bowler had got him out in the series. You could tell how short of answers Smith was when he claimed that as a victory for morale.

The series was level and the temper was poor. Rabada fronted the media before being found guilty of both send-offs: one demerit point for Warner and three for Smith. The Australians muttered the right things about wanting to play the best, but were deeply relieved by his suspension. Tension remained between the boards, and anger in the dressing rooms.

As if there hadn't been flashpoints enough, a final point would grow in retrospect. Neil Manthorp is South Africa's answer to Maxwell, a broadcaster with distinctive tones and impeccable connections. On the third day, when de Villiers had finished up, Manthorp got on air and starting asking about medical tape. There had been suggestions, he said obliquely. Could Warner have sandpaper fixed into the strapping on his left hand?

Ridiculous, I said. Not a chance. He'd broken several digits on that hand, so he used silicon guards for batting, and strapping in the field. He'd also just moved back into the slip cordon after two years banished to mid-off for his own safety. There are pictures, Manthorp countered, that show areas of varying colour on the palm of his hand, like there are different materials involved. Doesn't that seem a little unusual? But Warner had used that tape for years – I'd been there when he started, coming back from his last broken finger.

At the innings break on the last day a familiar tune had come over the muffled PA. Fast and electronic, high synth notes in frantic succession. Cue flashbacks to an era when it would have churned a dancefloor and when half the New Zealand team had it as their walk-on music for one-dayers. 'Are they playing Sandstorm?' I asked hesitantly. 'What's Sandstorm?' Neil replied.

Not everyone expects a cricket broadcast on two national networks to go down a rabbit hole about pioneer 1990s rave-culture crossover tracks, but away it went. After so many tense days we had finally relaxed. The series was about to fall level. The disciplinary process was a foregone conclusion. The off-field politics had surely reached their end. There were nine free days ahead, stretching out across elephant parks and sunny beaches. We didn't know that at the other end, another sandstorm was coming our way.

Chapter 14

SHAME SHAME BUT DIFFERENT

As the Warner brawl prompted ongoing discussion and retribution, only a few contributors conveyed the problem with Candice Falzon's treatment. They included the vastly outnumbered women who write about cricket, such as Firdose Moonda and Melinda Farrell, and a disproportionate number of the sport's female followers. Most people focused on Warner, saying his conduct deserved the response. When the Sonny Bill Williams masks were banned, spectators made their jibes via signs, t-shirts, songs and shouts.

On the second night at Cape Town – the day before the tampering story would blot out all else like an ancient curse on the sun – Darren Lehmann gave the press conference. This wasn't unusual: the phenomenon known as Bad Day Boof has its equivalent with every team. But as the name indicates, it happens when no players have produced a performance of note. Runs for Bancroft and Lyon would normally have earned a nod, but Lehmann had a message to deliver.

I think it's been disgraceful. You're talking about abuse of various players and their families, personal abuse – it's not on, on a cricket ground. Anywhere around the world, it shouldn't happen. You can have the banter, and that's fine, banter's good-natured fun by crowds. But they've gone too far here.

We've written to Cricket South Africa – Cricket Australia have done that – and we'll see their response. But it's been poor. It was personal, it was poor. And [Warner] wasn't the only one. It has gone too far with the crowd here. They've got to be better than that when they're coming to international arenas to watch a game of two quality sides playing against each other.

They go hard on the ground, but you don't expect that when you're leaving the ground, or you're having a go at someone's family.

Outside the visiting dressing room was a balcony where players' families sat. Falzon had her daughters in tow. Over the first two days, spectators had shouted slurs of the type that men grab by instinct when scrabbling at the bottom of their mental lockers for a weapon against women. Several men had been kicked out. The Australian entourage was upset. But for opponents, Lehmann's response was more evidence of his team dishing it out but not taking it, especially given how many South Africans had worn racist slurs over the years.

Former wicketkeeper Mark Boucher burned his monthly ration of exclamation marks on Twitter. 'Correct Darren! Fully agree! But start cleaning up in your own country first! The personal, racial abuse I've witnessed in Aus was ridiculous. You guys don't live in a glass house! Why the fuss all of a sudden? Seems fine when the shoe is on the other foot!'

His captain Graeme Smith chimed in. 'Absolutely right, and I don't condone any of it. But blimey, I have never seen an Aussie team whinge and whine like this!' The polite and peaceable Morkel noted that 'When we play in Australia, I've played in Melbourne, I've copped the same sort of abuse.' Former England skipper Nasser Hussain jumped on Warner: 'Some of the stuff he was alleged to have said to England's players during the Ashes was way too personal. Yet the moment anyone has a go at him, he starts bleating about where the line is.'

Stuart Broad at that point had played 27 Ashes Tests. 'Any England player, even media, who have toured Australia can laugh at those comments because some of the things we hear on the pitch from Australian supporters, known as "banter", I know is worse than South Africa. It's such an interesting point but it looks like things might change for that team for a bit.'

Before the 2013–14 Ashes, Lehmann had urged spectators to target Broad for a grudge from the previous series: Broad had elected not to walk after edging a ball, which was itself an adventurous arena for Australian self-righteousness. Apparently deflecting off the wicketkeeper to slip made it special. 'Certainly our players haven't forgotten, they're calling him everything under the sun as they go past,' Lehmann had said in comments made light-heartedly on radio, but widely reported nonetheless.

'I just hope the Australian public give it to him right from the word go for the whole summer and I hope he cries and he goes home. I hope everyone gets stuck into him.'

'We lost the series but it didn't make me cry,' was Broad's riposte. 'From the outside it looks like Australia have started a lot of fights and then are moaning when someone comes back.'

The language above is instructive. Whingeing, moaning, whining, bleating. Bullies who couldn't digest their own product. It was true on its face that Warner didn't deserve status as an injured party. He had been explicit and enthusiastic in targeting opponents. It was true that Australian teams had the worst reputation and were the most broadly disliked. But in all the back and forth, no one seemed to grasp the deeper issue.

Start with the fact that the subjects of abuse were not players but women bystanders. Falzon's offence had been marrying someone people didn't like. Justifying an attack as a way of riling Warner glossed over needing to injure a different human being to do so. Hurting someone by punishing others is a form of hostage-taking. How the men in this scenario feel is irrelevant; the rights and wrongs have to do with women, and environments that permit them to be targeted.

Falzon's case was especially pernicious because it doubled down on existing abuse. The back story was nothing more substantial than she and Williams being young and drunk and hooking up at a pub. He was a rugby player, she was an ironwoman, both were recognisable, so when they had a moment in a bathroom stall, some charmer stuck his phone under the divider to snap a photo. The result – two clothed blurry figures standing next to each other – is more suggestive than demonstrative. The only salaciousness comes from the creep crawling around a toilet floor with a camera, something that could have got him two years' jail had anyone bothered chasing it up. Instead *The Daily Telegraph* banged the photo on its website, and a feeding frenzy began.

A gross invasion of privacy spawned an even grosser interpretation. In Australia, where we're mostly free to do as we like, it's been common for decades to go drinking and perhaps entertain a brief physical interest in someone you meet. It's not for everyone, but it's a normal part of life for lots of people, especially in their youth. Once published though, Falzon's story was twisted into a source of shame. With puritanical savagery she became fair game. As for the other half, no big deal: 'Sonny Bill and the slut' was how it ran on rugby forums. One got not only respect but affection via his given name, the other had her identity stripped entirely. Prisoners are given numbers for a reason: the most dehumanising thing you can do to a person is deny them their name.

For Williams the consequences were limited to driving round his neighbourhood buying every copy of the newspaper to prevent his girlfriend seeing the story – a strategy that was unfathomably ineffective. He became a star across codes, won a Rugby World Cup and made a pile of money. Falzon was sniped in gossip pages, slated online, yelled at in the street. She became miserable and withdrawn, thought about killing herself, and never stepped back into the public eye with the same confidence. Six years later when she met Warner the undercurrent of scorn swirled on. The pub photo still kicks around the internet like a dormant virus. South Africa saw a fresh breakout.

Across most human cultures, female sexuality is the most potent locus of shame. It's the basis of profanity so raucous that people find it hilarious, profanity so potent it leads to violence, and profanity so overused it becomes innocuous – most people saying 'motherfucker' would be bewildered if you took it literally. Any sex for any woman can be portrayed as transgressive. So women have their sexuality attacked directly; men are attacked via the sexuality of their mothers, sisters, daughters, wives. Where women are perceived as objects of purity, sex sullies the women and emasculates the men around them.

When someone aims that abuse at men, they claim they're not attacking women. What they're actually doing is positioning men as the owners of women. It's a throwback to repression and possessiveness, the legacy of male-dominated societies and male desire for control. This is what gets women murdered for family honour. This is what gets women murdered by jealous partners. This is the reality of the intense, corrosive sexism at the heart of the matter, where women aren't supposed to have a sexual existence at all.

Even Falzon felt the pressure to buy into it. 'I've made a mistake and I'm very, very sorry about it,' she said in 2008. 'I'm conscious of my image as a sportswoman and I've got a responsibility to young people. Young girls look up to me.' But the worst thing she had done was be mildly inconsiderate of anyone needing the bathroom. People should be able to make their own sexual choices with consenting participants without being censured, let alone attacked.

Cricket South Africa invited further attack. Leaking Warner's stairwell video made it certain the details would follow. So did a protracted, coordinated campaign of humiliation. Senior employees joined in like it was a jolly ruse. CSA capped things off with a milquetoast apology, that the organisation 'wishes to distance itself from the alleged action of certain officials'. Someone who had done nothing wrong was accepted collateral in hurting the hated opponent. Every other woman in cricket was told that she too could be the centre of contempt.

South African colleagues suggested their country was behind the times. 'There's no Me Too movement in South Africa', was one summary. But Australia was where Falzon was first pilloried. Australian spectators use similar abuse. As Warner was in the headlines, Australia's National Rugby League was supporting a contract for Matthew Lodge, a player with unresolved cases of assault and death threats against multiple women, who had fled the United States without paying damages awarded in one attack. This is a failing not of nationality but gender. Falzon's online abuse is a project in global cooperation. So many men are angrier at the concept of taking responsibility for men hurting women than they are about the reality of women being hurt. They refuse to see the inaction of the many as influencing the actions of the few.

When Warner flipped, it wasn't just about an insult to his wife. It was about years of her being bullied and belittled for something millions of people have freely done. It was about strangers deciding she was a target to shoot at whenever they liked. He'd seen what it had done to her. As much as you can build a carapace against repeat attack, there are moments when it breaks through.

So we're back to the multiple truths of David Warner. He personally didn't have a leg to stand on. He was also right about what was unacceptable. He was less right about approving his own contributions. All the ex-cricketers had a point about the reticence of genies to go back in bottles. Or as Greg Baum formulated it with more insight, 'Nastiness is a nasty business. If you choose to deal in it, you cannot expect to set the rules about what is acceptably nasty and what is not. And you cannot be surprised when it all spins out of control.'

No one knew this at the time, but Falzon had been pregnant through the tour. After weeks of abuse in person and online, after a previous humiliation was dragged open for people to pore through again, the strain of the Cape Town week, the long flight home, her husband's public apology, and blaming herself for all of the above, Falzon had a miscarriage. The abstract figure people thought they were attacking turned out to be a real human, flesh and blood, tough and fragile. In no world, under no justification, should she ever have been forced into the middle of this mess.

Chapter 15

EXCREMENT MEETS VENTILATOR

At the end of the coastal road from the south, Table Mountain is waiting. It's been waiting since long before there was a city to watch. Now it looms silent over Cape Town, refusing to be drawn on endorsement or disapproval. It permits the city on its skirts but no higher. Wind scours it at night, howls of exultation, tracking the curve of highways round its flanks in a mad ribbon ballet. Below them, strands of light in matching circles make a neckpiece for the king. Slopes climb until they become vertical, deep green fading into greys and reds to the crumbling top. Clouds clamber, fog ascends and trails, then both are stripped by sun and breeze to start days bare and new. The summit is omnipresent, a thing of impossible bulk, watching so close over every shoulder it startles you on turning around. A stone rolled from the top would surely hurry straight into the sea.

Its dangling peninsula ends in the Cape of Good Hope, target for any sailor to go round. Cape Town's centre feels like a European city tacked onto the coast. White locals and travellers burble out from pricey venues, black drivers circulate for fares. Money makes its own apartheid: in the residential streets of each city, see the high walls, the barbed wire, the armed guards, the mirrors and cameras and lights in blinding array. Every house is a compound set in defence. As white Australians with an exchange rate on our side, we fitted right in and felt ill at ease with the fact. This is Africa, Danny, after all.

Cape Town means drama for Australian cricket. Bowled out for 47 after rolling South Africa for 96. Ryan Harris winning a series with four overs to go. Peter Roebuck's death at the Southern Sun Hotel. This time, Kagiso Rabada was appealing his suspension, meaning a new hearing in front of an independent judge. This brought not the slightest surprise. 'South Africans' knee-jerk response to any attack, legitimate or not, is resolute defence,' wrote Telford Vice for *Wisden Cricket Monthly*. 'This has been true since 1652, when Europeans arrived on our shores to stay and considered the place theirs. They were, of course met with resistance.'

The cricket team was an exemplar. ICC bans don't get overturned; charges are levied based on convention rather than the letter of regulations. But one team fights them as an expression of grievance. Faf du Plessis contested his mint-based tampering charge not on the basis that he didn't do it, but that everyone else does. In Durban the argument was that de Kock hadn't said anything on the few available seconds of leaked video. 'Our strike rate is zero per cent at the moment with trying to challenge these cases, it will probably stay at zero,' said du Plessis of Rabada.

His team scrambled to defend its strike bowler nonetheless. The South African internet lit up with #RabadaMustPlay. Philander stirred that pot with the midnight Twitter action of a man at the wrong end of twenty Castle Lagers, likening Smith to a footballer diving for a penalty. The Philander who awoke next morning claimed his account had been hacked. Andrew Wu noted that it was an unusual hacker whose aim was to slightly inflame cricketing tensions via a solitary tweet, and a punctilious hacker to perfectly mimic Philander's sentence structure and punctuation.

Rabada had form. In barely over a year, he had collected three points for bumping Sri Lankan wicketkeeper Niroshan Dickwella, one for a screaming send-off of England's Ben Stokes, and another for the same against India's Shikhar Dhawan. Then in one match came his charges for Smith and Warner. His first conviction had involved a nudge of his forearm against Dickwella's bicep while walking back to bowl, so he knew how strictly this was policed. He wasn't learning. Michael Holding spoke on Cricinfo like a no-nonsense patriarch clipping young bucks round the ear: 'You can shout and go after your teammates and hug them or kiss them or whatever you want to do. But leave the opposition alone.'

It was no coincidence that Rabada's anger was at Warner and Smith. In the Durban video, he cruises into the stairwell as Warner is shoved into the dressing room, the bowler moving as if to follow and lifting his chin as if to shout. Paine rests his fingers gently on Rabada's chest and motions to keep calm, while du Plessis also bars his way. After the South African captain and his towel move out of shot, Rabada stares after the departed opponent with a look of contempt. 'Never in my 14 years of refereeing,' wrote Jeff Crowe of Rabada's bump, 'have I seen such animosity between two teams that was mainly a result of the debacle in the previous Test in Durban. This I have no doubt is a contributing factor to the events that occurred under this Code of Conduct charge.'

In Port Elizabeth, Rabada admitted he was culpable. 'It's going to have to stop. I can't keep doing this because I'm letting the team down and I'm also letting myself down. I would've loved to have been playing the next game.' It took several moments of thought before a revision to 'Actually, I don't know if I'll be playing or not. It's not looking good.' But it was worth making the case. He was the best fast bowler in the world, in a huge series poised at 1–1. And in South Africa's legal scene, Dali Mpofu was his equivalent.

It worked. The star lawyer and his supporting team convinced another star lawyer – New Zealand QC Mike Heron, who was hearing the appeal – that he could not prove the bump was deliberate. Heron's judgement exonerated Smith: 'Mr Rabada could have avoided the contact. Mr Smith was walking towards the batsman at the other end … and was not at fault in any way in continuing his line. It was Mr Rabada who moved towards Mr Smith.' But for Mr Rabada, Heron overturned years of convention that had papered over a poorly written clause.

Players had always been held responsible for contact if they created a situation that made it likely. Officials in Port Elizabeth followed that precedent. The relevant article, though, called it 'inappropriate and deliberate physical contact'. Heron interpreted that legalistically: Rabada's actions were 'provocative, disrespectful and involved getting close enough that the risk of physical contact was high', but these qualities did not make contact 'deliberate'. Smith's testimony was not requested.

The Level 2 charge was replaced by a lighter Level 1 for inappropriate behaviour. With the bowler on six demerit points and suspension due at eight, Heron discussed how many points he should impose and whether the code permitted him to consider the consequences. He didn't mention that a star player missing a title fight wasn't something Test cricket could afford. After making everyone sweat, he decided on a one-point penalty, wagging a finger with 'Mr Rabada will be well aware of the consequences of any further breaches.' Two days out from the Test, Rabada was free. Every sportswriter in the city glanced at Robben Island and resisted a howler of an analogy.

Smith was furious. The uncertainty had kept the Aussies on edge for their whole break, before falling against them in unprecedented fashion. For them it felt like another injustice, leaving both sides stewing over perceived wrongs. The next day Smith Instagrammed a shot of Newlands and its mountain backdrop. 'Excited to play at this beautiful ground tomorrow. It's in my top 3 grounds in the world. Can you guess my other 2 favourites?' (Probably Lord's and the SCG, that's his wheelhouse.) But at Newlands, his preview press conference was held in filthy mood.

Smith is cautious in speech, sensitive to how words appear in print, but his tone and body language broadcast in semaphore. At the press conference and his ABC interview to follow, he expressed polite disagreement but the resentment was obvious. 'The ICC have set the standard, haven't they? There was clearly contact out in the middle. I certainly won't be telling my bowlers to go out there and after you take a wicket go and get in their space. I don't think that is on and part of the game.'

He felt the legal process had made a fool of him. 'Particularly being the person Rabada came in contact with, I was a little bit surprised that I wasn't questioned at all about what happened out in the middle ... When you're looking for evidence and those kind of things, the other person involved not getting asked about it is pretty interesting.' As for Crowe being publicly overruled, 'I'd be feeling a bit annoyed if I was him, to be perfectly honest.' The grudge would weigh on Smith into his next appointment.

Day one dawned perfect and clear, the mountain crisp against blue. Overnight scorecards showed England had collapsed for 58 in Auckland. There was that buzz of anticipation before a new contest. All the controversy hadn't been able to swamp that. What mattered now was that scores were level between some of the best in the world.

The game delivered, Elgar and de Villiers batting in their contrasting styles until after tea, when Cummins turned in a tireless and brilliant spell. The junior bowler who always operated under threat of injury sent down eight overs straight without dropping pace or swing, taking four wickets for eight runs. Australia kept the old ball past 80 overs as it reversed, helping Mitch Marsh and a tiring Starc. South Africa's 2–220 became 311 all out. The opener carried his bat for the third time in Tests, a tally matched only by the Bajan king Desmond Haynes. Elgar's 141 along with 64 for de Villiers had saved an innings otherwise rich with single figures.

Come the second innings on the second morning, the animosity with Rabada could finally be expressed. In the 2000s, TV cameras sometimes showed close-ups of Damien Martyn whispering as the bowler ran in, 'Watch the ball. Watch the ball.' Warner apparently faced up to Rabada mouthing the batting mantra of 'Put him on the fucking moon.' After five balls that saw Warner get hit, drive four, and edge past his stumps, the next five went to the boundary or over it: a square punch with no footwork, a descent to one knee for a cover extravagance, a midwicket flick, a fairground pull on a steeply rising diagonal onto the upper deck behind fine leg, then hurling the bat at a no-ball past gully. Rabada's follow-up was a heatseeker at the stumps, with Warner expecting a bouncer and stranded in back-foot defence. 'I wouldn't say Dave did anything out of the ordinary to attack him or anything like that,' was Bancroft's translation of opening a Test innings with 30 from fourteen balls.

For Daniel Brettig on Cricinfo it 'told a rather different tale'.

It spoke of a batsman and a team stung by a fast and fiery adversary, mounting an attempt to fight fire with fire that left the Australian first innings a smoking wreck on a deteriorating Newlands pitch. Warner, undoubtedly, was trying to assert himself; Rabada, definitely, put a stop to it ...

Across this series, Rabada's duel with Warner has been critical to its direction, both tilting further and further towards South Africa the longer they have gone on ... There was no send-off from Rabada, but utter glee from the hosts; a heavyweight bout ended by knockout. ['Rabada puts Warner, Australia in fight-or-flight mode', Cricinfo, March 2019.]

As Warner walked up the race he was followed and berated by one of those corpulent middle-management heroes who sits in the bar announcing that if he were a few years younger he'd just pop this Starc joker back over his head. Morkel was back in the team for Ngidi and grabbed a wicket either side of lunch: Khawaja flapping at a hook; Smith in the most un-Smith-like fashion, fending at short wide nothingness that could have been belted or left alone. Morkel had started his penultimate Test on 297 wickets and the Aussies were throwing donations into the tin. Shaun Marsh got him home, genuflecting to flail cross-batted at some more wide dross against a bowler whose danger was bounce. Alongside Steyn, Ntini, Donald and Pollock, the South African 300 Club could no longer fit in a taxi.

Bancroft went into combat mode on a wicket giving assistance, playing edgily at times but watchful enough to survive the scares and cash in the opportunities. It took a fearful working over from Philander to trap him after his half-century swelled to 77, with several overs shaping and jagging away before one ball cut in just before tea. Three wickets went quickly afterwards, and the score was a dangerous 8–173 when Lyon started slapping cleanly on the pull and through the covers. The resulting 47 was his highest Test score, his chance of a milestone disappearing with one too many off-side lofts to give Morkel another soft win. Paine nailed down the other end, Hazlewood made it to the next morning, and the last two wickets shrank the deficit from 138 to 56.

By lunch on the third day, which Smith would claim was when the tampering plan was hatched, South Africa had taken that lead back out to 121 for the loss of Elgar. The ball was 22 overs old. In the session to follow, as Bancroft was testing his DIY skills, Amla mistimed serious pace to cover. Cummins had been the match's most dangerous bowler, de Villiers the series' most dangerous batsman. Cummins was sending down high 140s on a gloomy afternoon in a Test match. De Villiers got off the mark fourth ball he'd faced with a six. From a cut shot. Flat. Over cover point. He was batting on a different planet, different atmosphere, different gravity. We settled in for another special. Then the Supersport producers launched the Bancroft sting, and we saw what really happens when excrement meets ventilator.

Smith and Bancroft crossed the ground in dark that had nearly finished falling, the gallows walk towards the distant light. Up the lift and down the breezeway, entering the press box still dressed in grass-stained whites, spikes clip-clopping on the floor. The players took seats at the front, negotiating the lux of the spotlights. Media manager Kate Hutchison stood to the side to direct traffic.

Right from the jump, everything about the presser was wrong. The players hadn't even taken their baggy green caps off to avoid terrible optics in the news. Clearly there was only one topic – we weren't so much dealing with an elephant in the room as scrabbling for room inside an elephant – but Smith still had Hutchison throw to the floor for a question rather than tackling it head-on. When Peter Lalor did the formalities, Smith handballed to Bancroft like a disappointed parent: 'Do you want to explain?'

The team's junior member, fronting an intimidating if attentive room, tried to formulate a line around his stammers. His cleaned-up quotes were widely circulated, but the raggedness of what he actually said is telling.

'Yep, so, I've been, I've just had discussions with the match officials and, um, I have been charged with attempting to ah, um, ahhhgh. [Here he shakes his head and his voice drops almost into a growl.] To change the condition of the ball. Um, yeah look, we, we had a, um, yeah, a discussion during the break to, and um, yeah I, on my, on myself, I saw an opportunity to potentially use some, use some tape, get some, um, y'know, granules from the rough patches on the wicket, and try to, I guess, change the, yeah, change the ball condition. Um, it didn't work, the umpires obviously didn't change the ball, but I guess once I was, y'know, sighted on the, on the screen, and having done that, I panicked quite a lot, and ah, that obviously resulted in me shoving it down my, um, my trousers.'

'It was tape, was it?' interjected Lalor.

'Yeah. Yeah, so we have this, um, yellow tape in our kit and, um, it's connected to actually some, some padding, but the actual sticky stuff itself is, it's very sticky and I felt like it could be used to collect some stuff from the side of the pitch.'

Lalor switched to Smith to ask where the idea came from.

'Yep, the leadership group knew about it. We spoke about it at lunch. I'm not proud of what's happened. You know, it's not within the spirit of the game. My integrity, the team's integrity, the leadership group's integrity has come into question, and rightfully so. It's not on. [He also loses his thread, shaking his head.] It's certainly not on and it won't happen again, I can promise you that, under my leadership.'

When Rob Forsaith pressed Smith for detail, the evasions began. 'I'm not naming names, but the leadership group were what talked about it, and Bangers was around at the time.' None of it washed. A dance of passive language followed. Tampering was a 'mistake' and a 'poor action'. The pair were 'not proud' rather than ashamed. A plan to cheat was 'a possible way to get an advantage'. Both mentioned that it hadn't worked, indicating they'd rehearsed that line for mitigation.

Regret or embarrassment got sixteen mentions next to one apology. Remorse was less a feature than redemption; it was apparently time we moved on from something we'd only just discovered. There were three mentions of Smith's leadership and three promises of no repeats. 'I won't be considering stepping down. I still think I'm the right person for the job,' he offered with bewildering conviction. 'It's a big error in judgement but we'll learn from it and move past it.'

In the effort not to implicate anyone, Smith implicated everyone. The plan came from 'purely the players' he said in defending his coach. Then: 'I know the boys in the shed are embarrassed as well.' And: 'It's a poor reflection on everyone in that dressing room.' The 'leadership group' had six mentions and zero identified members. The last time such a group was mentioned had been a season earlier, when Glenn Maxwell was reprimanded by Smith, Warner, Hazlewood and Starc. Take them for a start, but that was in the ODI team. In a fluctuating Test side, Lyon had the most matches, Paine had started earliest, Shaun Marsh was the oldest, Mitch Marsh captained Western Australia, Khawaja captained Queensland. Really the only player exonerated was Cummins.

Smith even mustered a bit of chippiness, like at questions over Starc's reverse swing in Durban. 'You can ask questions as much as you like, but I can promise you that this is the first time it's happened. I think I've made it clear.' How dare you reproach the word of the Australian captain. 'Even if we weren't caught, I'd still feel incredibly bad about it,' he said when asked how much his remorse hinged on Supersport's camerawork. A few hours earlier he'd been on the same cameras lying to two Test umpires.

Having dragged in his teammates and admitted cheating, Smith seemed to think he could carry on without naming the culprits, without any detail on how it happened, and without sanction. His commitment to never again doing what should never have been done was supposed to be inspiring enough. His only convincing statement came from a Freudian slip. 'We're very regrettable, in our actions,' said Australia's captain.

Nine reporters managed a question in eight and a half minutes before Hutchison pulled her players from the room. It was the final blunder in a media disaster. Players are treated as a resource so valuable that their time and energy must be strictly rationed. But this time, the players desperately needed the press. My colleague Adam Collins channelled his previous career as a political adviser. 'When you're sprung, you've just got to eat the shit sandwich,' he said, shaking his head. 'The bit that fucks you is the cover-up. You run a till-they-drop press conference, you take your hit, you get everything out there, you get shit all over you, and you say you're sorry. It's the only way to get through.' Instead there were thickets of questions unanswered and confusion unclarified. An explanation that was half-arsed, half-hearted and ultimately half-witted would never pass autopsy.

As it would turn out, Smith and Bancroft were lying through their teeth. The tampering idea had come from Warner, who they were trying to shelter with their vagueness. So had Bancroft's recruitment, a question the batsman sidestepped. His tampering tool had been sandpaper, but tape and dirt sounded more impromptu. Especially among the Australian press, we took them at face value, as they took advantage of that to ameliorate the offence.

At that stage, crazy as it sounds, the players thought they could play down the story enough to soften the hit. Their level of concern was that Warner might miss one match on demerit points. Their level of delusion was that they could cover for him. Their level of hubris made them think Smith's captaincy would be secured with some solemn words. The Australian cricket team looked after its own.

The press conference should never have happened. Someone in team management should have been sharp enough to knock it on the head. Players faced the media while panicked enough to lie. This would end up more damaging than the original sin; there's not much less dignified than trying to squirm out of trouble. Had the team refused comment until the ICC hearings were done it would have given them time to compose themselves. There would still have been a storm during the silence, but things couldn't have gone any worse.

In the moment, most of Australia was asleep. Our African evening was nine hours behind the east coast of home. The high-ups at Cricket Australia snoozed soundly. Media outlets had overnight subs throw up holding pieces on websites, while breakfast radio producers punched their alarm clocks and rubbed their eyes while printing off the wires. Only the insomniacs and die-hards who had sat up all night with their pay TV or radio streams were buzzing with news they couldn't share, isolated in their pockets of the night. We knew this was big, but not how big it would become. Night had fallen on Newlands, and even the mountain was gone.

Chapter 16

SANDSTORM

For an hour or two after the press conference everything was quiet. People banged together articles, shot videos, fired off updates. Then the calls started coming in. New Zealand breakfast radio kicked off from their monitoring outpost near the International Date Line. East coast Australia followed, then Perth. The Brits were close to South African time, so they were planning for our morning. Across continents, producers searched their offices for someone who liked sport, checking in bathrooms or poking heads into smoking areas: 'Do you know anyone in cricket?' With half a dozen Australians on this tour, outlets would grab any one of us.

Papers back home had missed the story – the day's print editions were already on trucks by the time it broke – so they bridged the gap with online blasts. Cricket Australia's first communiqué was a masterwork in understatement, offering in its entirety: 'South Africa currently hold a 294 run lead at stumps on the third day in Cape Town. Captain Steve Smith and Cameron Bancroft addressed media at the close of play, with vision available below for editorial broadcast use.' By 9 am Jolimont time they announced James Sutherland would front the media at midday. At our end that meant staying up till 3 am to give a radio response.

Gerard Whateley did a special Sunday edition of his morning show from Melbourne, doubtless stewing that football season had called him home from the scene of the story. 'Australia's cricket team cheated,' was how he began. 'Blatantly, wantonly, brazenly. It was premeditated and unsophisticated, as stunningly naive as it is deeply shameful.' As SEN threw open the lines, in came call after classic talkback call – Matt in Officer, Courtney in Ivanhoe. But it wasn't the usual anger; their voices were bewildered, hurt, defeated. Whateley isn't the type to pump one side of the story. He loves the contrarian view. On that morning there wasn't one.

'Gerard, it's good to talk to you but under awful circumstances. It's just so sad.'

'Complete embarrassment. It reeks of such desperation. It's plunged cricket to an all-time low. Steve Smith should be sacked, he should never captain Australia again.'

'The most shameful incident in cricket in my lifetime. This is a blatant disregard of the spirit of cricket.'

'I'll tell you what, I listened to Steve Smith, and two or three occasions he said this isn't what Australian cricket's about. If they've got together and thought about it and decided to go ahead and do it, it is what Australian cricket's about.'

There was no way to justify it, nowhere to hide. No Australian had ever been caught ball-tampering. No one from any country had been caught so cold. Former players sighed before stating the same conclusion.

'I think when Cricket Australia front the media, they've got no option but to stand down and then sack Smith, Warner and Lehmann,' Simon Katich said to Whateley. A former New South Wales captain, Katich had mentored and adored Smith. 'They've got no option because this was premeditated and calculated at the break and those guys are in charge of Cameron Bancroft behaving the way he did ... If CA come out of this and condone sledging, they condone blatant cheating, then the message they send to the thousands of kids that they want to aspire to wear the baggy green is a far worse message than a few guys losing their jobs.'

Jason Gillespie, the nicest man in cricket, axed Smith in *The Guardian*. So did the Australian Sports Commission in a statement. Shane Warne dug deep to find his ethical core: 'Forget the ball-tampering issue, the bottom line for me is the captain sat there and took a decision to go out there and cheat.' Prime Minister Malcolm Turnbull took the wheel of the bandwagon, tooting the horn in delight at finding an issue where he could extract broad electoral agreement.

'We all woke up this morning shocked and bitterly disappointed by the news from South Africa. After all, our cricketers are role models, and cricket is synonymous with fair play. How can our team be engaged in cheating like this?' The firefighter in the background of Turnbull's video-op had no answer. 'I look forward to Cricket Australia taking decisive action very soon,' concluded a politician who had just spent weeks trying to avoid sacking his scandal-plagued deputy.

Sutherland offered his style of underwhelmingly competent management talk that followed caution and satisfied nobody. 'Australian cricket fans want to be proud of their cricket team, and this morning they have every reason to wake up and not be proud', was as strong as it got. No, he didn't know what had happened. Sorry, he hadn't spoken to Smith. No, he wouldn't go to South Africa. You'll understand he couldn't comment before an investigation. One would be conducted by Iain Roy, head of CA's previously unknown integrity department, and Pat Howard, who had some housekeeping to do as director of team performance. 'I understand that's not necessarily the fullness of response that everyone is looking for right know, but you will understand there's an element of process that needs to be undertaken.'

With no answers and no action, public anger kept building. A bemused ESPN writer who also happened to be named Steve Smith was having his Twitter account blown up by abusive messages. In Cape Town it was four in the morning and we had phone calls at seven. We headed back to the ground because there was no point doing anything else. It was going to be a rugged day. Before play Sutherland said that Smith and Warner had 'agreed to stand down' from leadership jobs for the rest of the Test, which was generous of them. The board had approved Paine as a replacement without feeling the need to consult him.

Australia's comeback wicketkeeper was in the nets, having taken the early bus to the grounds, and his mad few months were about to get madder. Paine had avoided the internet overnight, reasoning it wasn't going to improve his existence. Instead he'd hung out with his baby daughter and had an early night. 'I knew it was big,' he said of the furore, 'but I didn't know it was that big. I didn't know that Steve and David had spoken to James and that was the decision that was made. I had no idea. I hadn't seen them that morning. So, yeah, the first I even got wind of it at all was when Cracker [selector Trevor Hohns] said they had stepped down. I remember looking around the room and thinking "Well, who's going to be captain?" And, yeah, Cracker said it was me and off we went.' Talk about a hospital pass.

If the third afternoon had been the rollercoaster stomach-drop, the fourth morning was the hollow feeling when you've finished chucking up a couple of hot dogs. The match seemed pointless. The moment mattered but the action didn't. I'd never described a delivery or a shot without feeling its significance; no matter how one-sided there was always a buzz at calling cricket. Now it felt like training. An unknown number of players had cheated, as bluntly as if they had rewritten the scorecard. Reckoning was imminent. This was a strange interim in which their feats meant nothing. Sporting teams are like fairies: they only exist if people believe in them.

Jim Maxwell had been deluged. We scrolled through message after message from friends, acquaintances, punters, club stalwarts, all the enthusiasts he had met in 68 years of bat and ball. As the voice of cricket for so many, he became a centre in which its goodness was seen to reside. People turned to him for comfort as troubled villagers to a priest. Jim embodied the enjoyment of the game, sharing the brass warmth of his enthusiasm however modest the player or contest. If there was love to be given, he would be the last well to dry out. Surely Jim could explain to the bewildered? Retrace steps for the strayed? If anyone, Jim could understand a feeling of loss that made little sense in the light of rationality?

When he got on air, the cumulative effect caught up: having to find a response to something without precedent in the nearly 300 Australian Tests he'd spent behind the microphone. 'I do not remember,' he began slowly, 'being as disappointed in an Australian team as I feel, and I know a number of Australians and a number of my colleagues here would feel at the moment, about what they did yesterday.' His voice caught, needle snagging in the groove, and he was as surprised as anyone to find he was close to tears. Quinton Friend froze in the co-caller's chair. 'I think it was so blatant and so stupid – immature, naive, I could go on. It was disappointing.' Maxwell nearly lost it, Pavlovian conditioning wrestling back composure as the ball was bowled. 'Cummins goes around the wicket – ooh, bouncer! That was a sharp one too, just outside the line of the off stump, and he let it go through to the keeper in the end. The lead is 310. Sorry, I'm getting a bit emotional myself.' Scorer Julia Scully came to the rescue with stats. A recording of the moment was listened to 65,000 times.

The Australian players were listless and lost. 'It was good, hard cricket and it was a pretty even contest,' Cummins recalled later. 'Then from day three onwards it was such a different match.' During tea after Bancroft was sprung, they had tried to retain focus. While the tamperers talked to management, Paine said, the rest 'were still having a general team talk about how we are going about this. I remember Boof coming in and saying not to worry about it, that the most important thing was the next two hours, going out and sticking to what our plans were for certain batters and then we'd worry about what we'd have to worry about after the two hours.'

It didn't work. South Africa ended that day 294 ahead. Australia got de Villiers on the fourth morning for 63, but de Kock and Philander smashed fifties, pushing the innings past lunch and the lead past 400. Catches went begging, including Hazlewood stepping on the boundary rope. Starc was belted by Philander and Rabada. Lyon took his 300th Test wicket, but where Morkel had soaked in adulation and done interviews with a beaming smile, Lyon got a quick hug from Shaun Marsh and some low-key high fives. He was ranked among Australians with Lee, Johnson, Lillee, McGrath and Warne, but would never want to remember when he got there.

Australia's final collapse was apt, a physical manifestation of a spiritual state. At first you thought Warner and Bancroft were not the pair you'd want opening the batting, preoccupied as they must have been. For Bancroft, though, the middle seemed to offer an island of calm. Here he could do nothing but watch the ball, standing in the sunshine in a Test match for what might be the last time. It was better than sitting in the stands, avoiding eye contact and agonising over what he'd done.

Concentration was Bancroft's best asset. He'd shrugged off blows and distractions before. Here he did the same, facing up to the first ball, watching and leaving well, soaking up Rabada's first three overs to spare Warner, absorbing a hit to the box before driving through cover. The pair made it to tea, then to 50. The junior member looked the steady one, the senior more streaky, and having already pulled Bancroft into trouble, Warner did him in again.

Anxious facing Maharaj across two full overs, Warner started the third by tapping to cover and running without a glance. Bancroft did the team thing in responding, having to hope that du Plessis would miss. So it began, Warner following Bancroft back to the pavilion so fast that they started a conga line.

1–57.

2–59.

3–59.

4–59.

5–75.

Rabada had a final chuckle against Warner, a swat to gully. Khawaja prodded at Maharaj way outside his stumps. Shaun Marsh punched him tamely to short leg for yet another Golden Globe. Smith flailed Rabada off his top edge for a desperate six, then produced an identical dismissal to his first innings, chasing Morkel short and wide, forcing with an upright bat rather than forming a stable base for a cut, tentative and led by the bowler in a manner antithetical to Steve Smith.

6–86.

7–86.

8–94.

9–94.

10–107.

Pull shots toed to gully. Ramps to third man. Two golden ducks and a diamond, nine scores in single figures. Ten batsmen for 50 runs, a collapse outdoing England's 58 a few days earlier. Morkel had seldom troubled Australia – he went into that match averaging nearly 39 versus 26 against all others. His 2014 assault on Clarke caused the 'broken fucken arm' ordered by karma, but Clarke still finished 161 not out and Morkel finished wicketless. His only five-for included Warner after a ton, Clarke after a double, and the great Bobby Quiney for a duck. Until now, when he took five in 32 balls. He had nine in the match, including the best Test batsman in the world twice to trash. A furious contest ended with a whimper, and the irony that a team's own desperation to win had brought such abject surrender.

After the crowd had gone and everything was done, the SABC crew got hold of the ball-bazooka from the teatime catching competition. A contest between groups of commentators broke out, complete with Steadicam operators getting close-ups, Natalie Germanos hosting, and Kass Naidoo interviewing the entrants. Former pros Quinton Friend and Ed Rainsford took theirs with nonchalance, non-pros like Neil Manthorp and Mluleki Ntsabo put theirs down. TV scorer Sue Abbott kicked off her heels and did it barefoot, Aslam Khota in his socks. No one at my club would call me comfortable under the high ball, but I held one in the crook of my elbow to seal a tie.

With people laughing and cheering in the deepening dusk, and Table Mountain our backdrop one last time, there was a minute where the gloom engulfing Australia was forgotten. It was a reminder that for South Africans the story was no big deal. There had been coverage, but not the vitriol that either Ashes side would have given the other. Most people locally couldn't understand the fuss. The next few days they would only grow more bewildered.

While Australia's batting was collapsing, the ICC verdict was handed down. Bancroft got three demerit points and a fine, consistent with recent cases. Smith got four demerits under a broader misconduct charge, meaning a one-Test ban. That manifestly wasn't going to cut it, not when the front pages in Australia finally had their chance to launch.

The headlines traded on variants of disgrace and shame, aside from the *NT News* with a trademark rhyming penis-related composition. Queensland's gleefully partisan *Courier-Mail* – the paper that in 2013 had led the Stuart Broad is a Shit Bloke campaign during the Gabba Test – sentenced its little battling Aussie Ashes heroes to unemployment. Melbourne stablemate the *Herald-Sun* agreed that someone had to 'SACK THEM ALL'.

Subcontinent papers played it straight while the British couldn't contain their delight. *The Mirror* went with 'CLOWN UNDER', *The Times* with 'CHEATS' in a font bigger than the paper itself, *The Sun* chose 'HYPOCRITES', and of course the key interest for all was whether Australia had also cheated in the Ashes.

As the story snowballed, the rest of the world got involved. There was a major spread in the UAE. The *New York Times* ran an explainer. CNN started coverage on cable and online. In Sweden, the *Aftonbladet* led its bus-stop billboards with 'Stornationen skakas av byx-fusket', or 'Country shaken by panty-cheating'. Run through an online translator, the report was strangely perceptive.

> The players in Baggy Green, Australia's cricket team, are usually some of Australia's most beloved athletes. But after the weekend's meeting with South Africa, the image of the stars has been transformed from idols to cheats.
>
> Everything exploded when the cameras caught Cameron Bancroft's stuffing down a piece of tape inside the trousers. The judges also became aware of the tape and asked Bancroft to answer. He first blamed that he put down a cleaning cloth for the sunglasses but later got crawled to the cross.
>
> The truth was a most conscious cheating to make the ball court untouchable to the South Africans. With the tape bit he had picked up gravel from the ground and, in secret, tried to stick the gravel on one side of the ball to change the course.
>
> 'When I saw myself on the big screen, I panicked and tried to put down the tape in the trophy,' he says. Next to him lay team captain Steve Smith … But the storm that was under sealing could not resist Smith. In Australia, cricket experts, fans and even the Prime Minister broke themselves.
>
> Around the cricket world, it is now competing to criticise Australia's cricket cheater. Hardest are the British newspapers. Steve Smith and Viceroy David Warner were forced against their willingness to leave the so-called Test match against South Africa.

'So-called Test match' was bang on. While day five should have been underway, CA was issuing denials that players were being sent home. The detective team of Howard and Roy hadn't landed in Cape Town before Sutherland wised up to public mood and announced he would meet them in Johannesburg.

The calls didn't stop. The ABC and BBC have hundreds of stations, and they were all keen. Wake up for Australian drive slots or English mornings. Pre-records through the day for Kiwi or South African talk shows. A World Service cross at 6 pm, stay up late for ABC Breakfast, get grilled by Jon Faine as though I'd done the cheating myself, or a more amicable Jonathan Agnew from New Zealand. The wee small hours for Australian lunch, back up soon afterwards for BBC Breakfast.

We made little broadcast nests in bombsite hotel rooms, finding patches of blank wall and balancing lamps and devices on chairs. Modern networks would Skype our phones and whack the feed straight on TV. Impostor syndrome kicked in hard – suddenly the handful of us reporting from South Africa were world experts on aerodynamics and laminar flow, the history of relative ethics, and the psychology both macro and micro of the entire Australian national project as well as each individual cricketer.

The internet was going feral, and back home anyone who had ever fired off a cricket tweet was winding up on American cable or issuing a white paper to the Zambian government. A guy messaged me on Twitter to swear that Bancroft was holding 1100 grit sandpaper: 'I'm not a cricket expert but I know my abrasives', was a memorable line. This was the world we now lived in, where random online carpenters offering crank theories could turn out to be correct.

As we travelled to Johannesburg at the same time as the team, body language placed Warner very much on the outer.

Word was leaking that Starc and Hazlewood were furious at being implicated. Bancroft walked past swaddled in giant headphones to shut out the world, looking airsick. Smith hid behind the largest shades he could find. We were all on our way to see the boss.

Sandton is a weird place. It's in Johannesburg, undeniably: you can walk right out or drive right in. But it sits completely apart, hermetically sealed at the edges by money: a Boer wagon laager made of marble and gloss. A few blocks of hotels and apartments draw together, facing each other with their backs to the world outside. High-rise homes have gyms and shops and tunnels to the mall so you never have to see the street. All the luxury show-off brands are represented. The hotels are punishingly expensive. The whole place is set up for rich visitors to leave some wealth behind while rich locals enjoy the subsidised amenity. It only became a white enclave after its residents left downtown Johannesburg after apartheid. In a final twist its central plaza is named for Nelson Mandela.

The Australian team was at the InterContinental, the schmickest hotel on the block, but Sutherland could only get a conference room at the less upmarket Holiday Inn. It was March 27th, the day after the Test should have finished, and he'd gone straight from the airport to meet his investigators. TV crews had arrived from Australia, and the ABC's Africa correspondent Sally Sara from Nairobi. The press pack kicked its heels. Websites filled the time with nothing stories. 'Someone has posted a photo of Darren Lehmann smoking a cigarette and reading tweets at the team hotel,' said one of our number about a report. 'That could literally be any day of his life,' came the reply.

Sutherland entered the bland grey conference room that evening looking worn and weary, but worn and weary is his mode. At the start of his tenure he was Greg Baum's 'sombre young accountant in his dark suit and tie'; near the end he was Peter Lalor's 'funeral director wringing his hands as he explains to the bereaved that the chapel is on fire'. For twenty years the man managing a loved and vibrant sport had given the impression that he had recently stared into the abyss and found it returning the favour.

His presentation was another half measure: the investigation was incomplete, but complete enough to exonerate everyone bar three players. They would be sent home and charged under CA Code of Conduct Article 2.3.5 for acts against the spirit of the game, unbecoming of its representatives, harming its interests and bringing it into disrepute. 'I want to stress that we are contemplating significant sanctions in each case. These sanctions will reflect the gravity with which we view what has occurred, and the damage it has done to the standing of Australian cricket.' Previous discards Matthew Renshaw, Joe Burns and Glenn Maxwell would replace them, Paine would captain the final Test, and Lehmann would continue as coach. There would be a review into the 'conduct and culture of our national teams'.

Outside the stern announcements the proceeding teetered on farce. Most of question time was spent finding ways to decline answers. TV reporters badgered Sutherland to say 'cheat' so they could get a grab for their bulletins, while he channelled his days as a tailender blocking yorkers. A mummified shape in the hallway as we left was Sally Sara under a curtain trying to record a voice piece. Few vocations have such a gulf between their reality and their perceived glamour.

The investigation was finished next afternoon. By now the Aussie press pack was all but camped in the lobby of the team hotel. It was the easiest way to share updates, divide transcripts and uphold morale. None of us had slept in days. Slumped on couches round a table that was a mare's nest of charger cords and dictaphones, we ordered the odd coffee or club sandwich to keep the house happy while we churned out updates. Lalor announced with an official air that day-drinking was legitimate. It felt more like essential. We'd become blasé about television, wearing the same rumpled shirts on consecutive days, hair askew, hand-holding the video phone, waving down a waiter mid-interview. 'There's a bit of noise interference in the background?' said one producer politely. 'Yep, that's a very large fountain and a busload of tourists,' I replied cheerfully.

The CA report filled in some blanks. The yellow object had been sandpaper after all, and we'd been played for chumps. Smith had known tampering was being discussed beforehand and had tried to cover up afterwards, first with the umpires and then with the press. Warner had come up with the idea and recruited his junior colleague, including giving him a demonstration of technique. Collins pictured that scene 'like a Danoz Direct infomercial on *Good Morning Australia* with

Bert Newton', while others reimagined Patrick Swayze's pottery work from *Ghost*.

Smith and Warner would be suspended for a year from state and international cricket, Bancroft for nine months. Smith and Bancroft were banned for two years from leadership, Warner was banned for good. It reflected not only his instigating the plot but that he'd denied involvement for the longest. All three could accept the sanction or take it to a hearing. The press release ended by leaving the next move to the players. In the meantime, South Africa's media manager was putting out releases about car parking at the Wanderers.

What the report didn't do was tell the story of what had happened, only leaving it to be inferred from the charges laid. There was no timeline and no detail. What had Smith known, and how early? What did he tell the coach at the tea break, or stumps? Who came up with the lies about sticky tape and the leadership group? Was Warner in those discussions or pretending to be innocent? How could anyone be confident it was a first offence? There was still an evasiveness, as CA referred back to the report when asked questions that the report hadn't answered.

Lehmann answered one when he finally made an appearance, having not been sighted since day two in Cape Town. 'Appearance' might be a bit strong – Australian reporters were led down a staircase into the basement of the hotel, through a car park and into a storeroom full of spring water, like we were meeting someone under witness protection. After plenty of asking, Lehmann eventually said the players had used the sticky-tape lie to him and that he'd found out about sandpaper once the investigation was done.

Aside from apologies, most of his statement was about sympathy. 'We love all our players, and they're going through a really tough time … They have made a grave mistake but they are not bad people. There's a human side to this. These are young men, and I hope that people will give them a second chance.' Under questioning, he abruptly conceded what had never been conceded under his reign: that there was in fact a problem with Australia's conduct on the field. Having championed it, Lehmann maintained he was now the one to reform it. 'I'm not going to resign. We need to change how we play. Previously we've butted heads with the line, but that's not the way for us to play going forward. I need to change.'

Sutherland stopped by for his own discreet interview, saying CA had corroboration of Lehmann's innocence. 'You guys probably saw it, the first time anyone knew about it was when it came up on the vision screen. He saw that and he radioed down and he said "What the fuck is going on?"' But it was hard to have confidence in an investigation of respondents who had lied at multiple stages, that was completed in two days, and had no brief to look further back than one match. 'I certainly hope it's an isolated incident,' Sutherland said, but CA had no intention of finding out. It was a strange dance of minimising liability while performing lament.

The storm blew on. Magellan cancelled its sponsorship months after plastering its moniker all over the Ashes, costing CA $24 million and the impression that an early Portuguese explorer was especially keen on bat and ball. Smith was airbrushed off Weet-Bix boxes. Warner would no longer flog LG televisions, Toyota had no use for him without his leaping celebrations, and ASICS apparel punted both him and Bancroft.

Smith and Warner stepped down as captains of their Indian Premier League franchises but had their playing contracts torn up regardless. The IPL, with its corruption scandals and power struggles, could stomach Ben Stokes after his street brawl but not a bit of sandpaper. Bancroft's county deal was also cancelled. One wondered whether CA had been on the phone to the Indian and English boards. The sight of these players earning big money in front of cheering crowds would have gone down poorly with a public wanting repentance.

Then, in the space of a day, the narrative turned on its head. On the morning of March 29th, the day before the Johannesburg Test, Smith arrived home. It was evening in Sydney, and he fronted the media at the airport with former journo Malcolm Conn running a hectic press conference as the Cricket New South Wales media rep. They weren't facing cricket journalists who knew the context: the story was too big for that now. It was an audience of prime-time newshounds and commercial radio hacks. Smith completely lost control.

That image, of an Australian cricket captain choking off his speech halfway through apologies, unable to finish promises for the future, shoulders heaving with sobs, stopped people dead. The image of his old man standing behind him, one hand on his son's shoulder, sealed the deal. It was the human side Lehmann had implored us to see. Whether it was media drive or public mood, the tide suddenly changed from demanding vengeance on these vandals who had ruined Australia's reputation to sparing these poor young men who'd surely had enough.

At least that was the case for Smith, and for Bancroft, who spoke in Perth. Warner arrived later that night on a different flight, him and Falzon carrying their zonked-out daughters through a camera pack and saying they needed to get home. Where the others admitted culpability and remorse, Warner clearly had legal advice not to do the same in case he contested his charge. As public mood softened against the first two, it hardened correspondingly against the hold-out.

At the Wanderers ground a couple of hours later, when Lehmann walked into the captain's conference instead of Paine, we knew what was coming. It was the day before the game, so all the South African crews and Australian TV blow-ins were there. 'Thanks for joining me, everyone. I just want to let you know this is my last Test as coach of the Australian cricket team as I'm stepping down.'

Smith had finished him off. A player who had flourished under Lehmann from bit-part curiosity to the best in the world was crushed. A day earlier the coach was adamant he would lead the rebuild, a day later he couldn't. 'I'm ultimately responsible for the culture of the team, and I've been thinking about my position for a while. This will allow Cricket Australia to complete a full review, and allow them to implement changes to regain the trust of the cricketing public. As a team we know we've let so many people down. For that, we're extremely sorry.'

There had always been affection for Lehmann the player: a cricketer whose talent defied his look, and unlucky not to play more for Australia. Lehmann the coach soon disenchanted: flippant with decisions, dismissive of feedback, representative of a bloke-hood whose time had passed. But in this moment you couldn't help feeling for him, a man who wouldn't have wanted to show emotion and who had little love for the press, his thick fingers wiping red-rimmed eyes as his voice caught in his throat in front of a room of strangers.

'No sleep last night again. No one's slept, that's the biggest challenge fronting up tomorrow. I don't think I've slept since Saturday, to be perfectly honest, couple of hours here and there, playing it round in your head about what's right. I thought this was tough, but speaking to the players and telling them the news, saying goodbye, that was the toughest thing I've ever had to do.'

We were off again, racing back and forth from the ground, to Sutherland's response at the hotel, to the BBC studio in Johannesburg, to writing articles in the back of a cab, to the ground for training, to the hotel for the next development. Three emotional statements in a couple of hours. Everyone from CA looked utterly shot. In a week of human turmoil, high prices had been paid.

That night Collins and I recorded a *Final Word* on a suburban Johannesburg rooftop. The sound of beer caps and cigarette lighters is clearly audible. We had no plan, no structure and no energy for either. We were bone-tired beyond the point where sleep felt possible. 'You could tell me it was four days ago, you could tell me it was ten days ago, and I'd believe either,' he said. All we could do was fumble for articulation, trying to process and explain what we'd seen. A story whose hype had been absurd, but had still mattered. Where real lives had fallen into chaos. A few people had suggested we were lucky to be in the middle of it. It had been fascinating, but nothing about it had been enjoyable.

Sleep came somehow, then the surreality of showing up to a cricket match like it was a normal day. Throughout the Test, like a closing tap, the phone calls slowed and finally plinked to a stop. In the broader world, the howling in the trees dropped back to a rustle. The sandstorm in all its fury was over.

Chapter 17

ORDERS OF MAGNITUDE

'How does former prime minister and cricket tragic John Howard feel about the cricket imbroglio? Joining me live on the phone from his home in Bennelong is Mr Howard. Good evening Mr Howard. We've never actually had you on the phone before, it's usually just me doing a bad impression ... How do you think Don Bradman would have reacted to this whole ball-tampering fiasco brouhaha?'

'Uh, knowing The Don as well as I did, which was pretty well considering we barely met, I think, uh, uh, I think he'd have been spinning in his grave, uh, like a turbine. He'd have been burrowing his way out of his grave to rise again from the earth and wreak vengeance on all those who had sullied the name of Australia's greatest sport.'

'He would have haunted them, do you think?'

'He would not rest until they had paid for their sins in blood.'

'Mr Howard, would he have done this as a skeleton or a ghost, do you think?'

'It's hard to be certain about these sorts of things, Shaun. His body was previously interred in Centennial Park cemetery in Adelaide, so uh, I think not having a corporeal presence would allow him to travel interstate with greater ease.'

'It would be fair to say then that you think The Don would be disappointed in what's happened?'

'Not inconsolably, of course Shaun. You've got to keep a sense of proportion about these things. After all, it's only a game.'

Really, comedian Shaun Micallef's take was no more ridiculous than the fact that real prime ministers of Australia, New Zealand and the United Kingdom had issued statements about ball-tampering. For a week the story monopolised discussion. The drip-feed of revelations helped spin it out, but it would have been potent anyway. Sport stories in Australia usually draw counter-commentary asking why anyone cares, but most of the non-enthusiasts grasped the principles and emotion of this one.

'You know it's big news but don't really know the magnitude. Then the next morning when I woke up and checked my phone, that's when it hit me. That's when the reaction was unprecedented. We'd never seen anything like it before.' Patrick Cummins still looked a bit stunned weeks after the event. 'We thought, hang on, we're just cricketers playing a little cricket game over here in Cape Town, and suddenly this has just blown up all around the world. Suddenly everyone at home who's maybe not even following the cricket, or mates who don't watch that much cricket, are checking in going, "Mate, hope you're ok."'

Why was it like this? What caused what Barney Ronay called 'the extraordinary tide of mawkish grief and opportunist outrage'? What made it so difficult 'to distinguish the basic facts from their overpowering resonance'? Ball-tampering, after all, was in the ICC Code of Conduct as a Level 2 offence – the same as Kagiso Rabada's shoulder-bump or an upraised middle finger.

South Africa had been done for tampering three times from 2013 to 2016, including their current captain twice. A Sri Lankan seamer was pinged four months before Cape Town. None of Faf du Plessis, Vernon Philander nor Dasun Shanaka received more than a fine. Historically there had been tampering charges against big names like Rahul Dravid, Sachin Tendulkar, Michael Atherton, Shahid Afridi. None found it any threat to his contemporary standing in the game.

AB de Villiers thought Australia's case was 'blown up massively'. His captain agreed: 'We're not sitting in a glass house where we think we're better than them,' said du Plessis with good reason. 'It is difficult to understand, certainly from the way the Australian people and the media reacted, it's all been from an Australian point of view. How they view it is very strong, it's an absolute no-go for them.' The Australians on tour kept being asked why, as though we held the key to our nation's psyche.

'South Africa are champion ball-tamperers,' wrote local correspondent Telford Vice. 'Or are South Africa bad at ball-tampering considering they keep getting caught? Whatever. Not once out of those three times did a high-ranking suit get on a plane to find out what the hell was going on.' Sure, Faf got chased around in Australia by TV types trying to provoke some push-and-shove for the news. But ultimately he got his ICC scolding and carried on. Not for a second did his board consider adding to it.

Rather, when charges are laid most countries circle the wagons. In South Africa, wrote *Vice*, 'much of the coverage was sympathetic, dismissive or even aggressive towards proven transgressions of the laws of the game.' Fans defend those like Tendulkar and Dravid with whatever combination comes to hand of protested innocence, conspiracy theory, vendetta or deflection. Boards back players in contesting bans or refusing to take the field in protest. As Andy Bull wrote in *The Guardian*, 'it's not the offence that seems so very startling but the response to it. Because – and I'll admit I haven't checked the archives here – when Shanaka was caught I can't recall Theresa May's people feeling the need to provide a hot take on the topic.'

Ball-tampering happens all the time. Everyone in cricket knows this. Everyone concedes it, but in the most general terms. It's always fuzzy and plausibly deniable. Examples abounded after Cape Town. Start with former wicketkeeper Adam Gilchrist: 'Every single team in the cricketing world has probably had a crack at something ... to work out how to get the ball to swing.' T20 powerhouse Chris Lynn: 'I reckon every cricketer's probably done it throughout their career in grade cricket or whatever level.' South African quick Fanie de Villiers about Pakistan: 'It was obvious that it was a tactic that's been used for quite a while in their system, and not one of us knew how to do it, or we would probably have done the same, to be honest with you.' Former England skipper Mike Brearley: 'It was almost accepted. Nobody thought of it as a terrible crime.'

Not all tampering is created equal. A lifted seam can get jag for a medium-pacer or act as a rudder for swing or help a spinner's grip. Lollies and lotions maintain new-ball shine. But opprobrium is saved for roughing up one side of the ball for reverse swing. Reverse is the most valuable, coming in the old-ball overs which otherwise make for easy batting. It is also the most disdained, because Pakistanis mastered it from the 1970s to 1990s and others resented their advantage.

In *The Cricket Monthly*, Vithushan Ehantharajah wrote an epic history of England's fractious relationship with the skill. 'For the longest time, reverse swing was something only Pakistan could do. Depending on who you spoke to, reverse swing was something only Pakistan *would* do.' Wasim Akram, Waqar Younis, Imran Khan, Aaqib Javed, all were brilliant practitioners, all knew methods to obtain it, and all spread the gospel across England county sides. Once reverse became a weapon that teams could use themselves, moral opposition among players subsided. So did opposition to the ways it came about. Ehantharajah showed a candid picture of the current state of play.

'Have you ever noticed that the counties – about six or seven of them – with zips in their whites tend to be the "best" at reverse swing?' says one senior county cricketer. Nails are back in vogue, complete with a sleight of hand that makes it look like fielders are simply applying saliva in an above-board manner when they are actually scuffing the other side. 'You've got no way of knowing, even if you're watching on TV,' says one fast bowler. 'Maybe by sound. Our overseas taught us it about four or five years ago, and it sounds like a huge fucking caterpillar munching some lettuce when he does it.' Tales of a handful of county players fashioning their nails into a 'smaller dagger' and applying nail hardener through the season are common. The story of one who, during an England Lions match a few years ago away from the cameras, managed to get the ball reversing in just ten overs, stands out. 'He's an artist,' said a former team-mate in admiration. ['Reverse swing – an English tale', *The Cricket Monthly*, April 2017.]

Likewise, every player I spoke to for this book said tampering happens in Australian domestic cricket. But everyone, every time, asks that their name be left out. No one will name anyone else. Everyone does it, everyone knows, and no one will stand by that knowledge. It might be the world's biggest secret society, this bizarre omerta of an entire industry, covering thousands of players across national lines with admirable completeness. You can count on one hand the elite cricketers who've expressly admitted doctoring the ball.

Imran was one, admitting in a biography to lifting the seam and scratching the leather. This led to an extraordinary 1994 interview with Darcus Howe, a Trinidadian who moved to England to study law, became a civil rights activist, and ended up decades later hosting an ethics debate show called *Devil's Advocate* on the BBC. Howe's uncle was the great post-colonial writer CLR James, a 1930s cricket correspondent for *The Guardian*, whose *Beyond the Boundary* is often called the best cricket book ever written, and who coined the famous 'What do they know of cricket who only cricket know?' It was no surprise his nephew had an interest and fluency in the game.

On the show, the sober Howe measures up against Imran like a priest, standing with his notes at a kind of pulpit, tall and black-clad, while the more stylish cricketer sits uneasily on a podium, trying to look nonchalant under the gaze of a studio audience. The proceedings are fascinatingly confrontational: 'This is my case against Imran Khan,' is the way Howe frames it in his Caribbean vowels.

Imran argues that lifting the seam only means restoring its normal protrusion, and scratching means restoring rough patches that have been smushed flat. This cuts no ice with Howe, who wields the Laws with a barrister's gravitas. Imran argues that all law is assumed by social convention, and that his actions were accepted practice among cricketers. Howe wants to hear names, and the omerta comes into effect. As it does when Howe calls on Don Oslear, a former umpire who reads from a report he made after a county match.

OSLEAR: 'The Warwickshire second innings finished quite suddenly with Imran Khan taking the last six wickets in a very short space of time with some very accurate bowling. As my colleague and I left the field I noticed that a piece of the ball was sticking up, and upon a closer inspection it could be seen that this piece was the triangle of leather that joins the cross-seam and quarter seam. The stitching did not appear to have been frayed but more as if it had been cut, and the piece that was proud of the ball was large enough to be able to hold the ball by it.'

IMRAN: Don, if you don't have proof of that, I mean if I was doing it – if you don't have proof, that is a serious doubt on my credibility. When I said that I picked the ball once, it's different, but when someone else comes and says 'No, he did it again', my credibility's affected by that.

HOWE: Imran, he didn't say you picked the seam, he said you removed it so completely that you could hold the ball by it! [Laughter. Even Imran smiles.]

OSLEAR: [interjecting] I'm sorry, Mr Howe, I said nothing of the sort. I said nothing of the sort, and wrote nothing of the sort. I brought out a certain matter which we had seen with the ball. I said he had taken the last six wickets, he bowled 4.3 overs, he took 6–6, he bowled five of them and the other was lbw if you want to know the facts. But I did not accuse him –

HOWE: But why are you bringing it up if you're not wanting to say Imran did it?

IMRAN: Darcus, there's one point I want to –

HOWE: This is serious, Imran! Did you or didn't you? Answer me.

[A tangent develops. They end up at a 1992 incident when Oslear was third umpire for a Pakistan–England ODI when his colleagues changed the ball.]

OSLEAR: It had certain scratch marks on it. I would rather say they were cut marks rather than scratch marks.

HOWE: You're saying that ball was badly tampered with by the Pakistanis.

OSLEAR: No, I'm not saying that at all.

HOWE: Why is everybody scared to talk? You think the whole cricketing establishment would collapse. If you're accusing Imran of ball-tampering, say so.

OSLEAR: I am not accusing Imran of ball-tampering, and never would.

HOWE: I'm puzzled by this failure to clarify. It's all obfuscated, it's all gloomy … These accusations come out in the press, though officials are always very quiet, nobody accuses anybody of anything, it's all innuendo. It's a huge grey area. Why is that?

Seated among the audience, former England opener Geoffrey Boycott pops up as a rather unexpected voice on fair-mindedness and prejudice.

BOYCOTT: The English press at that time, certainly, were looking for opportunities to get at Pakistanis. Imran calls it Paki-bashing. That stems through a number of incidents that have happened over a period of time with Pakistan and English cricket. Nobody made much of Derek Pringle's statements in *The Telegraph* at the end of his career last year when he retired and said he'd done all these things to the ball: no big deal, because he's white, he's Essex, he's not that good.

I can put my hand on my heart. I've seen players in my own teams I've played with, and it became an acceptable practice – wrong, they'd known it were wrong, else they wouldn't have been doing it secretively. But they do it like we all do when we drive our cars. We go 75, 80 mile an hour, if we can get away with it, 90. Until one day, a policeman catches you and you're done.

Except the tamper cops since 1994 have a scant apprehension rate, and reverse swing has not ruined cricket. The skill is one of the game's most spectacular, and various spells have become storied moments. Here is the paradox: people love reverse swing, and believing its exponents all stayed within the letter of the Laws is fanciful. Sarfraz Nawaz is at once revered as progenitor and joked about for proficiency with bottle tops. We rage at Bancroft and drool at replays of Wasim curving the ball into the stumps. England in the sacred 2005 Ashes aimed for reverse before the 30th over, going straight from Matthew Hoggard's conventional hoop to Simon Jones or Andrew Flintoff the other way. At the classic in Edgbaston, Flintoff reversed it in the thirteenth over – the same innings where he became the image of sportsmanship while consoling Brett Lee.

'Reverse is an art that anyone vaguely involved with cricket knows uses a mix of legal and illegal acts to prepare the ball. Not all reverse swing is illegal, but much of it is,' writes Jarrod Kimber. We accept the dubiousness and the result as part of the colour and joy of the game. Except in the present, where we love the result but claim to hate its method. It's not even loving the sinner and hating the sin – it's loving the product of the sin as well. This is a masterpiece but you painted it on the Sabbath.

Why not update the Laws? Why keep up feigned disapproval while authorities continue without meaningful monitoring and everyone covers each other's tracks? If all eyes are blind except for the odd cameraman, why shouldn't bowlers prime the ball however they prefer? Perhaps not with hardware, but if you can polish it with sweat and spit and clothing then why is it a moral failing to use a fingernail? Increasing the chance of bounce or seam or swing could be a boon in a sport tailored to batsmen, especially when so many surfaces offer bowlers little else.

Tampering is not a secret weapon. Scuffing a ball doesn't mean your opening batsman can swerve it around corners. When asked by Howe if his admissions cheapened his record, Imran's response was frosty. 'I used to bowl for Sussex. The whole team knew I could reverse swing. When the ball was old enough, my captain would call me and I would swing it. I would swing it from one side, and there was Garth Le Roux – at the time a South Africa fast bowler – Geoff Arnold, Ian Greig. There were English or international bowlers bowling from the other end. Why could they not swing it?'

'There was more than a passing element of jealousy,' wrote former Cricinfo boss Martin Williamson of English angst. 'The brilliance of Wasim and Waqar was undoubted and those who tried to copy them failed because they were not good enough.' Plenty of quality bowlers never get reverse, especially when so often it only comes at high pace. Then you still have to be good enough to land it. Hashim Amla said it in Port Elizabeth: 'I promise you, guys can have a reverse-swinging ball, but if you bowl half volley after half volley it's not going to be effective.'

If a global storm over sandpaper seems overblown, remember sport is good at creating scandal from mundanity. In 2015 Deflategate left the National Football League a step away from the United States Supreme Court: the New England Patriots were fined a million dollars, lost draft picks, and had quarterback Tom Brady miss a big chunk of a season. The District Court overturned his suspension, the Court of Appeals reinstated it. A frenzy of scientists and amateurs wrote elaborate reports incorporating ideal gas law, heat flow theory, incorrect amplitudes, and the effects of moisture surface content, devoting their lives to analyses with introductions like 'The Wells report's physics argument, based on multiple experiments as well as theoretical modeling, runs as follows'.

That was over someone letting air out of a football. Harlequins rugby coach Dean Richards got a three-year ban for giving players blood capsules, same as I used to skip school. Baseball pitchers have long been run out of town for nail files or pine tar. Outrage is half the fun: one YouTube compilation at the bottom of a dark spiral had its narrator sign off cheerily with 'Which one of these unscrupulous cheaters are you the most disgusted by?'

But surely there had been nothing so crazy in cricket? Consider these lines from Andrew Miller.

So when the Australians, of all people, were caught on camera manipulating the ball in a distinctly fishy manner, the pictures were flashed around the world in an instant. The Australian press were caught on the hop by what they saw, and exploded in a frenzy of righteous indignation. And barely a year after assuming the Australian captaincy at the tender age of 25, Steve Smith found himself being crushed by the weight of the moral majority.

By his own admission, Smith was called before the headmaster ... and panicked.

Meanwhile, back at the cricket, South Africa completed an historic 356-run victory with a day to spare. But the result was entirely lost in the melee.

'Melee', however, was not a strong enough word for the shambles that followed. A press conference was arranged in a hellishly airless cupboard, somewhere in the bowels of the pavilion, where Smith was fed to the lions.

Smith, however, was made of sterner stuff, and was determined to ride out the storm – even though the idea of being front-page news was absolute anathema to such an intensely private man.

It's all so recognisable. The only thing is, I swapped Smith into that quote for Atherton, along with their respective countries. The above describes 1994, after England's captain was filmed at Lord's rubbing dirt on the ball. He was so hounded by the press that at one stage he left a dinner by climbing over the rooftops of the surrounding suburb, like some nocturnal vigilante about to leap down and apprehend a bag-snatcher with a stylish pull shot followed by a back injury. Atherton didn't lose his captaincy, but would have if he'd been suspended; match referee Peter Burge only withheld a two-match ban because Atherton claimed he was using the dirt to dry his hand, and by the time Burge learned the truth it was too late to change the penalty.

Some cheating stories explode, some don't. There are reams of factors in each case. This time there were Australians in genuine distress. It traced back to ideas of integrity and honour associated with the country's only truly national game. 'It would be easy at this point to row back against this, to argue that a sense of proportion must be maintained,' wrote Ronay. 'But this would be to misunderstand the importance of cricket to the Australian soul. If the Shoeless Joe scandal shone a light on America's own great pastoral sport, reflecting a hackneyed vision of itself as a cloudless, youthful world of fecund greens and whites, then the ball-tampering affair appears to have twanged something similar in the Australian national psyche.'

On this at least, James Sutherland caught the mood. 'It's an issue of great proportion because of the standing of cricket in the eyes of the Australian public,' he said in Johannesburg. 'Those of us who know the game and love the game know it's beholden on everyone that plays the game to uphold the spirit of cricket. The responsibilities of the captain are higher than anyone, and the leaders as well. That's something that's really important to the game of cricket, and in some ways what separates it from other sports. That's part of what hurts right now.'

In truth Australia's team was credited with this spirit by vanishingly few opponents. But the ideal left something to strive for, a distant lighthouse. Those with faith in that navigation point felt the distress of seeing it wink out in the dark.

Partly that was down to how blatant the cheating was. Atherton had an alibi that he was only drying the ball. Umpire

Darrell Hair took on Pakistan over gouge marks but didn't see anyone making them. Afridi chomping a Kookaburra like Snow White with an apple was so brainless it was almost adorable. Du Plessis, Dravid, Chandimal used the sweets so many players chew, and when du Plessis wasn't doing that he used the zip on his pocket. Philander and Tendulkar used their nails. Mick Lewis as a Sheffield Shield coach used a concrete gutter, in the way that bowlers in the deep have long felt is fair trade for a batsman hitting a boundary.

None of these differ in substance. It was strange to keep hearing of Australia's 'premeditation' – aside perhaps from the chaos theory that is Afridi, all tampering is premeditated. Bowlers don't use their nails on a whim. Close catchers don't have perennial sore throats. Du Plessis said his mint charge was 'different' because polishing was better than degrading, but he didn't explore the distinction between sandpaper and zip teeth. But the fact remains that all the players above used the array of what was environmentally available. Bancroft was the only Test cricketer to be caught using something that could not have been there for anything else. 'This is not an unprecedented cricketing crime,' wrote Ronay. 'It happens – just not, perhaps, quite like this.'

Australia doesn't cheat – unless we're stealing gas from East Timor, or bribing Saddam Hussein to buy our wheat, or coaching Essendon Football Club. In sport the national sense of identity is built on punching above our weight. We love other countries cheating: that way we can feel smug when we beat them, and morally superior should the result fall the wrong way. At every football World Cup a workmanlike team gets squeezed out at the group stage while we announce that at least our blokes don't roll around on the floor clutching their limbs like these jokers who should frankly be embarrassed to win the thing. Cycling's chemical heart made it more enjoyable to savour the injustice when Cadel Evans kept losing the Tour de France than the year when a lull in doping finally let him win. That Evans was a clean beacon in a filthy sport was never to be questioned.

To Australians, cricket is rife with chuckers and dopers and match-fixers and tamperers, and we don't do any of those things (except Warnie a bit but those were all misunderstandings and he's a good bloke). They cheat and we beat them anyway, except overseas because those cheats all doctor their pitches. There's a racist aspect: Asian cricketers rarely get the same credit for their wickets or runs. Australia was and remains the world centre of discontent about Muttiah Muralitharan, no matter how many biomechanists explain the optical illusion of his bowling action, nor that he can spin his doosra with his arm in a steel cast. 'Nah, still reckon he's a chucker,' is the considered rebuttal. Did I mention he took more wickets than Warne?

It's all part of the psychological furniture. So when an Australian team was caught red-handed – or yellow-pantsed – there was no way to play it down. 'We don't cheat, it's as simple as that,' de Villiers said when his team was caught cheating for the first of three times. Australia couldn't even marshal a denial that flimsy. Supporters were made to feel stupid: idealists for believing, antagonists for their bombast. Nothing gets people angrier than being left no way out.

The final straw was that the entire enterprise looked so daft. Jamming evidence down sweaty underwear while everyone watches is cringe-inducing. It wasn't just that Australia had cheated, it was that Australia was *terrible* at cheating. It wasn't just that they'd been caught but that they'd launched a slapstick routine. It wasn't just a loss of integrity, it was a surrender of dignity.

All this in front of the world. Parts of the world loved it and took the chance at a few blows. Getting whacked by your own people is one thing, but having the neighbours jump in is another level. In England, Bull wrote of 'the ebb and swell of the public mood, which is a strange brew of puritan pillorying, lunatics indulging in their daily two-minute hate, Australian fans suffering from genuine shame and sorrow and everyone else's giddy schadenfreude.'

Schadenfreude is especially rich when that misfortune pays a karmic debt. Australia had been cricket's worst on-field citizen while also being its most self-righteous: Steve Waugh and Ricky Ponting proclaiming about spirit while leading teams that were loathed for its lack; Warner pausing a diatribe to give rulings on deportment. A cricket world that shrugged off everyone's indiscretions regarded a cricket nation that only shrugged off its own. Australians who had long objected suddenly felt heard. 'It is striking how unpopular the Australian team has become,' was Brearley's view from the outside. He didn't just mean with opponents. If the furious response showed one thing, it was that popularity was as much an issue from within.

Chapter 18

'WHAT THE FUCK IS GOING ON?'

Through the build-up and the sandstorm, it can't be said that Darren Lehmann often asked the right questions at the right times. Once, though, Australia's coach did offer the most pertinent query. What the fuck, indeed, was going on? A professional national representative team, paid in the upper echelon of athletes in the world, in a sport thick with talk of fair play and respect, cheating in a way that left no grey area, ham-fisted in the attempt, leaving a junior player to do the work, then being so startled when the high likelihood of being caught became real that they ducked their heads and tried to lie their way out. How did this possibly come to pass?

To answer, you first have to twist the question to an Ella Fitzgerald iteration: how long has this been going on? Cricket Australia's investigation exposed lies about sandpaper and Warner, but otherwise its conclusions mirrored Smith's initial claims: that only three people ever had an inkling, and that Cape Town was the only incidence. No Australian ever considered tampering until the inspiration struck in the second half of a Test in the second half of a series, then was exposed within an hour of that newborn idea taking its first slow blinks in the sunlight.

All series the ball had moved extravagantly. 'Australia's use of reverse swing left the realm of the fleeting and elusive to be something like a constant. It was … organised, unrelenting and highly professional,' wrote Cricinfo's Daniel Brettig. Yet halfway through the third match, Australia's ball conditioners had apparently lost their entirely legal ability to extract swing. Smith even offered the precedent as amelioration: 'We've seen the ball reversing quite a lot throughout this series, and our ball just didn't look like it was gonna go.'

At lunch on day three, when the plan was supposedly hatched, that ball was 22 overs old. It would barely have worn off the lacquer. Reverse swing generally kicks in after 40 or 50 overs. Even Durban was closer to 30, and that was played on an emery board. So we were asked to believe that in Cape Town, Smith agreed to a tampering plan because a ball wasn't doing something that it couldn't have been doing unless it had been tampered with. Australia was driven to desperation earlier in the innings than swing had started in either previous match, where conditions had been more conducive to swing. Was this really the company line?

It was true that Bancroft had been sufficiently unskilled that he was caught in quick time. But equally implausible was the insistence that Bancroft's first time was also Australia's. He was under surveillance because suspicions were high. What was the likelihood that in the very match when Warner handed over his ball-conditioning duties, he also suggested the new kid try a method of cheating that he himself had never given a whirl? Warner had spent a couple of years in the job and gave Bancroft a sandpapering tutorial, but had never tried it out on his own?

Scrutiny in Port Elizabeth was what made Warner recruit a new ball-shiner in the first place. No other explanation was advanced. Yet CA had no interest. 'The focus of Iain's investigation was very much about the incident in Cape Town and what happened,' James Sutherland said. 'If there's an element of truth to those allegations then they're obviously of severe concern. If there was more to that or more understanding then there would be action taken and further investigation.' So would he look into it? 'Not at this stage. But from our perspective, if there are credible allegations, and there is evidence to come to light, we have powers under our code of conduct to investigate that or any other matter.'

There was plenty of reason for suspicion. South African players believed they'd seen tampering first-hand. They had spoken to media connections, who had spoken on air. Television cameras had suspicious footage. A range of outlets reported it at the time. Anyone involved would have taken a phone call if Sutherland had a few questions. Was someone else supposed to collate the evidence on CA's behalf?

Similarly, there was a misleading impression that Roy's investigation covered the whole team when he had only interviewed Warner, Smith, Bancroft, Lehmann and Handscomb. No other player had to sit down with a trained cross-examiner exploring what they knew. Lehmann's supposed corroboration had no source. Assistant coach David Saker, a skilled reverse-swinger in his bowling days, wasn't questioned. There was urgency to release findings, but an investigation could have continued after preliminaries. It was either a huge oversight or a convenient omission. There was no reason to think Roy would suppress answers, but those above him had shown a willingness to avoid questions. Roy was restructured out of a job soon after the investigation.

Du Plessis was diplomatic but left the suggestion out there. 'Without having evidence of it, I think it's unfair for me to say. Whether it was just really, really good skill in trying to bounce the ball in on the right places to get it roughed up, or whether it was someone working the ball, definitely in this series the ball has reversed quite a bit.' Lehmann's comments after Durban looked bad in retrospect. 'Obviously, there are techniques used by both sides to get the ball to reverse and that's just the way the game goes. I have no problems with it, simple. You'd have to ask the umpires and ICC about [legalities]. I don't mind the ball moving, I have no problems with it at all.'

The trail of questions led back to the Ashes. It was a little bit suspicious, said a very deliberate Alastair Cook, 'certainly in Perth when the outfield was wet with rain they got the ball reversing. I didn't see anything ... We have to be very careful.

We were curious at certain moments but then we couldn't get the ball up to 90 miles per hour where they consistently could.'

Stuart Broad was more direct, questioning the idea that Australia would suddenly use sandpaper. 'You look through virtually all of those Test matches and they reverse swung the ball, in sometimes conditions that you wouldn't expect the ball to reverse. So I don't understand why they've changed their method for this one game. I don't know. Steve said it's the first time they've tried it, so he's saying they have.'

Reverse swing hadn't played a part in the Ashes result. An old video circulated of Bancroft at the SCG supposedly spooning sugar into his pocket – hardly a helpful device anyway – but Fairfax papers had found at the time it was a bowl of chewing gum pellets. Analysts didn't track much swing from either team. Smith took new balls as soon as they became available. Reverse wasn't a required weapon when Australia's attack relied on hard pitches, high pace and aggressive lengths.

Bouncers did over a third of the damage: of 89 English wickets in the summer, 30 fell to short balls, 21 to Lyon, 18 to nicks or pads while the ball was new, and only 16 to a fuller pitch from an older ball. There was a hint of reverse when Hazlewood trapped James Vince at the MCG inside 25 overs. Aside from that, Cummins getting Mark Stoneman in the 55th at the Gabba was about the only other wicket suggesting contrast movement.

One England player told UK journalists that at post-series drinks, Warner bragged that he'd scuffed the ball using his hand strapping. Was this a drunk misunderstanding, a very Warner joke, an attempt at needling? Was it the truth, with the series done and Warner feeling untouchable? Perhaps the idea had been in his head a while, or he'd been trying out a few early methods.

This may not survive the tell-all interviews of the future, but what seems likely is that even if he flirted with tampering, Warner didn't fully put it into practice until South Africa. Jim Maxwell gets excellent mail in Warner's home town, and he was confident enough to tell *The Sydney Morning Herald* that the sandpaper had been given three outings, starting in Durban. South Africans were suspicious too. While AB de Villiers was batting in Cape Town, Fanie de Villiers was whistling up the dogs. 'I said earlier on, that if they could get reverse swing in the 26th, 27th, 28th over then they're doing something different from what everyone else does,' boasted the bowler turned commentator to Melbourne radio station RSN. 'We actually said to our cameramen, "Go out and have a look boys, they're using something." They searched for an hour and a half until they saw something.'

The thing is, South Africa were reversing it just as early. That doesn't have to mean they were tampering, maybe they were managing the ball to perfection. But it raised the possibility. Did Australian suspicion have an influence before South African suspicion? Remember Warner's comment the first night of the series: 'the ball shifting after twenty-odd overs on the first day is incredible.' During warm-ups next morning, *The Australian* reported an unnamed player speaking to 'a commentator' and asking 'How the fuck could they get the ball to reverse after eighteen overs?' Peter Lalor didn't write that piece, but he was the tour reporter for that paper and a commentator for SEN. No prizes for guessing who the player was. Smith used similar wording after the match: 'the ball started reversing inside of twenty overs in the first innings of a Test match, which you don't see too often.'

Now consider Warner's pachydermal memory for grudges. He had history with South Africa and tampering. In 2014 when de Villiers was the wicketkeeper, Warner noticed he would collect throws from the outfield, then brush the rubber pimples of his glove over the rough side of the ball. The action wasn't dramatic but had an effect over time. The tourists tried it in the nets and decided it gained reverse. Warner made the accusation in a radio interview after losing the second Test. The ICC fined him for inappropriate comments, then umpires in the third Test told de Villiers to stop brushing the ball. It was a perfect demonstration of Darcus Howe's dilemma – when no one is allowed to implicate anyone, an action can simultaneously be inappropriate to question and inappropriate to carry out.

In that bad-tempered third Test of 2014, Warner led the 'pack of dogs' confrontation that saw du Plessis barked off the field. South Africa struggled for swing. Australia didn't. 'I was really surprised to see the ball reverse from their side. It was twenty overs old and with the damp conditions ... let's just leave it at that,' said du Plessis with an artful pause. Had Australia responded in more ways than verbally? That was Michael Clarke's team, and some of his former colleagues were privately satirical about his public condemnations of the sandpaper story.

'Obviously with coming out and saying the comment about AB de Villiers probably wasn't the smartest thing, and I regret saying that,' Warner said after that series. But what was Lalor's line again? 'If forced to a public act of contrition he will whisper moral relativisms and resentments in private.' Warner stewed over his sanction. After du Plessis' mint charge in 2016, Smith was conciliatory and said that everyone uses that technique, while Warner gave a speech about how disappointed he would be if his team ever stooped so low. In 2018, when South Africa got swing at Durban, what are the odds that Warner decided it was dodgy? What are the odds it started an arms race?

It fits an earlier theme: anyone getting away with something makes Warner want to even the score. Targeting Jonny Bairstow balanced a grudge over Joe Root. Kagiso Rabada beat an ICC charge after Warner accepted one. Both times Warner used a mateship code as pretext to go after opponents. Deciding the other mob were cheats would have given him perfect licence. There was Warner, a little engine of discontent forever thrumming away, always at some level wanting to tear the world apart. The de Kock brawl capped it off and gave him the fire of righteousness. He could consider his suspicions confirmed: he was on the good team, they were the bad team, they had to be punished.

Having just moved back into the slips, tape was a fair precaution for Warner's damaged fingers. Questioning it seemed an obvious confection, like with Jimmy Anderson cleaning the ball in Melbourne. 'The times I've played with Davey, he had all that strapping on his fingers,' said former bowler Ryan Harris. It was true – Warner routinely taped his left thumb and index finger, wrapping a sheath around the digits as he had through the Ashes. What he didn't have when he played with Harris was a cross-strap, a thick band of tape running across his palm below his fingers. Trainspotters had never seen it before. It made its debut at Durban. But so what, right? 'Unless there's something rough,' said Harris, 'sand or glass or something on that taping, that's not going to do anything to the ball.'

As they batted in Port Elizabeth, South African players swore things were amiss. The tape on Warner's palm, they started to think, was sticky side up. As the bowler ran in, with everyone's attention elsewhere, they thought they saw Warner reach into his pocket and press something into his hand – maybe a square of sandpaper. When the ball came to him, he could seat the rough side in his palm while polishing the shiny side on his trousers. On the bowler's next approach, he would remove the object from his hand and stash it again. Just an occasional application, fine-grained.

That theory got passed on to broadcasters. You had to admit, the photos of how hard Warner gripped the ball were odd. Other photos of his strapping showed a curious patchwork, with alternating substances overlapping one another, even if they were just two sides of the same tape. Through de Villiers' defiance on the second day, Australia kept the old ball for 89.3 overs, only changing it near stumps when they got Philander on strike. Reports began to circulate questioning Warner's bandages, and the following morning camera close-ups found the names of Candice and his daughters freshly inked onto the new tape. Recasting an object of controversy as a sweet family tribute was a clever riposte.

Family was the central factor, anyway. If Warner hadn't been tampering before the stairwell fight in Durban, surely it was the catalyst. If he had been, it would have made him feel justified. Through the second and third Tests, as abuse of his wife intensified, Warner was coming back to the hotel each night to find her crying and blaming herself for the drama. I can't emphasise this enough: Warner loves Candice Falzon more than anything. He credits her with making his life worthwhile, like he was nothing and she was his salvation.

'If people could understand … if they could just sympathise just slightly with the month that he's had,' she said after the series. 'I always put on a strong front and I turn out to the games. But seeing them wearing the masks, to have people staring and pointing and laughing at me, to have the signs, to have, you know, the songs made up about me, I would have to sit there and cop that. And he had to just cope with it, he was protecting me as much as he could and protecting the girls.'

They were both besieged. The ugliness leached through the touring party and the series. The Rabada conflict and social media snipes and every other little thing turned into the deepest grievance. You couldn't understate the experienced match referee Jeff Crowe saying it was the angriest series he'd ever seen. The players' union boss Alistair Nicholson thought the same when he arrived: 'The environment that I encountered prior to the Test at Newlands was the most hostile I have witnessed since I began this role.'

Under all this, Smith was falling apart. He'd come right out and said during the tour that he wasn't mentally right: 'I didn't feel I was hitting the ball that well but my mind was in a good place, maybe now my mind is not in as good a space as it was but I'm hitting the ball better.' And, 'It got to the point where I actually didn't want to pick my cricket bat up for a bit which is very rare for me.' No one picked up on the significance.

There were signs. South Africa swarmed him as they'd done before. A fifty at first, then a thirty, then lower, lower. He hadn't made a ton against them since his first attempt in 2014. He was so plumb in Port Elizabeth that he started walking, then stopped and reviewed it just in case. He knew he was carrying the team. Two dismissals to left-arm spinners had him trying to wring even more from that strange head: 'perhaps I got a bit lazy at times and didn't have the same concentration levels that I had in India at the start of last year.' But the tank was dry. In Cape Town he was out twice to a trash shot at a trash ball from a bowler who rarely threatened. People would remember the second innings, when a broken Smith played one of the worst shots of his career. More telling was that he'd already played the same shot in the first innings, before the shit had hit the fan.

I wasn't fit. I mean, I was mentally wrung out, I was physically wrung out, and I was fed up with the whole system, things that seemed to be just closing in on us, and I suppose in my own case I felt they were closing in on me, and it was a cry for help ... I didn't recognise just how far down I was ... I was disappointed that there was nobody else either within the playing group or within the administration who seemed to understand.

That's not Smith, that's Greg Chappell recalling the lead-up to the underarm ball of 1981. When the river runs dry ... Later Smith would speak about the one-dayers he'd played after the Ashes. 'I don't think I've ever hit the ball that bad in my life. I was making horrible decisions and I just felt horrible at the crease. I think it all comes down to the mental part of the game and just putting so much into the Ashes back home that it took so much out of me.'

Small wonder that horrible decisions were being made in the dressing room as well. It also revealed that Smith had never been much of a leader to begin with. A great cricketer, a decent tactician, but not someone who would set the path or demand the behavioural standard. Having lacked the gumption to shut down Warner's handyman operation, and having allowed his most junior player to wear the risk, we finally saw how little control Smith had.

The 2015 clear-out that made him captain also stripped senior experience from his side. Lyon had played the most but never quite believed he belonged. Starc and Hazlewood were good-natured and played along. Khawaja was quiet, Shaun Marsh was silent, Mitch Marsh was a cheerful goof. Some of the players who might have showed some steel ended up on the fringes. New boys only wanted to impress, Bancroft to his detriment, Handscomb grinning and chirping like one of those schoolkids wanting to win favour with bullies. None of them would stop Warner doing as he pleased.

And so to the final piece of the puzzle. In November 2016, when Australia was shot out for 85 by South Africa in Hobart, the game's authorities hit a well-worn Crisis button. Rod Marsh resigned as chairman of selectors while his colleagues sacked five of eleven players. Sutherland made an emergency visit to the Bellerive Oval dressing room. It wasn't Smith's fault; he'd been the poor sod on 48 not out. But the captain was put up against a wall and barrelled: it was not acceptable for Australia to lose like this, it would not be tolerated, and it would not be repeated. The heads on pikes rather drove the point home. The narrative was about a lack of fight, a team that went down unacceptably meekly, as though edging balls on a green track was fundamentally a matter of morality. The 'quiet' wicketkeeper Peter Nevill was ditched, the new man Matthew Wade would 'bring back the mongrel'. In short: Nevill didn't sledge and Wade didn't stop.

The clear lesson was that management demanded aggression. When Wade was dropped a year later, Warner resumed the role, reportedly encouraged by senior management. And no matter what happened or how bad it got, Smith kept fronting up with his platitudes about good hard cricket and not crossing lines. That kid again, repeating what he thought he was supposed to. 'Oh, I'll say the sponsor's product, VB.'

That kid who just wanted to play cricket. The one who wanted to bat forever. The one whose agent told his headmaster that he could be making a million a year, so what use was study. 'His boyish exterior hides ... well, a boyish interior,' wrote Gideon Haigh. Leaders demand better; Smith covered shortcomings. He didn't know how to lay down the law or even what he thought the law should be. There was no team identity, no beliefs reflecting him. He reflected whatever was closest.

Repeatedly he dismissed what the public thought as long as his players approved of their own behaviour. There was no understanding of what it means to be representative. After Warner's fight, Smith had a philosophical ponder: 'whether I could have done anything to change the events of what happened in the last Test, I'm not sure, but I do take responsibility.' Of course he could have done something, had he controlled his players at any stage in the preceding two years. Warner had operated with impunity under a captain afraid to tell him no. 'It's about continuing to play our hard, aggressive brand and making sure we stay within the parameters of the game,' Smith said days before allowing his players to sandpaper the ball. His leadership had looked weak; in the end it was homeopathic.

Success covers a multitude of flaws. With Smith playing so well that his mental health was never questioned, his captaincy sure wouldn't be. Through 34 matches in charge he made 3659 runs, better than a hundred per Test, as his team's culture grew fetid. No one – not the people who appointed him, the coaches supposed to support him, the media reporting on him – was honest about his weaknesses. We all assumed the best batsman in the world was the only choice.

So when things got dark in South Africa, the captain didn't have a guiding store of principles to draw on. All CA had drilled into him was to win and back up your mates, the classic Australian way. There had been directives to be aggressive and directives to avoid losing, both carrying the implication to do whatever it took. Warner's mad ideas had caused the first directive to blow up in their faces, but Warner's mad ideas might help the second directive be achieved.

The pair's former batting coach, Michael Di Venuto, summed it up tightly. 'If you look at the whole series, it was pretty volatile. I suppose it was building up to something. Maybe the headspace of where they were at that particular moment in time. When you are in a different country and you're copping it from all angles, you don't know what sort of state the players were in to make that sort of decision. And the will to win, the Australian cricket team just wins. It is not allowed to lose.'

Smith was crumbling, strung out, manic. Warner was enraged, acting out, and had the longest track record in the game. Yet none of the managers and coaches, health professionals or media liaisons attending to the team over the course of five months saw anything sufficiently wrong to take action. The team's leaders were cooked but no one followed the smell of burning.

From the start there were rumblings from Warner's camp that he wasn't to blame. CA's report indicated that he'd made the plan, Bancroft was the stooge, and Smith didn't snuff it out. Warner took several more days to make a public appearance than the others, and did so with careful scripting that limited admission of liability. He was getting intensive legal advice and was close to contesting his punishment. Only the goodwill that Smith and Bancroft attracted for their apologies saw Warner accept his sanction, as the PR advisers pipped the lawyers.

Privately he maintained he had been, to use his brother's prescient neologism, the escape goat.

None of which is surprising given Warner's precedent with accepting fault, but it may have some basis. Whether tacit or explicit, CA staff had encouraged him to push for any advantage. Warner openly spoke of his sledging as a service for the team. Even if he did it discreetly for safety's sake, he could easily see tampering the same way. Perhaps to his mind everyone appreciated his work. As in 2015, when Clarke and Lehmann denied asking him to sledge, Warner remained adamant that he had done what they wanted. Is this a moral relativism, or did others actually know?

On Lehmann, most notable is that none of the three suspended players made a point of apologising to their coach. Had he been an innocent bystander who they had lied to, you would expect some savage guilt after they trashed his reputation and cost his job. That made two Australian coaches to have their careers ended by Warner. But in all the remorse, Boof barely rated a mention. It's also notable that Lehmann never uttered a cross word at the players who had, if you believed their version, deceived him and forced him to resign. But if he'd known about the tampering, and had the players volunteered to cover for him, you can imagine guilt driving him to quit when he saw them breaking down.

Had Smith driven the idea, Smith would have worn the blame. Implicating Warner but no one else suggests there was no other player to implicate. Paine confirmed that the players implicated went into a separate room to speak with management on the evening they were caught. Hazlewood and

Starc were both angry at the 'leadership group' terminology. Sutherland, when asked about the reactions of other players, said, 'I've spoken to a limited few. But I can only imagine.'

A couple of weeks after the tour, Starc was unexpectedly a participant at the Women in Banking and Finance forum in Sydney, speaking on a panel with a corporate adviser, a banking exec, and the editor of *Vogue*. With the topic 'Reputation: Your Most Valuable Asset?' there was little doubt what questions the bowler would face. He answered freely that when it came to issues that were 'about being up front and tackling a problem head on, that's something the group who decided to go into a press conference didn't really think about. They obviously didn't see how big the reaction was going to be at that time and then went down the path of not telling the whole truth and then I guess involving another group, which ruined – well, not ruined, but affected – other reputations.'

Scepticism was widespread that bowlers wouldn't know what was happening to a ball, given the way despotic quicks have historically guarded their weapon's condition. The Pakistani maestros fiercely drilled their English teams in not licking fingers, wiping brows, or catching the wrong side. Hazlewood, though, suggested a more casual approach: 'We obviously have ball maintenance people in the team … We pretty much get it at the top of our mark, one second before we start running in. So we have a quick look, see which side's a bit worn.'

Paine indicated that methods were entirely at Warner's discretion: 'all teams try and get the ball to reverse. That's a given and teams have certain guys who have that role. From our perspective, Davey has always been the guy we go to for shining the ball. So yep, people are going to say that everyone knew, and that's fine, but the facts are that people knew we were trying to get the ball to reverse, but how we do that is normally up to certain individuals.'

Warner's seniority and stubbornness could easily have made others leave him alone. Maybe it fell under 'don't ask, don't tell'. If any player could have made a unilateral decision to tamper, it would have been Warner. If any player could have convinced himself it was altruism, that would have been Warner too. If there is more to come out, it could be along these lines. Being who he is, any grievance will eventually emerge. It would be an interesting factor in reviving his Australian career if Warner happens to be sitting on something explosive enough to blow the joint up.

When the sandpaper story broke, Sutherland adopted his basset-hound air. 'In recent times, as I think most of you know, I've had reason to speak to Steve about the team's behaviour, and we put a media release out recently about that. I have very strong and clear views about the responsibility of the Australian cricket team to play the game in the right spirit, and I don't think anyone would be under any illusions within the team as to what I think about this.'

He could have recycled his line from the Walkabout. 'David Warner has done a despicable thing, but I also hold the team to account here.' Lalor wrote about the moment in 2013 when CA first heard about Warner drunkenly swinging fists: it 'sent a shiver through the organisation. They were wary of his headstrong ways and worried that one day it could land everybody in serious trouble'.

Call that a bullseye. But CA fired the shot. Talk of being held to account was hollow; Warner never was. He was encouraged and enabled through the intervening years. It didn't matter whether anyone started telling him to stick the boot in. It mattered that no one had stopped him doing it before. Australia wanted to use Warner's temperament but ignored an ancient lesson: elemental forces are never fully controlled. Fire, water, electricity, gravity, velocity: all can be bent to your purpose, but you respect their damaging potential and you never ease your vigilance. Those running the game could have worked towards better awareness, better standards, an aim of being better people, but had failed at each. All that remained was the poor theatre of condemning one's own creation.

Chapter 19

THE WANDERERS ALBATROSS

'The first thing is we have to listen. We've maybe had our head in the sand a bit over the last twelve months – that if we continue to win, we can act and behave how we like and the Australian public will be ok with that. What we've found out in the past month or so is that the Australian public and our fans don't necessarily like the way we go about it. It's pretty simple. We have to listen. We have to take it on board and we have to improve our behaviour in the way we play the game.'

Not many captains would have marked their first full match in charge with a statement like this. But Tim Paine's ascent didn't have many precedents. In Cape Town on the third day he'd been just another player. On the fourth he was a stand-in leader delivering an apology from the team to a country. Within a week he was formally Test captain number 46 in a turn of events so fast there was no time to get him a blazer for the Johannesburg toss. Warner still had the reserve coat in his luggage, and Smith hadn't left his. The day before that toss, Paine got bumped from his press conference so his coach could resign.

Welcome to the job. Early morning South African time, Smith heaving for breath on television sets, then late morning Lehmann choking up. A few mad days of endless shift and turmoil. We were all rolled thin enough for the light to come through. And on the main oval, training was underway.

It felt like the hours after a funeral. Not in terms of tragedy, though there had been farewells, but when it seems impossible that the world is carrying on. There had to be a match tomorrow. There was a different Australian team. Joe Burns was one of the Hobart discards, Matthew Renshaw a victim of Ashes panic. They'd just jumped on a plane after opening the batting for Queensland in the Sheffield Shield final. Glenn Maxwell had come, the perennial reserve. Peter Handscomb had ridden the pine for months and would bat four. Starc would join the missing with a leg injury.

Players did drills, perhaps comforted by the normality. But it was Stepford normality, surface smiles. There's no clear way to describe the feeling, but people know it: a hollowness, a detachment, the floating unreality after something immense. When the world must be a stage backdrop you could poke fingers through, blocks of painted polystyrene you could kick over, because it couldn't be normal right now.

The Wanderers – twenty-four hours before the final Test there was that magic quiet of an empty stadium. A perfect day, African autumn, gold and green and blue with the heat taken out. Players loosed occasional shouts, background traffic burred, then on the public address system a playlist of vintage Australiana fired up. Out from the vertiginous Unity Stand, with its canopy billows that could be sails on an impossibly high mast or whitecaps seen from its top, a cascade of chords began an echo-avalanche. The Church, Under the Milky Way, fanning out its sparse and lovely emptiness. 'Wish I knew what you were looking for. Might have known what you would find.'

The tone was set. Wide Open Road, The Triffids: 'Well, the drums rolled off in my forehead and the guns went off in my chest.' Whether the nod to patriotism was satirical or earnest, what washed through was a nostalgic poignancy, tangled as it was with feelings of tainted pride, drawing out each song's elements of wistfulness or yearning, absence or regret. Australian Crawl: 'She don't like that kind of behaviour. So throw down your guns. Don't be so reckless. Throw down your guns.'

Nick Cave haunting an abandoned church with Into My Arms. Crowded House with Don't Dream It's Over: 'Try to catch the deluge in a paper cup.' The Reels: 'Fame won't alleviate heartache,' giving way to 'I do the best I can to make things right. And I don't understand how I got here anyway.'

There was Throw Your Arms Around Me, no song more appropriate for the departing cricketer at summer's end: 'So if you disappear out of view, you know I will never say goodbye.' As the last reserve bowlers hurled down their wares, it was You

Am I, Heavy Heart: 'I miss you like sleep, and there's nothing romantic about the hours I keep.'

But best of all was Paul Kelly jangling in, the man who gets something at Australia's heart in a way few others can. 'Kelly doesn't seem to be interested in authenticity at all – it just comes naturally to him,' wrote Robert Forster of the Go-Betweens, 'and it reaches further because of that, to the campfires and the bush, the suburbs and suburban pub, and the inner-city sophisticates. His voice – sly and warm, laconic and sometimes frail – may be the closest thing we have to a national one.'

The song was How To Make Gravy, the story of a man who's done wrong and is taken away from those he loves. His missive from jail is about the pain of missing Christmas, remorse shot through with joy and the promise to make things right. The sportswriter Jack Quigley recast it syllable for syllable to feature Smith contemplating the next home summer.

Hello, Tim. It's Smudge here. I hope you're 'keeping well.
It's the 17th of November, and now they're picking the last twelve.
For all this misbehaviour, I'll be outta here 'til July.
When you see Milo kids on Boxing Day,
please don't let 'em cry for me.

I guess the Marsh brothers will fly into Queensland,
Matty Renshaw must be close.
They say AB can bat three hundred degrees, even more maybe,
but that won't stop the GOAT.

Who's gonna play like Davey now?
I bet it won't move the same.
Just add sunscreen, sweat, a little sugar from your pocket,
and don't forget the Flexovit 600 grit for roughness
    and that extra swing.

And give some runs to Usman. And some poles for Joshy.
Tell 'em all I'm sorry, I screwed up this time.
And look after Peter, I'll be thinking of him,
on those new-ball mornings, when me and Cam
    serve our time.

I hear Justin's got a new job now. I hope he can hold his own.
Do you remember the last bloke? What was his name again?
Uhh, just a bit too much Jack & Coke.
And Maxi – you know I'm even gonna miss Maxi,
cause there's sure as hell no one in grade cricket
    I want to fight.

Say hey to baby Moises, wish him merry Crickmas.
I'm really gonna miss it, all the pleasure and the cash.
And later in the season, I can just imagine,
when the Tests are over, you'll go and play Big Bash.

And you'll bat with Peter. I know you really like him.
Just don't bat for too long, oh brother,
I need to get my spot back –
I didn't mean to say that! It's just my mind it plays up.
It shouldn't even matter, I know you'll never match my stats.

You know I'll miss it badly, I'll bat against my family,

I'm gonna bat with Davey, I'm gonna take a catch.

Tell the game I'm sorry, yeah I love it madly,

tell 'em all I'm sorry, and kiss the badge of your helmet for me.

You know one of these days,

I'll be back with Davey.

We'll be making plenty.

I'm gonna pay 'em all back.

It was bizarre to think Australia was still a theoretical chance to draw the series. The likelihood was a million miles away. There were bright moments, like Chadd Sayers finally making his debut after spending more time in the twelve than an apostle. His face as he pulled on his cap said the match still meant something, plus it let me use the Doctor Zaius song on air. There was Paine asking du Plessis to have the teams start with a handshake: 'Sportsmanship was a really important part of what had gone wrong and I wanted to show that moving forward, from our very next game, that would be something the Australian team would be.'

South Africa batted five sessions, Australia lost half a dozen wickets in the sixth. The first day had been even, Sayers giving de Villiers an unlikely working over with swing and seam before drawing an inside edge for 69, but Markram made another ton and Bavuma was stranded a few short. Cummins refused to give in and finished with 5–83 at the ground where he was man of the match on debut a million years before. 'The boys have been getting into me that I only take five-fors here at this ground, but it's a pretty long couple of days so I'm not sure if it's right up on my favourites list at the moment.'

He bowled until tea and was batting by stumps. Paine matched him in defiance, the only two for Australia who looked like they could find their Test intensity. Both made fifties on the third morning but the top order had left them no base. The three new inclusions made a dozen runs between them; the Marsh brothers totalled 20. Australia made 221 replying to 488 – and South Africa batted on.

All of day three. Most of day four. Elgar relishing the chance, blocking and blunting his way to 81 from 250 balls. Mountains rose and kingdoms fell. The lead crept past 300, past 400. Du Plessis hadn't topped 20 in the series, had his finger split open by Cummins, then decided this was the day to make a hundred, most of it walloping Lyon with sweeps. Paine kept up to the stumps for Sayers, despite cracking his thumb that way in the first innings. Cummins kept up the heat for what would finish as 4–58. Lyon toiled towards 81 overs, Sayers to 49, Hazlewood to 47.

And so the match dreamed on, Mluleki Ntsabo in our commentary box tracking it in the melodic clicking and swaying of the isiXhosa language. Wilhelm on the Afrikaans update line taught us his terminology: short leg being *slagyster*, meaning bear trap; gully being *gengetjie*, meaning small hallway; yorker being *streepbal*, meaning stripe-ball. The SABC celebrated Jim Maxwell's 45th year in broadcasting with an imposing cake. Renshaw opened the bowling after a lunch break with some lanky off-spin.

The lead crawled past 500, past 600 for pity's sake, Bavuma and Philander having a bash. 'We don't always have to finish a Test in four days,' Elgar smiled, sounding so pleased with himself that his next line could have been 'Diplomatic immunity!' Mitch Marsh wasn't supposed to bowl with a groin strain: before tea on day four he was in his eighth over, trudging the slowest trudge back to his mark the game has ever seen. On declaring, South Africa's lead was 612. They'd batted nine of the first eleven sessions.

Australia had been reduced to a wisp. Three fell by stumps. With Handscomb and Shaun Marsh at the crease, Lehmann talked about how they'd batted out a Test in Ranchi a year earlier. Marsh was out first ball next morning. His brother was out to the fourth. It was all so inevitable that Philander took six wickets for three runs and I forgot to put him in my match report. Australia made 119, out not long after 11 am.

'It's an early beer, that's for sure. It might be a coffee,' said Paine of the post-match mingling. 'I think the enormity of the week potentially caught up with the guys, and when you're off your game five or ten per cent in a mental aspect in cricket you get exposed.' It had been a 'brutal week. Really difficult. I've never been in a situation when you've got your whole group, your whole staff flattened.'

Australia had won the first Test then been smashed. They'd bowled 738 overs in the series to South Africa's 562. They hadn't scored a century while South Africa scored five. Starc had opened with a bang then dropped off with his fitness. Shaun Marsh had returned to flake: one ball in Cape Town, five balls in Port Elizabeth, first of the day in Joburg. His brother had bossed the first Test, looked good in the second, then slipped away. Paine had kept cleanly and battled with the lower order, averaging 45 since his comeback. Lyon and Hazlewood had toiled. Cummins had been the light on the hill – even du Plessis singled him out.

'He's an exceptional player. We would sit on the side of the field and just admire what he does. We'd say, "Look at the guy, he's still running in and bowling quick." Diving at balls when he's just finished an eight-over spell, runs in the series. As a batter I definitely felt he was the biggest challenge. He's a nice guy, Pat. You enjoy it when nice guys do well, even opposition, the good people of the game. We're looking forward to having a beer now with the Australian team.'

A marked contrast to 2014 when no gathering took place, or 2006 of which Mark Boucher said 'We did share a few beers [but that] may be just for the sake of it because that's the right thing to do.' This time the teams held a joint fines meeting – that good-hearted cricket ritual where teammates look back over a match or season and rib each other with token penalties for invented offences. Paine's outreach had drawn a response in kind.

Australians were focused on their own disaster, but the result was huge for South Africa. They hadn't beaten Australia at home since coming back to international cricket. Senior members of the current team had failed at several attempts. And to win 3–1 from a game down in any series was almost unheard of. Normally player interviews for radio are perfunctory, a couple of minutes with an eye on the clock. Now du Plessis was relaxed and contemplative, standing under the shade of a eucalypt for better than ten minutes, wanting to go into topics in depth.

'It'll probably take a few days to understand how special it is. What has sunk in is we've played an unbelievable Test match, this last one. I've played a lot of cricket against Australia and I've never been in the position where I can look up at the scoreboard and see a lead of 600. To win by 490 runs against any Australian team is an unbelievable performance, and I'm really proud of that.' De Villiers later echoed his awe: 'it was the best series I have been a part of. There were scandals that weren't called for but cricket-wise, the way we dominated was – well, I haven't been part of a team that has done *that* to them.'

On the pitch when the crowds had ebbed, the two of them and Morkel posed with their collection of babies while their families took photos. It was a gentle moment in lives that exist under a magnifying glass. Morkel had played his last Test to acclaim. De Villiers had played his last Test discreetly. 'I think he thought, If I'm getting out to this bloke, then I probably should hang them up,' Sayers deadpanned later. The reality was that this demolition made a perfect end.

'When I was growing up it was always Australia,' de Villiers had told me in Port Elizabeth. 'South Africa's biggest challenge in my eyes. In the backyard we always had games as Australians against South Africans. As a youngster growing up I always wanted to play the best, and in my mind that was always Australia. I just feel that extra bit of magic against the Aussies.' He'd made six of his 22 Test hundreds against them, the most of any South African, and finished at a crest. 'All I know is when I came back, it was like I was twenty-three again.

It was a dream. That's how I want to play. You're not supposed to be going through the motions.'

So ended a series played at such intensity that Cummins, Starc and Rabada wound up with stress fractures. A series whose ramifications would extend for years. You could only marvel again at how such desperation to win had led to such devastation in defeat. Warner's attempt to aid his team had brought down everyone in it. Its more thoughtful members were left to plot a way forward. 'This is a moment where we can really have a think about how we play the game,' said Cummins mid-match. Paine echoed him after it: 'The positive for us is that we really do in the next series have a clean slate. We've got to learn our lessons from this series and where we can improve, and if guys aren't already thinking about that I'd be surprised.'

That afternoon the ground was empty again. Way up in the Wanderers press box, at the top of the high stand, you strain to see the players while you call the game. When it's done by lunch, though, you can roll back the floor-to-ceiling windows, let the breeze stream in, and write your columns in the warmth reflecting off the stands.

The most magic part of following cricket around the world has always been the ground when it's over. The Oval in 2013 was a fairyland marquee, lit up and twinkling in the dark late hours as I dodged a few damp patches across the square. The Wanderers was basking in sun. Every time is different. But it's amazing that the centre of so much action and attention becomes a place to wander across once the action is done.

The focus of millions moves on, dissipating before converging somewhere else. You're left with the site, the echoes of what has gone, the few things remembered and many forgotten. You know something happened here, however silent the witness, the way you can stand in an amphitheatre and swear you feel the potency of those who went thousands of years before. Ghosts soak into stone and sleep. A cricket ground at its heaving peak, then at repose. Another contest over, another layer bedded into the strata that form the story of the game.

Chapter 20

CAMERON

Looking back over Cameron Bancroft's Test career is like waiting through the setup of a movie where you know everything is about to go to shit. Dustin Hoffman in *Papillon* making a prison break; Rose and Jack having an art class on the *Titanic*. Roll the tape: Bancroft is under pressure after an ordinary Ashes, does himself over in Durban while walking at Philander, then scraps out a half-century in the second innings. He works hard in Port Elizabeth for good starts but can't turn them into something. Then through the first innings at Cape Town, as wickets go down around him, the junior player sticks it out; his 77 is more than the other five specialists make between them. Scores end up close to level and he looks like he's finally clicked. The reel turns.

There's a lot of love for Bancroft in domestic cricket. 'He's a beauty,' a few players have said, in the Paul Hogan sense rather than the Rita Hayworth. Like his captain, he was obsessed with playing for Australia and worked endlessly at his game. He was known, to his eventual detriment, as the kind of player who would do anything for a teammate.

He won you over easily. Making people laugh does. As annoyed as the English got about his press conference in Brisbane there was something pure about seeing him look back at the room, starting out intimidated, then responding to the audience, growing in confidence, like a plant reaching for the light. That room embraced him because here was a cricketer willing to shape whole sentences, who had a sense of the enjoyment of words in their application. Smith wasn't laughing at England, he was enjoying an Australian player communicating in a way Australian players don't. He was a spectator at the circus watching tricks he couldn't imagine how to do himself.

The night before doomsday in Cape Town, while Lehmann was up in the press box talking about the crowds, Bancroft was doing the ABC interview down on the ground. He was relaxed, happy to have made a total but annoyed not to have gone bigger. 'I always felt like if I was patient enough, I was going to get opportunities to score. It was just about trusting that.' It's strange listening back to that recording, knowing it's almost the last thing before his world falls apart. I asked who he'd found most difficult to face. 'Everyone,' he laughed, then in another nice piece of phrasing, 'It's been a very topsy-turvy game, hasn't it? We've ridden the waves.' Iceberg, right ahead.

Warner hadn't been a fan of his last opening partner. Matthew Renshaw may only have been twenty when he made the team, but he wasn't an acolyte. They called him Turtle for not coming out of his shell – the kind of nickname that conveys more resentment than affection. Bancroft was the opposite, agog at having made the team, the one thing he'd always wanted to achieve. After a lifetime of being talked down to, Warner loved having someone look up to him. Take this from Bancroft:

> Some of the boys might say I took one for the team and spent a bit of time with him and took him away from the group. He's a great feller, he's scored a lot of Test runs and he's a guy that is worth sitting down and listening to about the game. It wasn't just cricket we talked about, it was an array of topics that came up. But particularly regarding the game of cricket I find him very refreshing to listen to. He plays the game full of energy and with a lot of confidence and a lot of positivity and I find that something that's really worth listening to and learning from to improve on for my own game. If I can sit there and digest something that he's got to say then I'll listen to it. He's been great for me.

It was easy for Warner to talk that player into his plan. You can imagine him making the pitch like an Avon salesman: want to try something that will really change your life? You wonder what Renshaw would have done, or anyone else. Who might have laughed it off? Who would have made an excuse? Who would actually have had the self-possession to say it was wrong? Any time someone corners you with a proposition, refusal can be difficult. Among the first picked for IPL deals, central contracts, sponsorships, Warner was one of the biggest names in the sport.

After leading off the tampering press conference, the younger man sat very still while his captain fielded the questions to follow. Not quite a statue, Bancroft seemed to have turned a gentle shade of grey. When the focus came back to him he couldn't have asked for a kindlier inquisitor than SABC host Kass Naidoo, whose commentary has more empathy than the norm. 'Cameron, you're young in your career,' she said, 'and I can see you're absolutely distraught about this. How do you move on?'

A flicker of his eloquence came back to life. 'In my short career so far I've felt like I've sat here and been asked a lot of big questions a couple of times now. It's just, unfortunately I was in the wrong place at the wrong time, and I want to be here because I'm accountable for my actions as well. Like the captain said, I'm not proud of what's happened and I have to live with the consequences and the damage to my own reputation that that comes with.' That intelligence sparkling away, mica in the shale. But then, his way with words was being used to reinforce the lie he'd agreed to tell.

That week, Gideon Haigh wrote about interviewing Bancroft a year before. 'Nice lad. Courteous. Thoughtful. Had played trumpet at high school. Cherished the opportunity to play The Last Post because of an uncle who had served in Vietnam. Interesting things to say. Said them well. Also desperately perfectionistic; to an almost disconcerting degree consumed by his career. As we parted, I felt strangely worried for him. How would he cope if he did not achieve what he wanted? How would he cope if he did?'

Consumed by his career to the point of this line in his homecoming *mea culpa*: 'Through the last few days, sitting in my own company, the thing that breaks my heart the most is that I have given up my spot in the team for somebody else for free.' Or channelling a bit of Cher, 'Not a second has gone by where I haven't wanted to turn back time.'

None of us can, of course; it's all look and no touch. All you can do is scan back through the sequence, watch the ship steam in reverse away from the ice. Try to make some sense of a past imprisoned in the frame. There is Bancroft, finding his way at Durban. There he is, taking control in Cape Town. There he is, waiting for his interview, a lonely figure by the boundary line at dusk.

Chapter 21

AUSTRALIA'S CRICKET CULTURE

We want to go out there and play aggressive and hard cricket and not cross the line. There are some times you do nudge that line a fair bit and the odd occasion you might step over that, but you do have to realise that we're out there to win.

– DAVID WARNER

It's about continuing to play a good, hard aggressive brand but knowing we don't want to cross the line.

– STEVE SMITH

We've got to make sure we play hard but fair, and don't cross the line. We're always going to teeter pretty close to it, that's just the way we play, but we've got to make sure we don't cross it.

– DARREN LEHMANN

I probably say this every series but we respect there's a line you can't cross.

– MICHAEL CLARKE

The Australian way is always to be combative, to be positive and to have a bit of a chat out on the field. As long as it doesn't cross the line ....

– STEVE WAUGH

I believe it's part of the game. But players do have to understand where the line is. They should never cross the line.

– RICKY PONTING

For those wondering where the line is, take a look at Warner: he is almost always on it or has just crossed it.

– PETER LALOR

I always felt that as an Australian team member, we should be nowhere near the line.

– ED COWAN

If we talk about abuse it's certainly over the line, and that's not pure emotion, that's pre-planned bullying sometimes, and we've all been guilty of that.

– PAT CUMMINS

I always liked the team I captained – there was a line, I liked us to headbutt that line.

– CLARKE

I'm all for it. There's a line, we'll headbutt the line but we won't go over it.

– NATHAN LYON

The team has sounded almost cult-like, repeating a monotonous chant about good hard Test cricket, opening scars, and our old friend the line, the headbutting thereof.

– GIDEON HAIGH

'Ball tampering is becoming similar to crossing the line comment. Needs to be defined.'
'Yep. And then head-butted repeatedly.'

– ANDREW MCGLASHAN AND CORRESPONDENT

There are only two countries in the world: dick, and not a dick. The line goes right the way around.

– DOUG STANHOPE

Well, hello there. Remember 'The Line', that sacred mark in the sand that Australian cricketers make it their duty to push, needle, headbutt and generally challenge as part of their commitment to hard, clean competition?

– ANDREW MILLER

Well, it looks like that Australian hierarchy are on the wrong side of the line here.

– NASSER HUSSAIN

You know this moment has come and gone, but you are not yet willing to concede that you have crossed the line beyond which all is gratuitous damage … Somewhere back there you could have cut your losses, but you rode past that moment on a comet trail of white powder and now you are trying to hang on to the rush.

– JAY MCINERNEY

Getting personal on the field is not on, and that's crossing the line in my opinion.

– SMITH

As I said, I play with aggression on the field and I try not to cross that line and it has been in the past that I have sort of been fiery, but I don't think whatsoever there on the field that I have ever crossed that line.

– WARNER

I've only ever heard one thing that has ever crossed the line and that was when we were coming up that stairwell.

– TIM PAINE

I can't even remember the last time someone's crossed the line.

– BRAD HADDIN

Oh, that bloody line.

– ADAM COLLINS

We have gone in search of The Line and we have found a bloke who might know a bloke who saw it once. Back in a month or so.

– LALOR

There is no doubt the urge to pile in has a lot to do with the attitude of this Aussie team, the unpleasant way it has presented itself over the last few years, all the while preaching about the imaginary 'line' Australia alone is qualified to police.

– BARNEY RONAY

There's this thing and I've seen it recently now about the line. They're saying they didn't cross the line, but where is the line? Who sets the line? Where does the line come from?

– OTTIS GIBSON

I don't decide where that line is. We don't look to push that line. I don't know who owns that line. Definitely not us.

– FAF DU PLESSIS

Whose line is it anyway?

– DREW CAREY

The Australian public has a line, too. And with their culture of sledging, whingeing, hypocrisy and arrogance, our cricketers have been head-butting it for so long that they have become an insufferable national migraine.

– BRYDON COVERDALE

We're so comfortable being the moral arbiter of where the line is. The line is where we want it to be.

– ROBERT CRADDOCK

I walk the line.

– JOHNNY CASH

One of the hardest things in the world is to get an Australian cricketer to criticise an Australian cricketer. We're not even talking those who've played for Australia, just those who play in Australia. First class, first grade – they'll snipe like any insular community, and the competitive resentments run deep and long. But to publicly say a fellow player has done wrong, without qualification or excuse? Only those well out of the tent will even consider it.

Take the Sydney cricketers who named Warner and his brother as the hardest sledgers they'd known: all of them ultimately defended the pair. The Warners were nice fellers over a beer, and the on-field invective was normalised. These players didn't want to be seen as complaining, but were simultaneously marking something as extreme. There's a fascinating cognitive dissonance in approving behaviour that you would never engage in yourself.

On-field abuse – and let's call it what it is – is an ingrained part of cricket in Australia. There is sledging in its lighter form, the good-natured teasing that can pass time and keep focus for amateurs who find twenty overs in the field a long day. But it doesn't take high stakes to harden the tone: many a third-grade suburban game degenerates into unimaginative verbals. There's a reason the Grade Cricketer character born on Twitter became so popular: his stories of the nastiness at the game's mediocre levels resonated with those who've experienced both. That outward aggression reflects a stunted masculinity, endlessly trying to prove itself, or Samuel Johnson's idea 'that small things make mean men proud, and vanity catches small occasions'. It's not universal, only part of cricket's whole, but a part that goes largely unchallenged.

No surprise then that it lives incarnate in the national team. The lineage goes at least as far back as Ian Chappell's era in the early 1970s, through Lillee and Thompson, Allan Border and Merv Hughes, then to Steve Waugh. By the millennium it was multi-pronged: Glenn McGrath gobbing off as metronomically as he bowled, Ricky Ponting as heir apparent and enforcer, Matthew Hayden sledging bowlers from the crease and batsmen from the cordon, Justin Langer getting the key in his back twisted before going in at short leg, Shane Warne the provocateur in chief. Waugh no longer said much but puppet-mastered from cover, stubbled jaw working gum under his roadkill cap.

This was the far end of an evolution. Earlier loudmouths had acted on impulse. 'Ian Chappell was a kind of rough diamond,' said Mike Brearley, his England counterpart in some fierce contests. 'Yes, they did a bit of sledging and his side were a very militant, aggressive team but he was twice given out in a Test match in Melbourne against us caught at the wicket off his pad or hip and both times he got off the field without delay and no one in the crowd would have known ... There was usually a bit of humour in what went on between the teams which makes a big difference.' Players in the 1980s often found it safer to keep their mouths shut against a West Indian or Pakistani pace battery, and Border had more cause to yell at his own team than the opposition.

But when Australia became world-beaters from the late 1990s, the beaten became disdained. England were a joke. West Indies fell apart. South Africa growled but were brought to heel. Asian teams were easy at home and manageable away. The rest were minnows, barely granted a game. Verbals became a symptom of something broader, an attitude that Australia deserved to win, deserved to dominate, deserved to do whatever it damn well pleased. It was Waugh who parsed sledging as 'mental disintegration' and made it a deliberate arm of strategy. 'Look at the varnish of formality in dousing the true implication,' wrote Osman Samiuddin from a Pakistan ravaged by Waugh contemporary George W Bush. 'Does "illegal combatants" ring a bell?'

Cue Michael Slater screaming at Rahul Dravid when the batsman disputed a catch. Cue Glenn McGrath yelling at Ramnaresh Sarwan, 'What does Brian Lara's cock taste like?' Cue Mark Boucher in 2006: 'Nasty things have been said … I'm not going to mention names but I have lost respect for one or two of their players.' Or the previous South Africa tour in 2002, when Graeme Smith debuted a month after his 21st birthday, and later broke the omerta to recount meeting Hayden.

'You know, you're not fucking good enough,' he told me. 'How the fuck are you going to handle Shane Warne when he's bowling in the rough? What the fuck are you going to do?' And I hadn't even taken guard yet. He stood there right in my face, repeating it over and over. All I could manage was a shocked nervous smile. I'd taken a bit of banter before but this was something else. Hayden had obviously been told his job was to attack me … All Warne does is call you a cunt all day. When he walked past me he said 'You fucking cunt, what are you doing here?' And I remember looking at [the umpire] Rudi Koertzen and he just shrugged his shoulders.

After Smith bumped into Brett Lee, the bowler 'told me he would fucking kill me if I ever touched him again'. As for McGrath, 'the minute you hit him for a boundary he loses the plot and it never stops'.

James Sutherland at the start of his reign showed the same hunger for truth as he would near its end: 'If Australian players were breaking the code of conduct, I'm sure the officials at the match would take appropriate action', was the word from the boardroom. Whose team had won, after all?

The side-serving to abuse, each made less palatable by the other, was sanctimony. Australians were assiduous at complaining when they felt wronged. In 2003, Waugh edited the MCC's Spirit of Cricket document to 'define a set of standards of behaviour and values'. The year after the joint attack on Graeme Smith, the year of McGrath's query about penis flavours, the year of Lehmann yelling 'black cunts!' when Sri Lanka got him out, Australia thought it credible to sign provisions against 'on-field abuse and sledging'. Ponting over the years expressed affront when teams declined an honour agreement for low catches. Indian captain Anil Kumble accepted it in 2008 only to see Ponting and Clarke claim extremely dubious takes, while Clarke stood his ground after India claimed one. Ponting bristled at journalists for 'questioning my integrity'.

These were among a buffet of incidents in a filthy-tempered match at the SCG won by Australia in the dying minutes. The next day's *Sydney Morning Herald* took the unusual step of running Peter Roebuck on the front page, as he launched in unprecedented fashion.

Ricky Ponting must be sacked as captain of the Australian cricket team. If Cricket Australia cares a fig for the tattered reputation of our national team in our national sport, it will not for a moment longer tolerate the sort of arrogant and abrasive conduct seen from the captain and his senior players over the past few days ... He has shown not the slightest interest in the well-being of the game, not the slightest sign of diplomatic skills, not a single mark of respect for his accomplished and widely admired opponents ...

He turned a group of professional cricketers into a pack of wild dogs. As much can be told from the conduct of his closest allies in the team. As usual, Matthew Hayden crossed himself upon reaching three figures in his commanding second innings, a gesture he does not perform while wearing the colours of his state. Exactly how he combines his faith with throwing his weight around on the field has long bemused opposing sides, whose fondness for him ran out a long time ago. ['Arrogant Ponting must be fired', *The Sydney Morning Herald*, January 2008.]

The broadside had some effect – Ponting was more careful in his final few years. But the champion era was already over. Hayden and Gilchrist soon departed and he was the final link. Declining Australian teams started to look to the abrasive past as a necessary ingredient of success. And what do you know, it was the easiest part to emulate. If you couldn't play like them, you could at least act like them and hope the rest followed.

Like in the 2013–14 Ashes, and not just Clarke's 'Get ready for a broken fucken arm' immortalised through the stump mics. Mitchell Johnson didn't talk much but the rest yapped through the breach he made, emboldened by the vanguard leader. Smith got his example, and the taste of his first winning series from five attempts. That team took the approach on to South Africa, hearing no alarms when the hosts skipped the ritual of alcoholic absolution at series end. Confrontation meant success.

If there was any ambiguity about whether this attitude was cultivated, it ended when selectors dumped Peter Nevill. Former fast bowler Geoff Lawson was incredulous in *The Sydney Morning Herald*. 'There was no ambivalence about it. They *said* it: "We are picking Matthew Wade because he is a more abusive voice behind the stumps."' Wade's own slant was that 'there was a lot of media and public stir about how they wanted the team to have a crack through that period. They felt like we were rolling over.' Having a crack meant directly at the opposition.

'Every single match you play against Australia, you expect it,' said Faf du Plessis in 2018. 'So I'm certainly not sitting here complaining about it. For me that's not a surprise, that's a normal day of business for us.' When Wade was dropped, Ponting smiled on an Ashes preview video. 'I'm sure Davey can pick up the slack if the wicketkeeper goes quiet.'

Back to Plan A, then. 'A serial minor offender, Warner is Australia's pit bull, licensed to sledge and intimidate opposition batsmen and bowlers,' Lalor had written before the dog began his bark break in 2015. 'His aggressive, confrontational behaviour is uncomfortable for many, but is clearly sanctioned by the team hierarchy, who forever go on about knowing where lines are and accepting punishments when they are crossed ... At times his behaviour is hard to excuse, but the Australian team has little time for people who want to win friends. They want to win games of cricket.'

Such was the false equation: that only one of those was possible, that decency was a sacrifice to victory. It was, in its capitalised splendour, The Australian Way. It was also a recent and convenient fiction. 'Does the management of the Australian team really believe the call of "it's the way we play" does justice to all those who have gone before?' asked Mark Nicholas. 'Cricket is the cruellest game, mainly unfair and frequently exasperating: players are stripped to the bone over five days of competition, and have long boiled over in moments of duress. Thank goodness for that. It is not a softer game we look for but a kinder one.'

Of course even social games have tempers flare at umpiring errors or perceived liberties or just having to watch a batsman towel you up for too long. Of course every international team has players behave poorly, sometimes appallingly; Australia is not alone in aggression or anger. 'Which is true,' qualified the Pakistani writer Ahmer Naqvi, 'but it is unique in making a virtue out of it.' Unique in fetishising it, in perhaps even believing that anger and unpleasantness *form* a kind of fairness, in that a contest is played in the cleansing fire of fury, and so any opponent emerging as the winner is proved truly worthy.

Few within professional Australian cricket grasp how broadly and deeply the men's team is disliked. A few women players parrot the same nonsense, but most on that side of the game know they're pulling together. The men's game buys into its hard-but-fair mantra, then suffers the delusion that the world respects it. Of course Australian players and coaches go to foreign leagues and make friendships – sport is a results business and humans are humans. But as Ronay wrote, Australia's behaviour as a group 'has a corrosive effect on everyone concerned'. The resulting dislike isn't about rivalry. It gnaws at plenty of home supporters equally.

All the ill feeling centres on current teams. Players in commentary boxes have to get along. Nostalgia affords fondness for former antagonists. Merv Hughes and his moustache form a public teddy bear, an 'All 90s kids will remember this' meme made flesh. Border grudgingly bumbles about media centres like a puzzled uncle – the sweetest thing I've seen in cricket was the willowy Michael Holding having to get Border's jacket down after someone hung it on a hook too high. Warne zooms around on a hovercraft of self-regard, but it must be hard to be a normal person when drunk dickheads give a mass cheer every time you walk outside.

Mix the lack of consequence with a sure belief in the Australian way, the insularity of team sport, and the idea that supporting a mate means letting things slide, and it makes a hell of a bubble. No wonder it took a rocket to burst Ponting's. Roebuck addressed this too: 'That the senior players in the Australian team are oblivious to the fury they raised among many followers of the game in this country and beyond merely confirms their own narrow and self-obsessed viewpoint. Doubtless they were not exposed to the messages that poured in from distressed enthusiasts … Pained past players rang to express their disgust.'

Smith and company caused the same sort of flood after ignoring the water level through their own years of rain. In Durban, reporter Ben Horne asked Smith a carefully worded question. 'Long before you were playing, the aggressive stigma has followed the Australian team around, their reputation. Do you think there is an image issue with the way the Australian team is perceived and how they've behaved?'

The answer to anyone who had paid attention in two decades was clear. Even if you didn't think the behaviour was a problem, you couldn't deny the perception was.

'Not as far as I'm concerned,' Smith said blandly. 'I think that's when we play our best cricket: when we're aggressive, we're in the fight together, we're hunting as a pack as one, and we're working for each other and backing up our mates on the field. That's part of being an Australian, in my opinion. I'm comfortable where it's all at. As I said, it's just about ensuring that we're staying within the spirit of the game.'

It was classic Smith: the view from outside the camp didn't matter. Insiders can see more but not if they insist on keeping their eyes shut. 'I haven't played any matches, very few, where the players have gone too far,' said fielding coach Haddin. Former batting coach Michael Di Venuto said there hadn't been 'any cultural issues during my involvement with the Australian team for three years … I loved being a coach under Darren Lehmann and I love the culture he created … Take it back a couple of months when we won the Ashes, there wasn't too many people complaining about anything then.'

The blue ribbon for denial went to Mark Waugh, at that point still a selector with Lehmann, Greg Chappell and Trevor Hohns. 'I might be missing something,' he posted after the sandpaper bust, 'but I don't see this team as any different as any other team from previous eras.' Public scientist Mark West shot back, 'Current four selectors took money from bookies [Waugh], ordered underarm incident [Chappell], broke South African apartheid ban [Hohns] and got done for racial abuse [Lehmann].'

Self-justification is the culture's defining feature. Most groups that assert moral authority will instinctively cover or rationalise their own breaches. The upshot is the permissiveness we've noted throughout; using 'the line' to paint transgressions as momentary, listing the virtues of the guy spewing filth from short leg. 'Australia's notoriously soft on disciplinary measures,' said an incredulous Craddock on radio when the tampering story broke. 'It was Lehmann who was part of the group who wound up Warner to be the attack dog that was the start of all this.'

It was always the coach saying there was no problem with Warner's latest escapade, no problem with his methods of extracting reverse, no problem with anything much except the odd loss. Shrugging and smiling and cracking a beer like good blokes do. 'Lehmann may or may not get away with the suggestion he had nothing to do with this,' wrote Ronay. 'But he has overseen an infantilised team culture where such a plot was so easily conceived and where fear of being discovered by good old Boof was clearly not much of an issue. He should be profoundly embarrassed already, although past conduct suggests this may not be the case.'

The Good Bloke Doctrine was central to Lehmann's tenure, as arbitrated by him and senior players. Selection for Australia was based on whose personality made them comfortable more than whose results deserved reward. Some on the outer weren't liked, some just weren't rated, in a gut-feel ruling that overrode stats or performance. Many on the margins, like George Bailey, Michael Klinger, Glenn Maxwell or Ed Cowan, had consistent traits of independent thought and questioning orthodoxy.

Cowan was the Test opener when Lehmann took over, but he wrote books and liked Mickey Arthur. He got one more match. Bailey was T20 captain before Lehmann arrived, but got dropped from the team entirely when he asked to give up the leadership. His Test career lasted five straight wins. He made himself undroppable from ODIs for two years with an insane scoring streak, but was ditched as soon as it normalised. Maxwell might be the most talented ball-striker of his generation, dominating the 2015 World Cup, but was pushed to the fringes when Smith took over. The antipathy was obvious: Smith criticised Maxwell's training, stopped using his bowling, and made him run drinks for a series after an innocuous media comment about Wade.

That was just in the one-day team; by 2018 Maxwell had still never played a Test in Australia despite explosiveness most suited to the pitches of home. In the 2016 rebuild after Hobart, selectors said they wanted an attacking option at six, someone who could change the game in a session. With a dead rubber against South Africa and three Tests against Pakistan, there couldn't have been a better chance to ease someone in. So they picked ... Nic Maddinson, one of Smith's mates from New South Wales. A good bloke, by all accounts, with a mediocre career and a first-class average under 35.

Renshaw dropped off the approved list. Bancroft? Good Bloke™. It was notable how his coach and teammates rallied when his spot was at risk. He'd had middling returns through a thumping Ashes win, just like Bailey under the same coach four years earlier. Bailey tallied 183 runs at 26 and never played again, Bancroft tallied 179 at 26 and got a ticket to South Africa. He was, we were assured, a great fit in the team. Bailey got replaced by Shaun Marsh, who hadn't made a first-class run in two years.

When selectors wanted a Renshaw replacement, Cowan had been the top scorer domestically across the previous three seasons. But through three Shield rounds before the Ashes, he couldn't get a game to press his case. The NSW player of the year, having averaged 74 and topped the country for runs the season before, had Smith personally intervene to get him dropped. Australia's captain and vice-captain were warming up in the state team, which meant pushing out a middle order player – unless one was promoted to Cowan's spot. Hello Maddinson, with eight career hundreds to Cowan's 25.

'All this rubbish about me picking my mates is absolute garbage,' was Smith's response, dismissing the discrepancy as casually as Fat Tony asking 'What's a truck?' The excuse from NSW was self-incriminating: Maddinson had to play because he was a chance for Tests if he made runs. Which was an admission that Cowan could score a thousand and not get picked. Another line was that Cowan was too old at 35. Selectors then picked Marsh, aged 34, citing a need for experience.

Marsh was the ultimate good bloke – says nothing, objects to nothing, gets wild on the piss. Vacancies appeared around him as if by magic. Infantilised as the Son of Swampy, he was still being described as a player of potential at 32. When his perpetual adolescence finally ran out he skipped straight to veteran status, thanks to all the times he'd already been picked. Good bloke, but. Absolutely ripping bloke.

The fault, it must be stressed, is not with Marsh or Maddinson or anyone preferred under this system. It lies with those doing the preferring. It lies with a tribal setup where the impulse is to control admission. After 2010–11, the Argus review ordered it was 'critical that superior performance is rewarded' domestically, and 'players must earn their positions in the time-honoured way of making runs'. In no way, in no form, has that policy been honoured in the Australian cricket team since.

An insular and permissive society makes it easy for things to deteriorate. Good old Boof had your back. Administrators stayed out of it, or winked in the hallway, while the marketers designed a bright new banner. 'We got greedy,' said Haddin of Australia's bowling in Durban, and it seemed a good enough descriptor for everything else. Naqvi wrote of the tampering that 'it isn't impossible to imagine that at some level they felt entitled to push further into a grey area because that's what gives them their edge.' For Craddock, 'This was not an isolated incident. It was the deterioration of a win-at-all-costs culture that has been getting progressively seedier, and dirtier, and grubbier.'

When a furious public finally fired home the idea that not all was right with the good hard Australian brand, the coach was lost. The day before resigning, he insisted he was the man to lead a change that until that moment he'd dismissed the need for.

'How do you get the balance right, Darren?' asked Sally Sara when Lehmann pitched Sensitive New Age Boof. 'In a practical sense, what do you do?' There was a long pause, then an air of bewilderment. 'That's a good question. The thing for me would be if we take a leaf out of someone like New Zealand's book, the way they play and respect the opposition. We do respect the opposition but we push the boundaries on the ground.'

New Zealand – the team that had defined the 2015 World Cup by being overtly the nicest in the tournament while also winning matches with fearless cricket, whose semi-final epic against South Africa was capped with an enduring image of sportsmanship as Grant Elliott extended a glove to the fallen Dale Steyn. New Zealand, who Lehmann's team had beaten in a petulant final, giving send-offs to departing batsmen, Haddin clapping his gloves in their faces before deriding them drunkenly on a radio station for being 'too nice'. That New Zealand?

Back home, Wade's ears pricked up like a sheepdog hearing the farm is about to go vegan. 'I hope now we don't go too far the other way and lose all our drive,' he said. 'I just think we need to be careful about what direction we go in from here.' That's right, slow down fellers. What if we don't call people cunts *enough*?

The Wade attitude won't go away. Permissiveness still flowers wild and free over the hills of home – within a month of the ball-tamperers being suspended, everyone in Australian cricket was talking redemption. Langer, the new coach, described them as 'good kids'. There's a widespread platitude about giving them credit for putting their hands up and taking responsibility. Just like Clarke after Warner at the Walkabout: 'I respect the fact David has put his hand up and wants to move forward, has apologised to Joe, and acknowledged he has made a big mistake. He does deserve credit for putting his hand up.'

Does he? Do they? Do you get credit for saying you did things after you're caught doing them? No hands were put up in Cape Town: hands were forced up after multiple lies, when proof made denial untenable. Warner's hand stayed down until he was picked out of a line-up. The details, meanwhile, remained undisclosed. No one has actually told the public what happened. The many holes in the story remained unexplored. Most likely the players will dodge those questions by saying it's all behind them and they're looking to the future – the same evasive political tactics they used before.

The doublespeak would be funny if it wasn't so damaging. On it goes, along with the belief in antagonism, clung to like a life raft in rough seas. As though being an arsehole counts as having an identity. What probably grates most is that it's all so unnecessary. 'I don't think that sledging has that much influence on the way that people play,' said du Plessis. Teams keep quiet when they're losing. They sledge when they're on top, but they're already on top. We've made it this far with no Shakespeare, but how better to describe the quote-unquote banter at backward point than a tale told by an idiot, full of sound and fury, signifying nothing?

The new captain Paine gets it: 'guys were knackered and some of that energy could have been saved through not getting involved in that kind of stuff,' he said after South Africa. 'It really does take its toll after a while, both on and off the field. There's media around it, you're in trouble with the umpires, there are meetings you need to go to for that. So it spirals on and on.'

He also wants to break away from the abridged history that dooms players to bad re-enactments. 'We don't want to pretend we are like ex-Australian cricketers … What we've got caught up with over the years is trying to play a way that people have always perceived Australian teams to be, and that probably doesn't suit this current side.'

It doesn't suit any. Would Warne's mountain of wickets have lost any altitude if he'd been pleasant on the field? Would McGrath have shaved any off his 563? Take Moeen Ali, with a hard blink if you need it: 'I'd rather be nice to be honest. I set out in cricket to make friends. I'd rather people say they enjoyed playing with him and he's a good guy, not he's a good player but a bit of a so-and-so.' Sledging isn't just pointless. It cuts the good heart from something people play and watch for joy.

After the 2017–18 Ashes, BBC caller Daniel Norcross spoke beautifully on a *Final Word* podcast about his first tour down under.

The other thing that's really notable in Australia is that cricket is a game that's played by the people. It's not a class game. Everybody plays cricket. I was at an ODI warm-up game at Drummoyne in Sydney and I was looking out the back, and there was this greensward that was filled with kids, and it sent shivers down your spine. There's this nine-year-old, can't have been more than nine, ran in and bowled left-arm-over perfectly pitched yorkers, to another kid who was digging them out, and then naturally improvising and playing reverse swipes.

There were fifteen kids, and six or seven of them were girls, and when the girls batted they walloped it and they meant it and no boy expected not to be hit. It was equal, it was egalitarian, everyone was playing regardless of accent, class, colour, gender. And in England it isn't. It upsets me, because the sport I love is a narrow pastime in England. But it also thrills me that in Australia, it is a broad religion.

There is so much good. The way we can meet friends at some dodgy suburban oval and play a bunch of hungover pissheads and throw lunch on the public barbeques. The way we open the Esky under a gum tree afterwards like a proper national cliché and dig out handfuls of ice for our foreheads and our sunburn. The camaraderie and the comedy and the little achievements, making double figures for the first time, making a batsman fall into his stumps trying to sweep a wide. Being rubbish and being allowed to be. And of course it's different with livelihoods riding on it, but even the idea that cricket is something that *could* be enjoyed – for its own sake, rather than the grim satisfaction of having torn an opponent apart – is something that comes under threat well before you reach the professionals.

People who can't stand the ugliness are plentiful. 'This has been a culture that has developed over a generation,' wrote a fan named Matthew Beggs. 'It's not going to change quickly. Australian cricket culture has always listened to loud voices. Maybe it's time to listen to the quiet ones.' The loud ones will keep insisting that aggression is the way of the world. That's what they do. But accepting that means accepting cricket as another way to bring out the worst in people. Imagine if cricket was only a way to bring out the best.

Chapter 22

CRICKET AUSTRALIA'S CULTURE

As you trace back the causes of all we've seen, the trail ends at the top. Here the attitudes of Australian cricket and Cricket Australia sit in comfortable reflection. Board talk quickly becomes bored talk, so let's keep this punchy – but remember the yawn factor is how corporate structures get away with their excesses. It's easier to grab attention with a brick of coke or a firebombing than with creeping financial control and mismanagement. Where a flurry of wrongdoing can make society come down hard, a gradual accretion of wrongdoing can win the perpetrators respect for their influence.

The Australian Cricket Board used to just be the state associations having lunch. James Sutherland took over a modest operation in 2001. Then money happened. Kerry Packer had offered $1.5 million for broadcast rights in 1976, but under Sutherland that jumped to $270 million in 2006, then $590 million in 2013. The old ACB became the new CA, and the power structure flipped to top-down with the states as dependants. A few short years took it from semi-amateur administration to corporate monolith. Board members were recast as 'independent directors', and recruitment shifted accordingly to board-stackers from banks, mining, airlines. The attitude of the corporate headkicker spread through the ranks. Money brought the kind of people attracted to it.

Like the International Cricket Council, CA also has a lot of staff who do admirable work and love the game. They just tend to be well down the chain of command. Those at the helm are less intimate with their better natures. Because they steer CA, they also join the rich boards of England and India to steer the ICC. Again, power follows money.

To pre-empt the response that a business can do what it likes, CA is not a business. It's a non-profit organisation exempt from paying tax. Notionally sport has a social benefit, so CA's remit is to manage the game for the greatest public good. That makes it a public entity; effectively Australians own CA and are represented by the teams it manages.

Within its ranks, we'll keep our view to five characters. Sutherland was a cricketer who briefly won Victorian selection, and an accountant who won second-in-charge at the old ACB by negotiating its 1998 agreement with players after a pay dispute. David Peever worked for mining giant Rio Tinto; he was in CA's first batch of independent board members in 2012, became chair in 2015, and got another term in 2018.

Below them are eight executive managers, three of whom interest us. Kevin Roberts was an Adidas executive who joined the board with Peever, but moved to an executive role in 2015, meaning he'd be eligible to succeed Sutherland. Pat Howard was a rugby player and coach hired in 2011 as manager of team performance. Ben Amarfio ran commercial radio company Southern Cross Austereo before moving to CA to handle broadcast rights, marketing, communications and in-house media.

As we go you'll notice consistent themes: closed doors, closed shops, an absence of accountability. Like Mark Taylor sitting on the board while also leading the Nine Network's commentary team, appointing captains then praising them on TV. Or Mark Waugh commentating while employed as a selector. Like the behavioural non-standards for players. Like backing Lehmann as coach before even a pocket-sized investigation in Johannesburg. 'The written Laws of Cricket might tolerate Smith and Lehmann staying on as captain and coach, but the unwritten rules of Australia will not,' wrote Brydon Coverdale for Cricinfo, and it was Lehmann himself, hardly a master of introspection, who deciphered the markings daubed on the wall.

'I'm ultimately responsible for the culture of the team,' the coach had said when announcing his resignation. So what did CA do? Immediately gave Lehmann a job with the development squad at the National Cricket Centre. The man who had overseen the senior team while its foundations rotted out was next given charge of even more impressionable players as they crossed the rickety bridge to adulthood.

As for his replacement, writer Andrew Fernando said it best. CA 'suggested during the scandal that the Australian team was in for a complete culture change – the likes of which will wash all memory of the cheating away. No stone, it was implied, would be left unturned to right the team's course. And so, it transpired a month later, that with great courage, integrity, and willingness to see total transformation, they appointed Justin Langer, the literal next-in-line, avid follower of Steve Waugh's mental-disintegration philosophy, and the man Lehmann had himself groomed to be his successor.'

Langer, to be clear, was hired not just before a review into team culture had been held, but was hired to sit on the investigative panel that would conduct it. A culture he had contributed to for 25 years. After his playing days finished in 2007 he'd been assistant coach from 2009 to 2012 and interim coach when Lehmann took breaks in 2016 and 2017. Steve Waugh had been the Yoda to his Skywalker, even if Langer better fitted the role of diminutive martial artist. Singer of the team song, cultist of the baggy green, trembling with pride when he flipped tails on a 50-cent coin, Langer named his core value as 'elite mateship', and I wish I could remember who responded with 'That sounds like an Australian dating app.' His hiring was leaked weeks in advance, and Sutherland later said 'we have had a succession plan in place for this role for some time.' All the world's revelations couldn't stop them picking the next in line.

Langer the coach seemed a good-hearted man. He'd shown some development of ideas. He was willing to avoid sugar-coating when he took the job: 'There's been too many whispers the last twelve months or so about the abuse on the field, or dare I say it, playing like spoiled brats.' But he couldn't see a broader pattern of wrong. He leant on the flimsy rampart that 'everyone knows' the difference between good sledging and bad sledging. He voiced the delusion that people hadn't liked the team in his day because they won, not because they were insufferable. Ex-players don't all think alike, but they do come from the same parish.

It was often used against Pat Howard that he wasn't of that parish: cricketers resented a rugby outsider. After the 2010–11 Ashes thrashing, Howard was appointed to fine-tune Australia's national teams. He would track players of potential, find opportunities for their development, monitor injuries and trends, and go on tour to see what was working. He was the shuttle between teams and the system supporting them. No one could spend seven years in that job and learn nothing about cricket. But knowledge hasn't brought results.

'Australian cricket is in crisis.' People who work in the game are pretty used to writing that down. At least for the senior men's team – the women and the juniors keep their acts together. The first month of Howard's tenure off the back of that Ashes crisis saw the Test team rolled for 47 in Cape Town. In 2013 Australia got whitewashed in India, knocked out of the Champions Trophy, into a Birmingham bar-fight, and sacked the coach before an Ashes loss 3–0.

The death of Phillip Hughes in 2014 was bitter misfortune, but all the talk afterwards about how Australian cricket could be a kinder and better place was allowed to peter out. In 2015 another Ashes thrashing included the 60 all out at Trent Bridge and 136 at Edgbaston, with a subsequent player clean-out that required a full rebuild.

In 2016 came a Test whitewash against Sri Lanka, a one-day whitewash in South Africa, then a Test loss to the same side in Hobart that cost Australia five players and the chairman of selectors. Ball-tampering cost a coach, captain and vice-captain, plus a series thrashing, followed by another limited-overs whitewash in England.

Five crises in six and a half years. If we call him a high-performance manager, Howard failed at every word in his job title. He was responsible for selectors, players and coaches: the Good Bloke Doctrine flourished, players fell apart, and coaches rode the wreck into the ground. Howard had been central in installing Lehmann, and it was pure comedy when you recalled that 'Mickey Arthur was sacked over what Cricket Australia called failures of discipline, consistency of behaviour and accountability'. There were repercussions aplenty after the Cape Town sandstorm, but not for the man that the corporate structure deemed to be in charge.

Howard at least comes across as believing he's doing the right thing, even if his version of right is contestable. Amarfio seems less weighted by such concerns. He ran stations like the sports-schlock sausage factory of Triple M, and the former 2Day FM when it was home to some of the foulest trolls on air. 'It's not always such a bad thing to get negative press,' he announced at a marketing event in 2013. 'In the last twelve months, the NRL has had players assault women, players assault policemen, they've had drug, corruption and match fixing issues – the list goes on and on. And yet they've just signed a TV deal for over one billion dollars, which is almost fifty per cent bigger than their last TV deal.'

As long as someone's making money, right? Media partners and colleagues describe Amarfio's style as dismissive and antagonistic. CA staff leaked a small but indicative story to *Australian Financial Review* reporter Joe Aston: that while CA was promoting cricket as an inclusive sport for women, Amarfio was making his personal assistant cook him hot breakfasts and lunches at work each day. It was Amarfio who alienated the ABC in 2013 by banning it from providing online streams of its radio coverage, a disagreement that dragged on for years. In 2018 a well-sourced story said CA had strongly considered ditching the national broadcaster altogether. In a vast country, ABC networks reach corners where internet can't, not to mention the audience's connection with a broadcast that's been going since Bradman played. Recent entrants on the scene saw that relationship as expendable.

Amarfio's most bizarre episode was moonlighting as an agent for his friend James Brayshaw, a commentator who'd worked with him at Triple M. Predominantly a football caller who jarred with the rhythm of cricket, Brayshaw was Nine's least popular voice out of a largely unloved bunch. When his contract negotiations foundered in 2016, Amarfio suddenly appeared wanting to act on his behalf. The same person running Nine's broadcast rights negotiation wanted to represent its staff. Brayshaw wasn't retained, and Amarfio contacted at least one other company trying to find him a job.

Sutherland's response? 'I don't think it's right that one of our staff was acting as an agent. But let's just say they are things that we'll deal with behind closed doors at Cricket Australia. I don't think this is the place to be talking about that any further.' Of course not, talking in public about potential ethical breaches of highly paid executives subsidised by the public would be gauche. We could all rest easy that behind those doors lay CA's steely determination to get to the bottom of things.

It's a curious timeline. Brayshaw's peripheral role on Nine's cricket became central after Amarfio moved to CA in 2012. Amarfio's marketing department produced an ad campaign in 2014 centring Brayshaw's voice and promoted him as one of 'the Nine Network's favourite commentators'. Around the time Brayshaw's TV contract was stalling, Amarfio's old station Triple M made a late and unexpected deal for cricket rights. The lead caller was James Brayshaw. And as Triple M cancelled its coverage after two summers, the TV rights switched to Seven where Brayshaw was now calling football. Not to suggest that commentary jobs could decide a rights deal, but having a mate who runs the negotiations is an unusual quirk.

The Seven deal was a prime example of CA's general air of disregard for those they deal with. They were obsessed with topping a billion dollars to stand alongside the AFL and NRL. How to get there wasn't important. Nine was the stale old-school partner. Network Ten had done the game a service, growing the Big Bash from a joke fluorescent league that no one could watch on pay TV to a summer staple in a world that accepted 'the Brisbane Heat' as a reasonable concept. People found a new presentation refreshing, it was free to air, and the viewer average jumped from 236,000 a night to nearly a million on Ten. Now the BBL was successful, CA wanted every dollar back.

Nine and Ten offered a joint deal. Amarfio met them for less than fifteen minutes and dismissed it as 'non-compliant'. Peever asked Ten's American owner CBS not to 'include local management as I feel they are not prepared to challenge their operating model to be anything other than bottom feeders'. All totally normal and professional.

Ten went all in: $960 million for the lot. Their secondary channels would broadcast men's and women's Big Bash, domestic one-dayers, even the white elephant Sheffield Shield. It could have been an amazing coup for cricket. But you may have noticed that 960 million is less than a billion. So CA signed all the valuable games to Foxtel, as long as a free-to-air partner would simulcast Tests and some BBL.

Ten was told this was now all they could bid for. They offered $80 million a year and Sutherland shook on it. Then Seven was allowed another bid, worth $82 million. The network that had revitalised cricket broadcasting and made CA's risky Big Bash gamble a winner was punted over comparative pocket change. Sutherland made an appearance with the victorious network heads, the three of them trying to manage various bits of cricket gear in a photo as awkward as David Cameron posing with a pig.

The Australian limited-overs teams went behind a paywall. The future for 50-over cricket is bleaker than ever, but its demise has been predicted for so long that perhaps CA decided to wring the last cash from it while they could. A tax-exempt body would now privatise its output, making the people who subsidised it pay to watch teams that bore their name. It clearly circumvented anti-siphoning laws that keep national teams on free channels, because technically Seven bought the rights to games it would choose not to screen. The federal government shrugged, because who is the government to stop people making money doing whatever they like? The billion was banked. A month later, news emerged that CA had told Bangladesh not to bother coming for a scheduled Test tour because it would cost too much.

Of everything, the 2017 pay dispute illustrated CA's corporate culture best. It was a masterpiece, the Springfield Tyre Fire of sports administration. Sutherland this time was the honourable exception, but board members and executives managed to provoke an entirely unnecessary conflict, conduct it unconscionably, lose comprehensively, and reward themselves for the effort.

The dispute was never about international players getting more money. They would have received the same sweet deal either way. The players CA wanted to squeeze were at the bottom of the domestic game. Every state and national player since 1997 was part of a revenue share, collectively paid a quarter of CA income as their cut for helping create it. It was reviewed every five years with the union, the Australian Cricketers Association. Women's cricket would be included for the first time. The system meant players felt like partners rather than hired help. But sharing revenue with a unionised workforce is against every corporate impulse. Financial transparency involves ceding control. As new corporate players joined the board, they wanted it dead.

The driving force was a union antagonist with an industrial relations background. Peever is the archetypal charcoal suit, relishing powerful positions and the tiny world of connections and privilege they afford. One board seat spawned another as years went by: mining subsidiaries, investment companies, Business Council of Australia, Brisbane Airport, Melbourne Business School. He was vice-chair of the Minerals Council, the mob that spent millions fighting Kevin Rudd's government over the outrageous idea that mining companies might pay a bit of tax. When conservatives took office they appointed him to an Indigenous Advisory Council and a defence department review, before he chaired the committee implementing his recommendations. He joined French submarine maker DCNS the day it announced a $50 billion government contract in 2016. 'I know David well,' announced MP Stuart Robert when the Joint Standing Committee on Treaties examined the deal. (Robert had resigned as a minister a year earlier after dubious dealings with mining companies and the Chinese government.)

This was the worldview the cricketers were up against. Peever's offsider Kevin Roberts was tasked with bringing them to heel, his chance to make a claim on the top job. The opening tactic was to refuse any meetings with the players' union for months, insisting that the end of revenue sharing be accepted as a starting point. To fill the time, CA issued press releases about how the pay model was outdated and due for replacement. This was presented as both self-evident truth and foregone conclusion. When that didn't work they took up the wholesome shield of underfunded clubs, saying that pay changes were desperately needed to fund grassroots cricket. Media repeated the line without questioning it, so the conflict became framed by its instigator.

It was all PR – if a crisis had come so suddenly, the governing body must have been crushingly negligent. How would the quarter of revenue going to cricketers fix what the three quarters spent by administrators had not? Former batsman Simon Katich cited $1.9 billion in CA revenue over the previous five years: 'You can't tell us there is not enough to fund grassroots. The money is there, it's just being spent on other things.' Meanwhile, CA's cash reserve of $70 million remained untouched.

By May 2017, administrators were antsy. Player contracts would expire on July 1st, meaning CA couldn't stage matches and would lose intellectual property to names and images. Negotiators refused mediation and started making threats: that they would play hardball, let contracts expire, withhold back pay, blacklist players who signed with rival sponsors or played exhibition games, withhold the paperwork to join overseas leagues.

The previous December, CA had suspended talks saying they didn't want players to be distracted. By May players were bombarded with emails and personal approaches. Their repeated requests for all contact to go through the ACA were ignored.sa The worst effort was Roberts with a video missive: the man himself hanging out at the nets in a CA polo, reassuring everyone he was just a cool regular cricket guy. It was addressed to players but posted publicly in a passive-aggressive copy-all, rehashing arguments with all the charm and conviction of a

VHS safety demonstration tape. 'Some players have asked how CA's proposal differs from the current revenue-sharing model,' he said. 'The short answer is not very much.' Leaving, of course, the question of why they were pushing it.

The grassroots argument encouraged a perception of players as greedy millionaires in Lamborghinis. Friendly heads in commercial TV said they would play for Australia for free. It was dishonest, given that national players were only standing up for colleagues. 'We want to make sure that the female players and domestic players are in this revenue share model,' Warner said in a TV appearance. 'Through the decades gone past, the past players in our situation stood up for us. I was a domestic player, I was a young kid coming through. We're doing the same that they did.' CA put out figures that men's domestic cricketers averaged $200,000 a year, a number distorted by the top earners and foreign BBL stars when the median pay was under $100,000.

Howard emailed top players saying, 'I don't apologise for putting international players ahead of domestic.' He personally pitched rich three-year deals instead of the usual one year to Smith, Warner, Cummins, Starc and Hazlewood, anything to break the picket. It backfired: the big names only campaigned more actively. It was Warner's finest hour in an admittedly uncompetitive field.

Contracts expired. The Women's World Cup team got an extension until they lost their semi-final, then were unemployed before CA sent out a press release praising their efforts. Female players had just professionalised, giving up other jobs for a modest income that had now vanished. Domestic players could be on less than $20,000 a year. They were under the most pressure to agree to a deal, while CA blamed their situation on the union defending them. 'It is unfortunate that the ACA's hard line and inflexible position has not been conducive to delivering any positive outcomes or certainty for players, and this may place significant financial and emotional strain on them and their families.' It was classic gaslighting: I'm really upset that you made me do this to you.

The players held. High earners made a fund to tide over others. Bluffs were called. CA had threatened suspensions if anyone took on rival sponsors, so Starc went straight out and signed with an Audi dealership. The leaping Toyota mascot all over CA's website could land in a lake: there's no scab workforce of giant left-armers who reverse the ball two feet.

This was always the glaring flaw. Without cricketers there is no Cricket Australia. A reserve tour to South Africa was cancelled. There was a Test tour to Bangladesh due that August, India one-dayers in September, the Ashes in November. Cancelling series would mean financial ruin, and all the players had to do was stay in the sheds. Roberts and Peever had tried intimidation, but as soon as the players decided to resist there was no chance. Instead of admitting this, the board spent months torching its most valuable asset while imagining it could spy victory in the firelight.

Sutherland saw it clearly. He knew the players' unbeatable advantage and how the union would direct its members. He didn't object to revenue sharing; he'd agreed to it in four previous deals. But the board was insistent and had the power to oust him, and Roberts wanted to impress. Seeing the new man handed a grenade, Sutherland stepped back into the shadows and blocked his ears.

When the time was right, back he came to fix up the damage. He hammered out the deal and was proved to have been right all along. His colleagues had to perform a full retreat. Revenue-sharing was retained, back-pay came through in full, rival sponsorships were accommodated, and it was a shame no one had staged an exhibition match, because CA probably would have posted highlights.

The board had nearly wrecked the joint in a fight they picked themselves. Their bluff was called, limitations permanently exposed. Yet two months after his surrender was signed, Peever showed up to the October AGM as the quintessential Teflon Don. Perhaps it was held in Brisbane to avoid cricket media further south: Adam Collins, Robert Craddock and myself were the only representatives. We fired questions for twenty minutes while Peever played a dead bat, then made light conversation with us after the event. It was unsettling to see someone so unruffled to have created such epic failure.

'We didn't want to put players in the middle of the dispute and we hold our heads high that we didn't ever do that', was one of his lines, which as far as fantasy goes had a dozen dragons circling a distant tower ruled by psychic twins. He patted himself on the back that 'no player has gone without payment' even though CA had threatened exactly that. There was not the slightest admission of any problem with his objective or method.

Surely he had to admit it had gone badly, we asked? They would learn from it, he said; they would hold a review. Who will conduct that review? We will, internally. When will you do this? We'll take as long as it takes. When will the results be released? Oh, they won't be public. So you'll review yourselves, whenever you feel like it, and not tell anyone what you find out? Yes, we think that's best. A few months later Peever got a three-year extension and Roberts was promoted to second-in-charge.

This is Cricket Australia. The closed doors are nothing new. When Gideon Haigh and David Frith literally wrote the book in 2007 with *Inside Story*, 'the authors confirmed cover-ups and an attitude of evasiveness and secrecy'. They had access and transparency during a brief window of confidence, with Australia's team at the peak of its powers and self-regard. 'Haigh has continued to write fearlessly on the game and its discontents,' said Daniel Brettig in reviewing another of that author's books, 'and now finds himself once again the outsider to an administration increasingly committed to uninterrupted message control.'

That message is that they're never wrong, unless you happen to have them on camera. Even then, the Cape Town hammer only came down so hard because it had to match public anger. It was performative punishment with money riding on it. 'We've let them know that we want them to urgently complete the investigation and take the appropriate action,' was the message from Qantas boss and team sponsor Alan Joyce, a man who had no qualms grounding his airline and stranding thousands of people worldwide over a pay dispute in 2011.

Sutherland confirmed that some directors wanted harsher punishments. They wouldn't actively sabotage their best players, but once Smith and Warner opened themselves up for a whack it was an eager hand bringing down the cane. Crossing the board's agenda was a greater sin than crossing The Line, as Peter Lalor summarised: 'Cricket Australia were aware of Warner's nature when he was appointed vice-captain. The organisation was more offended by his role as spokesman for the players during the recent pay dispute than by anything he did in the field. If CA directors – they must approve captaincy appointments – had concerns over his appointment as T20 skipper, it was only because of this.'

The pledged cultural reviews – one into the team, one into the organisation – gave some hope, but slender. CA director Michelle Tredenick was also on the board of The Ethics Centre commissioned for the corporate review. The team review was run by a consultant who had worked for CA for a decade. Neither took public submissions. ACA president Greg Dyer chose his most passive tense: 'Recent disclosures to the banking Royal Commission indicate that a review which is commissioned and paid for by a board, with terms of reference set by that board and a reporting process that has a closed loop back to the same board, will be viewed with cynicism. The review's success and its broad acceptance as being truly independent will therefore be conditional on absolute transparency.'

Bob Every quit the board within his first term, unhappy with the reviews and Peever's extension. Iain Roy, the head of CA's integrity department who ran the Cape Town investigation, had a restructure eliminate his job. Glenn Maxwell spoke on radio about an Al-Jazeera documentary that implicated him in spot-fixing: the accusation seemed spurious, but no one at CA had even asked him if it was true. Finally, all within months of Cape Town, Sutherland announced in June 2018 that he would resign within a year.

At last, people might say. This paragraph from Aston could be a summary of his reign: 'Learning the truth of a matter – not wishfully believing incredible denials – should be highest on Sutherland's list of priorities should he wish to survive (and, frankly, even should he not). However limited, cowboy behaviour at the sport's governing body on his watch is totally out of step with community and corporate standards. And waving it away after the fact, despite overwhelming evidence, is as heedless as presiding over it in the first place.'

There are things worth praise about Sutherland if that were the point of the exercise. But in the end he looks like Steve Smith, a decent fellow in himself who lacked the tools or appetite to stop those around him who weren't. Complicity makes you culpable. But it's much bigger than Sutherland. He was just the face that people knew. Ask the man in the street to pick Kevin Roberts out of a line-up – hell, I've watched his video at the nets 40 times and can't remember what he looks like. He's so background they could paint him onto stealth jets.

You're not supposed to know the suits running a sport. They're supposed to be quietly effective behind the scenes. That's why the current mob enjoy impunity. Between them, a deep unpleasantness has been allowed to form. It's there in carving out money from poorer nations, refusing games against emerging teams, flipping big cardboard fingers to the rest of the world. It's there in Peever, Roberts, Howard, Lehmann, Amarfio: in their extensions, promotions, retentions, new jobs, new portfolios. One truth has become evident. At CA it's impossible to get fired.

Well, that's not quite true. In early 2018, CA staffer Angela Williamson had to travel to Melbourne for an abortion after the last provider in her home state of Tasmania shut down. She lobbied the state government to allow other women to access the procedure at state hospitals. The government shut down the proposal in parliament, and she wrote on her personal Twitter account criticising the policy. She was sacked in June.

That's what CA has become. Sutherland's departure won't improve it a bit. Some in the organisation have been edging him towards the door for years. He's too old school. Get him out of the way and this unelected tax-free non-profit can *really* get down to business.

And what'll that look like? Like Matthew Hayden coming in from gully to welcome a kid on debut. At its upper levels, CA has developed a culture where aggression isn't just tolerated, it's encouraged. Where accountability isn't just lax, it's eliminated. Where enemies are created and the culprits rewarded. The Cricket Australia of the last few years has been abrasive, selfish, and immune from consequence. It would have been a miracle if its cricket team had been anything else.

Chapter 23

TIMOTHY

Tim Paine should never have been there. He shouldn't have been close. By 2018 he should have been watching the Test side on the telly late at night before getting up for his office job. Or ignoring cricket altogether and sleeping through. Back in 2012, a young Matthew Wade in his first stint as Australian wicketkeeper expressed his sorrow for Paine's lost career. A Shield highlights video in 2014 described Paine as a 'former Aussie international'. He was a trivia answer, a blip like Graham Manou on a wicketkeeping timeline that went Healy, Gilchrist, Haddin.

Paine had been Haddin's injury filler in July 2010. He debuted alongside Smith against Pakistan, the two beaming and baby-faced in a photo, their skin as soft and undamaged as the green felt of their caps. Lord's and Headingley were the neutral English venues after Pakistani militants had tried to kill the Sri Lankan team in Lahore. Paine made 47 and 33, then

92 and 59 in India that October. Throw in sixteen catches and a stumping in his four Tests and he was flying. In November he was in a Cricket Australia exhibition team against a fan-voted side at the Gabba. It was a season opener, a bit of fun for retired or established players who had nothing to lose or prove. But it was nothing of the sort for others who did.

Three weeks earlier, Dirk Nannes played what would turn out to be his last match for Australia, a T20 in Perth. He'd been leading wicket-taker at the World T20 that year, and excelled in domestic competitions around the world, but was never embraced by national selectors. With one foot always over the drop, Nannes wasn't taking it easy against anyone. In this game he was up against the new generation's anointed kids in Paine and Warner, domestic guns Brad Hodge, George Bailey and Dan Christian, and the IPL's most expensive buy in Kieron Pollard.

Nannes bowled left-arm-seriously-fast, sometimes so wild he didn't know where it was heading, with unplayable yorkers and unpalatable bouncers. He had an angle over the wicket that bent in at right-hander's gloves. He was nasty. When he worked for the ABC, a drunk bloke once stopped us in an Adelaide street yelling, 'Hey! Dirk Nannes! You were quick, mate. You bowled *up de la gasolina*!' Turns out a quote from Puerto Rican rapper Daddy Yankee is one of the better descriptions of what Nannes did.

The game in question was halfway between being a spectacle and a contest. Being the former, they had Paine miked up chatting to commentators while he stood at the crease. Being the latter, Nannes bowled a brute at 150 kilometres an hour that crushed

Paine's hand against his bat. The poor bugger was still on air. How was he, asked the comm box. 'Oh, seriously no good,' he said with a heavy wince, trying to get his glove off. Was it broken? 'I think so,' said Paine. He retired immediately on 4.

'I was hoping he wouldn't retire, because as soon as I saw it I didn't want to get out there and face Dirk, no way,' said captain Hodge after the game. 'But I feel sorry for Painey, I think he's not real great. It's a shame because he's playing some real good cricket lately. I think he's out for a while, which is bad news for him.' The next day's ABC news bulletin announced he could be sidelined for up to eight weeks. Try seven years.

He re-broke it in training, and CA medicos delivered the diagnosis he would keep hearing. 'It is clear that the fracture has not healed as expected and the best course of action is for Tim to undergo further surgery.' Seven times he went under the knife, harvesting bits of bone from just about everywhere else in his body. Australia would play 78 Test matches between his injury and his eventual recall. Smith, who had stood alongside him at Lord's, would start in 53 of them.

There were always nerves that another whack was on the way. His confidence went to bits. When reporters sat around a table with him in Port Elizabeth and asked about his game going off a cliff, he was blunt. 'I don't think it was perception, it was actually happening. I couldn't get a run. I had some mental demons. I came back from my finger injury thinking it would be easier than it was, and when it didn't happen I started to panic. I couldn't score a run in club cricket three years ago.'

He almost hated the game, hated his inability to play it. So he went to England in 2015. While Smith was making hundreds in the Ashes, Paine was playing in the Home Counties Premier League and living with the club chairman. 'I had the previous thirteen years in the professional environment, and as much as I love it, at times it can be draining,' he said in an interview after South Africa with *Wisden Cricket Monthly*. 'I'm a real cricket nuffie and I was finding it hard to front up to training all the time, I was going so poorly. I think going over there and playing for Banbury and finding a bit of enjoyment in the game again, looking back, it was a real turning point.'

He battled in Tasmania for another couple of seasons, slipping in the pecking order as Tom Triffitt and Jake Doran came through. Then Wade announced he was moving back to Tassie, having left years before to get out of the queue behind Paine. Long-time gear sponsor Kookaburra offered Paine a job in Melbourne. It would have been bittersweet: he would have been running sponsorships as the liaison with current players, signing them up and organising their kit so they could go off and play the cricket he couldn't. But it was stability, his wife Bonnie was keen to move, and baby Milla was on the way.

'I was pretty much done and dusted at that point. I had a quick conversation with Greg Chappell, who had become a friend, and he said that maybe I should reconsider it, which made me think that I was around the mark for the Twenty20 stuff. And then, I suppose a bit of fate with whatever happened with a new coach and a new CEO, list manager, high performance manager. With a huge change in Tasmanian cricket those new guys were really keen for me to hang around, not only from a playing point of view but a leadership point of view. That's the full story.'

That incoming CEO was Nick Cummins, who backs this up. 'As I got the job things started to fall apart pretty badly on the field. There was concern about the lack of leadership and it was all falling on George Bailey's shoulders. From the outside looking in, I couldn't believe that a player like Tim didn't have something to give.'

Paine was indeed around the mark for Australian T20s. He came back against Sri Lanka in February 2017 and made a diamond duck. Luck wasn't his strong point. So it was a bold call to tour Pakistan with a World XI in September as a test case for its safety. Those games counted as T20 Internationals, taking him to seven for the year. Hardly anyone noticed: when fellow Tasmanian Ricky Ponting discussed Ashes wicketkeeping options, Paine didn't get a mention. But Haddin was watching, now a national coach. Runs were the required currency. None of the first-class keepers could get a score that season. Paine at least managed a fifty captaining a warm-up XI against England.

It came down to the last Shield match before the squad was picked. Tasmania were setting a target with rain forecast. Wade knew he had one more chance to bat. All he had to do was give selectors a reason to keep him. Problem was, Alex Doolan chose that innings to make his highest first-class score, soaking up 380 balls for 247 not out. For hours, Wade was due in next. For hours, Doolan's partner was Paine. 'The declaration in Melbourne was the turning point,' said Cummins. '[The coach] and George were arguing over when to declare. Matthew Wade was sitting between them saying "I don't think we've got enough runs."' It looked like Tasmania had delayed the declaration to help Paine, when in fact they were trying to get the other wicketkeeper picked. Wade never got to bat, Paine made 71 not out.

'That's the square-up, isn't it?' said Cummins. 'People were saying how lucky he was. I said to him, that makes up for all the bad luck. For someone who at the time it appeared had his best years taken away from him, it was really gratifying.' Wade took it similarly. 'They pretty much found out at the same time with the Ashes that one was in and one was out. They were both at the pub, Matt came straight over and gave him a hug and bought him a beer and told him good luck.'

Fair enough – it'd be hard to dislike Tim Paine. He's somehow inherently reassuring. As soon as he took over the Test team it felt like an adult was in charge. Where Smith gave the impression of reading a lifelong autocue, Paine just speaks. He's not a wordsmith; his sentences are littered with the diminutives that mark Australian discourse: maybe just potentially a little bit of a chance that they're possibly a fraction redundant. But he's straight up, not fumbling for consultancy cliché or Aussie macho bluster. He looks you in the eye with a bit of a smile in his. The shaggy blond look has aged to a darker brown quiff, but still casually pushed back. He's relaxed and manifestly pleasant; he could be an ex surf-rat who's opened a cafe.

In captaincy he took immediate ownership, asserting that things hadn't been good enough and would get better. This wasn't a high bar, but one that Australian players and captains had been failing to clear for a long time. His model for decency was Bailey, his long-time state leader, and one who couldn't be any more different to Michael Clarke, who led Smith's apprenticeship. The two acted this out in the 2015 World Cup:

for years Clarke hadn't bothered playing ODIs, but now wanted the glory of the prestige tournament. Bailey had spent those years getting the team running so beautifully that it had no place for Clarke. So Bailey himself made way without complaint and spent the tournament running drinks while Clarke took the spotlight.

Work ethic and decency was why Kookaburra wanted Paine. 'We were sponsoring him during that injury period,' said communications boss Shannon Gill, 'and he was self-aware enough to see that, even though it was through injury and no fault of his own, he wasn't giving the value of exposure the sponsorship was designed for. So he volunteered to do things over and above what was in his contract, like head out and speak at local cricket presentation nights and the like. We have great relationships with our players but it's not often we have someone offering to do that.'

The only part where Paine hasn't been upfront is about suspended players. Here we're back to the custom of looking after mates. He was upbeat about them coming back, and denied there would be tensions with the other players who had the tampering episode dumped on them. He even tried to link Smith with reform: 'Under Steve a few of us had sat around a few times and spoke about the need to change the way we were going about it ... those conversations around those type of things were already happening.'

Which was, frankly, an Inspector Gadget level of stretch. Those conversations were probably just Paine trying to tone things down. His work in the Durban stairwell springs to mind: clipping Warner in the face with his gloves to disrupt the rage, conferring with du Plessis, defusing Rabada. His comments since South Africa showed a man trying to balance being supportive with giving teammates an opportunity to be better.

'I think in sport winning covers over a lot of cracks,' he said at the Wanderers. 'There was probably some noise being made from the public in the last year or so and the guys thought maybe while we kept winning and playing a certain brand of cricket, while it was working we wouldn't change it. But I think it has got to the stage now where we need to listen to our fans and the Australian public and give them a cricket team that they are proud of, win, lose or draw.'

That was precisely the acknowledgement that Smith never had the perceptiveness or humility or courage to make, whichever of those may have been lacking. Another was an admission that had been buried under years of bullshit about good hard cricket. 'We don't want to be abusive and berating and belittling our opposition like at times we've attempted to. We want to be more respectful.'

For a long time Paine's Australian career was bitter, a scrap of history that spoke of missed chances. He hid his baggy green cap and never looked at it. All of a sudden, he wasn't just wearing it again but was leading out ten others doing the same. He had his own way of doing that, like when he stood up to the stumps in Johannesburg and Chadd Sayers cracked his hand.

'I remember thinking that I just wasn't going to go off. I was certain that I had broken my thumb that ball, but I also had in the back of my mind that I was the captain and we weren't going so well and it was the last Test of the series. I thought it would set a tone of how I want to play my cricket: I want to be tough and uncompromising and there are different ways to do that rather than sledging. I thought that was a good way to show that.' That included batting twice and coming back up to the stumps in the second dig.

Perhaps being outside the national setup for so long can make Paine better able to come in and change it. He's grown up elsewhere and has his own ideas of what's right. Considerate as he's been to the deposed, perhaps there'll be less deference to old power structures. 'I've been put into this leadership position because of how I've been previously,' was his simple take. 'So the important thing for me is to continue to be myself.'

It's hard to be confident in his chances. Teams don't win by being pricks but confirmation bias is strong. The myth will live on below the surface, a cold sore waiting to shoot through. These words are being set down in mid 2018, so an unclear future for the writer will become a certain past for the reader. As of now, Paine doesn't have a team. When the Australian contract list came out a week after Johannesburg, it didn't contain a single proven Test batsman. The most experienced were Usman Khawaja and the Marsh brothers, all of whom have patchy records and none of whom had an impact when things got rugged in South Africa.

With Paine making a point of prioritising decency, it will be the first thing blamed if he starts to lose. A bad home summer would take us from laments for Australian cricket's integrity to laments for Australian cricket's mongrel. And if the old way returns, any success that follows will be marked up to it.

Correlation and causation are famously not the same, but God, it's easy to imagine that they are. No story ever ends: every ride into a sunset has a cold night's camping ahead. At the time of writing, Australia has a decent man as captain. The question is how long he'll be allowed to continue being either.

Chapter 24

EPILOGUE

During Australia's winter, months after the curtain fell in Johannesburg, a new off-Broadway show started up in London. Tim Paine led an Australian one-day team onto The Oval to begin a series as low-key as you could get – the games ran late into the night Australian time, and two of the first three had the same start time as Australia's team in the football World Cup.

Only the captain and Shaun Marsh remained from the last Test outing, and Paine was straining every sinew to set an example for a green side. When a ball leapt off the turf behind the wicket into his face, cutting both outside and inside his mouth, he spat out blood for the rest of the innings but didn't get stitches until the break. When Jos Buttler edged high in the air and Paine lost the catch after a sprint into the deep, he lay inhaling the moist English turf for a long moment, wanting so desperately to have reeled it in.

Those were metaphors for his series. He won five tosses and lost five games. Twice his team crawled past 200 then nearly bowled England out. Twice they smashed over 300 and lost with ease. And once, right in the middle, he bowled first and England used a perfect batting track at tiny Trent Bridge to make the men's world record score of 481.

At least the crowds were gentle. The real ribbing was held over for the 2019 Ashes, with England fans hoping Warner and Smith would be back. On this tour it was limited to a local wag at The Oval handing out '4' and '6' cards printed on sandpaper. Commentator Alison Mitchell posted a photo and was chipped online by Lehmann: 'Your better than that?' ran his pithy if ungrammatical indignation. Boof still failed to get it, playing wounded that someone would dare tease his people about their wrongs.

The second game was up against Australia versus France in the football, so not many saw David Warner's commentary spot on Nine's secondary digital station. When Nine announced this one-game recruiting coup with a cheerful Twitter post, the replies ran at ten in favour and 239 telling them to get in the sea. Public opinion had firmly settled on Warner being the criminal and Smith the innocent bystander. If the team kept struggling though, Warner would be on the redemption list too. Ethics meet pragmatism very quickly.

Smith and Warner both headed to the fledgling and unglamorous Canada Global Twenty20, a lightning tournament in Toronto featuring teams like the Winnipeg Hawks. Australia notched a few T20 wins in Zimbabwe, though Paine wasn't there. Having made his way back to the longer formats by playing the shortest, he was now deemed unsuited for the shortest because he played the longest. Aaron Finch took the reins, broke his own record for the highest T20 International score, and played chasey with hordes of kids in Harare's poorest township, suggesting Australia did have leadership to draw on from some largely unexplored corners.

Life went on, with its stupidity and inconsistencies. Australia's worst newspaper ran a story when Steve Smith drank a beer in New York. The other Steve Smith, the ESPN writer, wrote tweets criticising two basketball teams for having a brawl, then got a lengthy roasting by a South African news website for being a hypocritical 'mastermind of organised sporting crimes'. Sri Lankan captain Dinesh Chandimal got pinged in St Lucia for rubbing confectionery on the ball. He was no more transparent than Smith, telling the referee he couldn't remember what he'd taken out of his own pocket and put in his own mouth. He got a one-match ban. If he hadn't refused to take the field for hours in a huff, no one would have paid it much attention at all.

Abraham Benjamin de Villiers announced his international retirement after 420 games. He'd been a constant in Warner's career, taking the catch to end his first international innings in 2009 and the catch to end his last before suspension in 2018. When Warner blazed a hundred in Adelaide in 2012, de Villiers made 33 from 220 balls for a draw. He riled Warner into accusing him of tampering in 2014, creating resentment over the resulting reprimand. On the final tour it was de Villiers' dismissal in Durban that saw Warner lose control, and de Villiers' century in Port Elizabeth that saw Warner draw suspicion. The fall-out meant Warner gave the maintenance job to Bancroft, and it was de Villiers at the crease in Cape Town when Australia's carpentry ruse took place.

By the time this book is published Australia will have played Test cricket again, in the UAE against Pakistan. The culture reviews might be critical or might paper the cracks; either way they'll be delivered to a body with no track record of enforcing standards. India will play the summer of 2018–19, and any Australian team should win at home, but strong visitors could upend that. The honouring of abrasive ways will cycle around – the fallacy of good hard cricket as a birthright rather than a costume to dress up something uglier. There are warnings about hubris, but the Greeks wrote them down for us thousands of years ago and we mostly fail to learn them. There's a chance things might change: they can when people try. It's our blessing and our curse that even a pessimistic future usually sparks a flicker of hope. 'Nothing is written,' said TE Lawrence to Sherif Ali. 'No fate,' Sarah Connor carved into a tabletop. Look at least to the wisdom of these ancients.

While one Australian team was being towelled up in England during Australia's winter, another two gave a better account of themselves. Dan Christian, who played with Paine in that exhibition match years before, captained the Men's Indigenous team as they retraced the steps of the Aboriginal team from Victoria's Western District 150 years earlier. On their backs, players wore the names of their predecessors: Unaarrimin, Yellanach, Grongarrong, Brimbunyah. The Women's Indigenous team was touring for the first time so players wore their own names as pioneers.

We say that Australia the cricket team pre-dates Australia the modern nation, with a game against England played in 1877 well before Federation in 1901. Early teams were drawn from disparate colonies in a collective spirit. But the Indigenous tour to England dated back a decade further than the match that was retrospectively deemed the first ever Test.

On the commemoration tour, the men's team recreated photographs from 1868: a group shot standing and reclining on a cricket ground, and a series of individual portraits collected in an oval frame. Each of the current players took the place of the man whose name they wore. The old portraits were action poses held with spears, boomerangs or cricket gear. The modern tour organisers tracked down some of these artefacts, so that players could match the poses of the past. There are things that Cricket Australia gets right.

Unaarrimin and his fellows have a complicated story: there's no fairy tale here. But the history that we have suggests they loved the game they played, and there's nothing to suggest they didn't play it fair. For all these years we've heard of the Australian way as our undeniable heritage, a game flint-eyed and wary by its most inherent nature. This one strand excludes a hundred others. Australian cricket also has a different heritage, any time it decides to look.

Acknowledgements

Mostly, thanks to the people in their dozens if not hundreds with a meal or a hug or a place to stay so that years on the road have felt more like home. To Jim Maxwell and Adam Collins for support through those years. Vithushan Ehantharajah, Will Macpherson, Melinda Farrell and Subash Jayaraman, for lifeguard duty. The whole Australian pack in South Africa, and our excellent colleagues round the world – too many to list. Particular gratitude to Phil Walker, Daniel Norcross, Mel Jones, Saurabh Somani, Jarrod Kimber, Charles Dagnall and Kritika Naidu. For the backing, Stuart Watt, Mike Hytner, Shannon Gill, Tim Verrall and Nick Morris. The SABC for hospitality, especially Aslam Khota, Mluleki Ntsabo, Hussein Manack, Melinda Lombard, Neil Manthorp and Kass Naidoo. At home, Karen Tighe with the light burning in the host studio. Tom Cowie, Andy Lane, Jonathan Woods and Ben Renick, for camaraderie. Daniel Brettig for sharp eyes, (the other) Steve Smith and Jessica Vovers for patient ones. Henry Moeran and Jay Mueller for saving various days. Glenn Mitchell for guidance, Zac Zavos and The Roar for the boost. Everyone at White Line Wireless and the Dan O'Connell Cricket Club. Pam Brewster, Emily Hart, and Hardie Grant for backing the kind of book I wanted to write. Lastly, to everyone who doesn't care about cricket but cares about me anyway, and to my family for a lifetime, never wavering.